DICK TAVERNE
Against the Tide

POLITICS AND BEYOND

A MEMOIR

Biteback Publishing

First published in Great Britain in 2014 by
Biteback Publishing Ltd
Westminster Tower
3 Albert Embankment
London SE1 7SP
Copyright © Dick Taverne 2014

ISBN 978-1-84954-669-0

10 9 8 7 6 5 4 3 2 1

A CIP catalogue record for this book is available from the British Library.

Set in Baskerville

Printed and bound in Great Britain by
CPI Group (UK) Ltd, Croydon CR0 4YY

CONTENTS

PREFACE

This is a memoir rather than a proper autobiography. It is mostly not about my private life, except for a fairly brief description of the background from which I came, but about those episodes in my public life that will, I hope, be of some general interest beyond the circle of my friends and acquaintances, perhaps even to historians. I have not mentioned the many people who are and have been a much-valued part of my personal life but who were themselves wise enough to live their own lives outside the attentions of the media.

I have never kept a diary. This memoir therefore relies mainly on my memory, which hardly rivals that of Samuel Johnson, who never had to rewrite any sentence that he ever wrote or reread any book that he had ever read. Where possible I have tried to confirm my account from public sources or other people's recollections. But it is likely that some inaccuracies have survived, for which I am solely responsible.

I owe a special debt to my wife Janice, who acted as editor, improved grammar and style, and prevented me from making howlers in any scientific subject mentioned; my two daughters, Suzanna and Caroline, and my son-in-law Michael Jermey, who all made invaluable comments; Ed Pearce, who was most generous with his corrections and erudite suggestions; my agent Ros Edwards; Hollie Teague, my editor at Biteback; Lord Stevenson of Coddenham, without whose early support Sense About Science might never have got off the ground; my long-standing friends in Parliament, Bill Rodgers and Bob Maclennan; and my friends in Lincoln, especially Pat Coates, Frank Goulding, and Linda and Biddy Richardson, who between them kept records of the principal events in the second Lincoln by-election.

CHAPTER 1

EARLY DAYS

I was born in a house on stilts in the jungle of Sumatra, in what was then called the Dutch East Indies. That was in October 1928. At the time, my father, Nicolaas Jacobus Marie Taverne, was employed as a geologist by the Bataafse Petroleum Maatschappij, the Dutch half of Royal Dutch Shell, which ran a big oil field nearby in Palembang. I have no recollection of this exotic start in life, as a year and a half later he was transferred back to his native land, the Netherlands, where the family lived until 1939, except for a period of eight months spent in America in 1936, where my father was sent by Shell on a special assignment.

My mother, Louise, was also born in the Dutch East Indies, where her father, John Koch, was a colonel in the Dutch army. I never met John Koch and know little about him except that his own father was a general, that he was highly decorated after a campaign against 'rebels' in Aceh (still a fiercely independent and rebellious part of Sumatra in today's Indonesia), and that he strongly held the view that the Dutch had no right to be in the Dutch East Indies. He was also a keen Francophile, but I never found out which of the many attractive qualities of France specially appealed to him. It seems he was a rather remote figure with whom my mother had no close relationship. In fact she had no close family ties. Her own mother died very young and she was sent 'home' to be brought up in Holland by a family acquaintance she did not particularly like. She did remember one of her grandmothers with affection, known as Oma Jenny, one of whose parents was a native of Java.

My parents, particularly my father, did not reveal a great deal to my three sisters or me about life in Dutch East Indies and were generally reticent about their past. I wish I had questioned them more closely. To his children my father was always the soul of respectability and for a while in the early 1930s he held strong right-wing views, which became more moderately conservative as the threat from Hitler grew. My mother told me that he had a rebellious past in his student days and once sang the Communist anthem *Internationale* in Batavia (now Jakarta) on Queen Wilhelmina's birthday, a rather sacred occasion in Dutch national life. He qualified with a doctorate in engineering and geology from Delft University of Technology and started his career as a vulcanologist employed by the Dutch government in the Dutch East Indies, but was soon lured away by Royal Dutch Shell. He was less happy there, since he started as a high flier but never quite reached the heights he hoped for.

After finishing her schooling in Holland, such as it was, my mother returned to live with the colonel and it was through him my parents met. Her father played chess with my father. When my parents announced their engagement, the colonel apparently expressed great surprise that such an intelligent man as my father could possibly want to marry such an uneducated girl as his daughter. She was twenty-one; he was thirteen years older. It was not a happy marriage and for some time in the mid-1930s they lived apart before settling on a modus vivendi that kept the family together. My older sister, Yvonne, and I gained from their reunion, because we were able to enjoy a stable and, on the whole, a happy home life. My two younger sisters, Joke and Tine, were born several years later.

One great piece of luck in my life is that I have always been surrounded by loving women: my mother, three sisters, two daughters and my wife, Janice. I was my mother's favourite and I loved her deeply. Yvonne and I were also very close. She was some twenty months older than me and (like my mother) very good looking, with a warm and sparkling personality and a bewitching and infectious laugh. I hardly dared introduce her to my friends because, when I did, droves of them were bowled over by her. Two of my best friends at Oxford, Robin Day, later the doyen of television journalism, and Keith Kyle, a distinguished historian and winner of several TV awards, fell briefly under her spell.

Yvonne was recklessly flirtatious in a very innocent sort of way (it was a relatively innocent era) and hopelessly fickle. None of her passions lasted long, until she met her future husband, Arthur Williams. She was a nurse, he a gynaecologist at the Radcliffe Infirmary, Oxford. Arthur was a devoted surgeon and a lovable man, but his reserved manner and socially conservative outlook were a sharp contrast with her effervescent personality and what he regarded as her 'continental' ways. She was a superb dancer, had a good singing voice and would have made a great musical star.

Joke was born in The Hague in 1938 and Tine in Leatherhead in 1941. I was not as close to them as to Yvonne, partly because of the age difference but mainly because after the war they went back to Holland with my parents while I attended board-ing school at Charterhouse and then went to Oxford before becoming a barrister. Yvonne qualified as a nurse at St Bartholomew's Hospital and also lived in England. We were both naturalised and regarded ourselves as British, while the younger siblings went to school in Holland and are Dutch. In the course of time I have got to know and appreciate them properly, especially after Yvonne died in 1999.

I have few clear memories of my early days in Holland. For three years I attended a school in The Hague called the Nut School ('nut' in Dutch means 'usefulness'). About all I remember is that we learned a lot of geography by rote, for example the names of all the world's major rivers, and were taught that the Dutch defeated the *Armada* with little help from the English or the weather. Twice in early life, before war loomed, politics entered my consciousness. One day, when I must have been about six or seven, some people came to the door to ask for money and my mother brusquely refused them. 'Why did you refuse poor people asking for money?' I protested. 'They were not poor. They were Communists.' 'But Mams [as we called her] I thought you said you were a Communist.' 'No, I'm not, only when I argue with Paps [as we called him] because he is so terribly right-wing.' The other occasion was in Bavaria where we spent some months in a delightful small town called Oberstdorf, probably in about 1933 or 1934 during my parents' temporary separation. There was a Nazi rally which got all the children excited. I jumped on a chair and like my young German friends raised my arm in the Hitler salute. I never saw my mother so furious. She warned that she'd kill me if ever I gave that salute again.

In the last days of August 1939 we were on holiday in the Veluwe, a pretty, relatively unpopulated, heather-covered part of Holland that even boasts a few gentle hills, when my father received a telegram urging him to return to The Hague at once and then leave for England within twenty-four hours. He was to be one of a small group of Dutch Shell executives entrusted with the task of keeping Shell Anglo-Dutch if Holland was invaded. I found the prospect enormously exciting. My mother was a strong Anglophile and even praised Chamberlain for his 'courage' in travelling to meet Hitler at Berchtesgaden! She was also, like many young women on the continent, half in love with the Prince of Wales, later Edward VIII.

So on the evening of 28 August 1939, when I was ten years old, a convoy of some dozen cars took our party from The Hague to the Hook of Holland to catch the night ferry to Harwich. The next morning we caught a train to Liverpool Street station, a taxi to Paddington and another train to Ross-on-Wye, regarded as a safe haven far from the bombs about to rain on London. My father and his colleagues would work in UK Shell's headquarters in Teddington and live in London or nearby during the week and visit us at weekends. It was in Ross-on-Wye that I heard Chamberlain declare war on 3 September. A few days later we moved to a hotel called Sedbury Park, a converted country mansion in Tutshill, Gloucestershire, by the junction of the rivers Severn and Wye. Our Dutch colony shared the hotel, which would later become a borstal, with some old ladies knitting sweaters for our brave soldiers, sailors and airmen, and we learned to sing 'Run Rabbit Run' and 'We're Going to Hang Out the Washing on the Siegfried Line, if the Siegfried Line's Still There'. Early in 1940, as no bombs had dropped on London, we moved to a house in Leatherhead, where we lived until 1946 when my parents and my younger sisters returned to The Hague.

Life in England met my mother's highest expectations. They

were the happiest years of her life. Wartime was of course a time
when the English dropped their reserve, felt united for a common
purpose and even talked to each other in railway carriages. Her
great regret was that when my father's job took the family back to
Holland after the war, she never realised her dream of opening
a tea shop in a Surrey village. She was a woman of very decided
opinions, as strong a Germanophobe as she was Anglophile.
Throughout the war she kept a scrapbook of German atrocities
in Holland, telling us never to forget, and vowed that if ever
she met a German after the war she would spit in their face.
Fortunately she did not keep her vow. In 1949 the family went
back for a holiday in Oberstdorf, where I once stood on a chair
and gave the Hitler salute, and met the lady in whose pension we
had stayed at that time and who had become my mother's good
friend. They met again and my mother embraced her warmly.
I did not inherit her anti-German views. I like Germany and
have regarded it as the least nationalist, indeed the most pacifist,
and one of the best-managed democracies in Europe since the
Second World War. Nor did I inherit her party political sympathies. She strongly favoured the Conservative Party in England
and would refer to Labour supporters, in her less than perfect
English, as 'Those Damned Labours'.

My father adapted less easily to informal English ways. On
one occasion soon after we settled in Leatherhead, he strolled
down the road on a Sunday morning dressed in his Sunday best,
as he would have been in Holland, and passed a rather scruffy
individual working in a garden. Seeing this immensely respect-
able figure, the gardener touched his forelock and greeted my
father deferentially with a 'good morning, sir'. My father was
most upset to learn that the gardener was an eminent Harley

Street surgeon and, never having read P. G. Wodehouse, felt the man had been rude and made fun of him.

At Sedbury Park I was sent to a nearby preparatory school called St John's-on-the-Hill just the other side of the bridge across the river Wye from Chepstow, first as a dayboy and, when my parents moved to Leatherhead and I was eleven years old, as a boarder. Mostly school was fun but the end of holidays and the first few days back at school always aroused an intense feeling of home-sickness. To the other boys I was an alien creature from another world (they had never met a foreigner), speaking a little American with a Dutch accent, learned during eight months in America in 1936. When Holland was invaded by the Germans in May 1940, I became a refugee from the land of a brave ally. I was not bullied, but they made fun of my Dutch accent. When I boasted of the feats of Admiral de Ruyter who sailed up the Thames and burnt some of the English fleet at Chatham in 1666, boys went round chanting 'Good old De Rotter'. The headmaster J. G. O. M. Meade and his wife (their son was an Olympic horse rider) were particularly kind to me, and his wife even knitted some baby clothes when my mother was expecting my youngest sister.

Three years of schooling on the borders of Wales left its mark in at least one respect. Most people don't know about my Dutch origins – which I never try to hide – as I gradually lost my Dutch accent during my schooldays. Once, many years later in adult life, a latter day Professor Higgins, whom I didn't know, happened to be present during a general conversation, which he interrupted to ask me, 'I can't place your accent, which baffles me. What is it?' 'What do you think?' After a long pause, 'Were you born in Monmouthshire?'

As some return for the kindness shown by the Meades, I won a scholarship to Charterhouse, the first scholarship to a major public school won at St John's. I was there from 1942 to 1947. It had not generally been regarded as a particularly intellectual school, unlike Winchester for instance. One distinguished Old Carthusian (as Charterhouse old boys were called), the historian Hugh Trevor-Roper, described it, before my time, as 'a thought-free zone'. I was once told it was the school for the sons of stockbrokers, not, as far as I know, a claim supported by any evidence. There was a lot of snobbery and some reference made to those going to state schools as 'oiks'. Sport was very important, as it is in most public schools, and probably the most admired of my contemporaries was Peter May, later one of England's most successful and stylish batsmen and captain of England. During a match against Eton I once made an undistinguished eight runs at one end while he scored one of his regular centuries at the other. My season's average as a dour opening batsman was a modest twenty; his over a hundred.

Unlike Trevor-Roper, I found Charterhouse intellectually inspiring. At that time a host of discussion societies flourished: a Lit and Pol (literary and political) society and a rival Thackeray Society, named after an Old Carthusian. There was a poetry society, a religious discussion society, a Shakespeare society and several more. We were encouraged to write papers and I produced a stream of them on topics as diverse as Plato and religion, why public schools like Charterhouse should be abolished because they were class-based, and even one in praise of Marxism, which I found attractive because it seemed to provide a single solution for all political, economic and social problems. Part of my broader intellectual awakening was due to Professor C. E. M. Joad, the star of a popular radio programme, *The Brains Trust*, and a noted populariser of philosophy. His catchphrase was, 'It all depends what you mean by...' – a very sensible observation. I was given his book *A Philosophy for Our Times*, which made me feel philosophy was the most exciting subject in the world and Plato its most exciting exponent. It became my ambition to be a philosophy don at Oxford.

There were a number of inspiring masters at that time, under an unorthodox headmaster, Robert Birley. Several not only tolerated but positively encouraged eccentricity and dissent from 'public school' orthodoxy. Sir Robert Birley, as he became, was a remarkable man. He was known as 'Bags Birley' at school because of big bags under his eyes, and later as 'Red Robert', not because of his liberal views, but because of mistaken identification. He left Charterhouse because he was asked to reorganise German education in the aftermath of the war and root out the influence of Nazism. In his office as education 'tsar', as no doubt he would now be called, there hung a Victorian photograph of a man with a big black beard. One of his less liberal critics reported that it was a picture of Karl Marx. The story stuck. In fact it was of Johannes Brahms.

I am not sure what he achieved by way of reorganisation, because he was not a great organiser or administrator, but many prominent people I later met in Germany praised his liberal influence on the ethos of German education after Hitler. He was certainly greatly respected by the German participants at the annual Anglo-German conferences at Königswinter that I twice attended. After Germany, Birley became headmaster of Eton and then, on his retirement, surprised everyone by taking up a post as Professor of English at the University of the Witwatersrand in apartheid South Africa. Perhaps that was the apotheosis of his career. He became a relentless scourge of the government, for example urging his students to study the nineteenth-century debates in the UK Parliament on the slave trade to bring home the message that black people had the same rights as whites. His assaults on apartheid were all the more effective because an ex-headmaster of Eton could not possibly be regarded by the public as revolutionary or subversive. On his return to England he used his many connections with influential old Etonians and Carthusians to help victims of the regime. When I was an MP and later a minister, I was frequently lobbied by him on behalf of refugees, or would-be refugees, many of them members of the Communist Party. In fact he once told me he advised some of the ANC leaders to 'read your Lenin' because the Bolshevik revolution was organised from outside Russia.

In 1976, when I was a member of the board of the BOC Group (originally known as British Oxygen), I was due to visit South Africa and arranged to see Birley for a briefing beforehand. One of my roles as a board member was to advise on politics. He gave me valuable contacts and particularly urged me to visit the headmaster of the Orlando High School in the black township, Soweto. BOC duly arranged for a car to drive me to the school. When I arrived, I was told that unfortunately the head was inter-viewing new pupils that day and could not see visitors. I could see there was a long line of children waiting so I wrote a brief note to send him Birley's regards. Just as we were about to leave a schoolgirl came running out with an urgent message: I had to see the head because any friend of Birley's took precedence over everything and everybody. The headmaster then told me that Birley had been a huge support to the school, so much so that they put up a picture of him in the most prominent place they could find. When the government found out, they said they would withdraw all funding unless the picture of this dangerous Communist was removed at once. The head refused and told them he would rather close the school. Eventually the government caved in and that day I was reverently shown the picture. Incidentally, the head also told me that demand for school places was so great that classes numbered well over fifty, as he never refused any applicant. There was no problem about discipline because every child was passionately keen to learn.

Two of my close contemporaries at Charterhouse achieved a degree of fame, for very different reasons. The first was a strange, tall, bespectacled figure who wandered into our classroom in my second term, wearing a waistcoat and Albert chain and speaking with a slight lisp, which someone later attributed to his early fascination with antiquarian books in which the letter 's' was written as a long 'f'. His name was William Rees-Mogg. He advised me to buy *Daily Mail* shares, as the price of the paper, he assured me, was about to be put up to one penny from a ha'penny (at the age of fourteen I had never heard of shares). I became friendly with him, although he was a year ahead of me, because he was one of the few boys interested in politics. His views were strongly conservative. In fact politics was his first love, next to journalism and antiquarian books, although later he made his name principally in journalism as editor of *The Times* from 1967 to 1981, and subsequently as a regular *Times* columnist. At school he was not only a clever eccentric but a precociously scheming politician, far more unscrupulous than in his later career when he was a model of rectitude and the least malicious and intolerant of men, although as a Catholic his tolerance did not extend to abortion, which he once described as a crime worse than the Holocaust.

However, at school he once took revenge on a master who had offended him. William and a close friend of his, Clive Wigram, also a Conservative, had been rather unfairly excluded from the Lit and Pol, then the most prestigious of the school societies, because the master who ran it, one Harry Iredale, disliked their intellectual pretensions. They persuaded two other masters, who were envious of the popularity among bright pupils of the eccentric Iredale, to form the rival Thackeray Society and at William's suggestion it recruited members at the age of fifteen, whereas the Lit and Pol had an entry age of sixteen. For a while the manoeuvre was successful and the Lit and Pol was eclipsed, but in time it recovered and it was found that there was room for both and membership often overlapped.

The other plotter, Clive Wigram, might well have become the most successful politician of my Carthusian contemporaries. He was very able, became president of the Oxford Union (as did William) and had a reputation as a rising young hope of the Conservative Party. He married the daughter of Tory grandee Sir David Maxwell Fife, a Conservative Attorney-General, later Home Secretary and finally, as Lord Kilmuir, Lord Chancellor. When Sir David practised as a barrister on the Northern Circuit there was a popular ditty: 'There is little worse in death or life / Than David Patrick Maxwell Fife.' He was known as a man whose intellect excelled more in its retentive than its creative faculties and he once told Bob Boothby, who was lobbying for the reform of homosexuality laws, 'I am not going down in history as the man who made sodomy legal.'[†] It should be mentioned, however, that he not only played a much-admired role as a

---

[†]   Roberts, A., *Eminent Churchillians* (London: Weidenfeld and Nicolson, 1994) p. 219.

prosecutor in the Nuremberg trial of leading Nazis, but was one of the principal architects of the European Convention on Human Rights, now denounced by Conservatives as an unwelcome foreign intrusion into British law. Sadly Wigram died from Hodgkin's disease in his twenties.

The other contemporary Carthusian who achieved fame, in his case mixed with notoriety, was the novelist Simon Raven. He was a year ahead of me and I did not know him well, although for a short time we were both members of the classical sixth form. He won a scholarship to King's College, Cambridge at an early age. We were only briefly together in the sixth form because soon after I joined it he became the only boy during my time to be expelled from Charterhouse for seducing younger boys.

He was well-known as the school rake and cast a strange spell over Robert Birley and several other masters. In fact, school gossip claimed that the final offence which led to his expulsion took place in the holidays when Simon and some younger boys were staying with the Birley family. Tall, red-haired, pale-skinned, with a high-pitched voice as if it had hardly broken, he was striking rather than handsome, and what I remember most vividly about him was his leer. It was his natural expression. He could out-leer all other leerers. Several years after we left school his exploits were a perpetual subject for discussion and fascination. It turned out he developed very catholic sexual tastes. There was, it was reported, a transition from white boys to black boys to black women to white women. He got married at Cambridge but only because he had made a girl pregnant and her father had threatened to horsewhip him if he did not make an honest woman of her. The marriage did not last long. He left King's heavily in debt and escaped his creditors by joining the army, which in time he also had to leave, reluctantly, because of his losses at the races. An essay he wrote about the army in the series *The Establishment* and a novel about it, *Feathers of Death*, were in my view among the best things he wrote. I was intrigued to learn from one of his obituaries that according to E. W. Swanton, the cricket correspondent of the *Daily Telegraph*, his book *Shadow on the Grass*, which I have not read, is the filthiest book about cricket ever written. In his novel-cum-memoirs about Charterhouse, he records that William Rees-Mogg warned him that hell was like a bad tooth that got worse and worse for eternity and Simon described him as a scheming Catholic opportunist.

I developed left-wing sympathies early in life, which were popular neither at home nor at school. I was one of three boys, as far as I was aware, in a school of over 400, who welcomed the Labour victory in 1945. To me the issue was quite simple. There were huge inequalities in our society between rich and poor and I was on the side of the poor. I was part of a privileged few at a private school which was likely to give me a big advantage in life and I was determined to fight privilege from the inside, which has been my aim ever since.

I look back at my time at Charterhouse with pleasure and appreciation. Proof of its tolerance and broadmindedness was that despite my subversive views I ended up as head boy. Perhaps the most important of its legacies was that it left me with a life-long zest for learning

There were two prizes which I won during my school career that I was particularly proud of, neither very ethically achieved nor in subjects in which I could boast or sought special expertise. On Sunday mornings we had a compulsory scripture lesson for all sixth formers, a time when I was keen to get away early to cycle to Leatherhead (fifteen miles away from Charterhouse, which is based in Godalming) and spend a few hours at home before I had to be back for evening chapel. I therefore played hookey when I thought no one would notice. In the summer of my penultimate year, Birley gave a series of scripture lectures for all sixth formers on St Paul, with special concentration, I gathered – for I did not attend them – on Paul's views about determinism. It transpired that at the end there was to be an exam with a valuable book prize for the best essay. What was I to do? I went to Birley and said I was particularly interested in determinism. Could I borrow his book about St Paul's views? He was delighted to find someone so interested and lent it to me. No one else had read the book. I won the prize.

The second was an achievement in unorthodox military tactics. One of the worst chores in our life in the summer term was a compulsory military competition involving house platoons of the cadet corps, supervised by cadets at Royal Military Academy Sandhurst. (This was a time just after the end of the war.) One afternoon for several weeks we had to train for an attack on an enemy post, which would be manned by other Sandhurst cadets, in the glorious countryside around Hindhead. The most successful attack won a prize, the Arthur Webster Cup. On the great day we were supposed to march off smartly as directed by one of the Sandhurst supervisors and when fired on from an unexpected quarter on top of a hill, storm up the hill in an immaculate straight line (so that we could be mowed down systematically by the enemy) and capture the hilltop. The attack was scheduled to take about half an hour.

Our house, Pageites, was known as a 'slack house', particularly in corps activities. Although not yet in my final year, I was the only one with any corps rank. The ranks rose from lowly lance corporals to corporal, sergeant and lofty under officers. I was an acting lance corporal, the lowest of the low. At the start I told our platoon that we were not going to waste our time on lovely summer afternoons training for this ridiculous exercise, but would find a nice hidden spot, post a sentry in case the officious master in charge of military training, one Major Morris, came to inspect us, and read books or do whatever we liked, as long as they followed my orders on the day.

When the day came I told one of the more capable members of our platoon house to trail the house ahead of us without being seen and to find out where the enemy was, which he did. The Sandhurst cadet then arrived and it was our turn to march into battle. Ignoring his instructions where to go, we ran off in a different direction, in a formation about as orderly as a pack of hounds, to the back of the hill where our scout told us the enemy was and started to rush up the hill. The breathless Sandhurst cadet yelled at us to stop: 'They won't know you are coming. Fire a shot to warn them.' We duly fired a blank and continued our onward rush. Before they realised what was happening, the enemy was overwhelmed and we captured the post without a shot fired, except our warning blank. It all took about five or ten minutes. We won the prize. Major Morris could not believe his ears. 'Pageites?' he kept shouting, 'Pageites?' It was as if Lincoln City had won the FA Cup. I was immediately promoted to sergeant and I still possess a pewter mug inscribed 'Arthur Webster Cup, Sergeant G [sic] Taverne', which shows how well known I was in military circles.

CHAPTER 2

STUDENT

From Charterhouse I went straight to Balliol College, Oxford in 1947. I am critical of many institutions I have been part of: public schools, the Bar, the House of Commons and the House of Lords, and the boards of publicly limited companies. But I have few criticisms of Balliol or, for that matter, of Oxford. Not that Balliol was perfect. It had a reputation for 'the arrogant display of effortless superiority' and the first was more in evidence than the second. Balliol alumni did tend to regard themselves as rather special:

> Balliol made me, Balliol fed me,
> Whatever she had she gave me again:
> And the best of Balliol loved and led me,
> God be with you, Balliol men
> *Hilaire Belloc*

Women undergraduates would have deflated these pretensions, but at the time women were restricted to five women's colleges. My older daughter, Suzanna, later went to Balliol.

Some of us, I confess, could behave like intolerable intellectual snobs. When the college rugby team uncharacteristically reached the university cup final, a group of us attended a rugby match for the first time to cheer on our opponents, University College, in case Balliol became known for sporting prowess. The president of the Junior Common Room complained that this showed a deplorable lack of college spirit. His remarks were greeted by loud laughter. In fact a bias against sport was not confined to a few snooty undergraduates. One of the Carthusians who applied to Balliol and who was academically sufficiently qualified was the cricketer Peter May, but the Master, Sandy Lindsay (later Lord Lindsay), preferred other candidates less preeminent in sport (preferably from state schools) and May went to Cambridge instead.

One of our Balliol contemporaries was a very tall, languid, elegant, handsome old Etonian ex-Guards Officer called Ian Gilmour. Of course, no old Etonian Guardsman could possibly be intelligent. One day when a group of us was sitting on the lawn, I mentioned that I had been to a political drinks party and had for the first time had a long conversation with Ian Gilmour. I said, 'You know, he is quite intelligent.' 'Well,' said Bernard Williams, later one of our best philosophers, 'he'd look good as a guard outside Buckingham Palace.' Ian proved to be one of the most distinguished and progressive Tory intellectuals, a successful editor of *The Spectator*, a maverick Cabinet minister and the author of two much-admired books: *Britain Can Work* and *Dancing with Dogma*, which had a picture on the front of Ian dancing with Mrs Thatcher.

Balliol was a wonderfully stimulating environment. It was a good time to be at Oxford – except for the shortage of women. Some, like me, came straight from school. Many others had been in the services and the war. My closest friends at Oxford, Robin

Day and Keith Kyle, and another friend, Peter Blaker (later Conservative MP for Blackpool), were Captain Day, Captain Kyle and, most impressive of all because of his rank, Major Blaker. My impression was that the more mature undergraduates benefited greatly from their experience of the world. They were more serious about their studies, less likely to get drunk, less theoretical in argument. It was a time of austerity. I heard there was a Bullingdon Club, but never came across any of its members. We often ate in a very cheap 'British restaurant', no place for gourmets, and although it was still a time of rationing, I personally was unaware of shortages and they certainly detracted in no way from the excitement of student life.

My Balliol colleagues reading the same subject were exceptionally talented. The subject was commonly known as 'Greats' (I do not know why), officially termed *Literae Humaniores*, and in fact consisted of four terms of Classics and eight terms of philosophy and ancient history, four years in all. People often asked what its practical use was. It had two great merits. First, it was a very practical course because it taught one to think more clearly. The final examinations in philosophy, for example, did not ask us to expound on Kant's *Critique of Pure Reason* or Descartes's logic, or expect us to show how many books we had read and absorbed, but tested intelligence. In my finals two of the questions I answered were 'If I have a right, what have I?' and 'What is a sentence?' I had not read the great philosophers very conscientiously, if at all, except Plato and Aristotle, who were the subject of a special exam paper, and attended few lectures, but I had the huge advantage of talking to my contemporaries and reading their essays for tutorials, especially the philosophy essays of Bernard Williams and another friend who also became

a distinguished philosophy don, John Lucas. Our moral philosophy tutor, Dick Hare, later Regius Professor of Moral Philosophy,
said Bernard was the best philosophical mind he had ever met
and Bernard lived up to his promise.

History, too, can be a rigorous intellectual training, especially
if it consists of trying to interpret evidence from sparse arcane
sources. Reading the history essays of my contemporary Robin
Nisbet, a brilliant classicist and a very good historian, later the
Regius Professor in Classics, proved far more useful than attending lectures on Greek or Roman history. Eight out of the ten
of us reading Greats at Balliol won first-class degrees. I was
rather lucky to get a first. I had not worked very hard, except in
a frantic last few months, and could not boast special intellectual
brilliance, but was fortunate in the sympathetic and tolerant attitude of my examiners at my viva, which they seemed to enjoy, as
I did. At one point, in questioning me about my knowledge of
Greek history, they asked 'would you like to discuss' some topic
about which I knew very little. I replied, 'Do you mean "would
I like to" or "do I have to"? If I have to, I shall try to make the
best of a bad job.' They smiled and asked, 'What would you like
to discuss?' I said I was quite good on the Helot revolt against
Sparta and they allowed me to hold forth. After that we got on
like a house on fire.

The second advantage of Greats was that the study of classical Greece introduced students to one of the great episodes in
the history of civilisation. In a short period in the fifth and fourth
centuries BC in Athens, then a tiny city state, it produced some
of the greatest poets, playwrights, philosophers and historians of
all time. To me, Thucydides is one of the greatest historians
and none have been more entertaining and captivating than

Herodotus. Rome never appealed to me as much as Greece, with many exceptions, especially Catullus and the great Lucretius who, in wonderful poetry, expounded the Epicurean philosophy of the atomists, Democritus and Leucippus. He argued that all nature was composed of tiny moving atoms, that we should not fear death because there was no afterlife, and excoriated, like a Christopher Hitchens or Stephen Pinker of classical times, the evil effects of religion. *Tantum religio potuit suadere malorum* ('so much harm has been inflicted on the world by religion') was one of his most famous lines, referring to Agamemnon's sacrifice of his daughter Iphigenia to appease Artemis who had calmed the winds and stopped him sailing to Troy.

The contemporary fashion for linguistic analysis, which seemed to have little to say about the real problems of life, cooled my schoolboy enthusiasm for philosophy. Discussions would focus on a sentence such as 'Smith left the room, but I don't believe it'. Was it a logically impermissible sentence? Was it as illogical as saying 'Smith left the room and Smith stayed in the room'? The reader may be as puzzled as I was, but it was a question seriously discussed. I wanted to discuss big subjects rather than try to solve academic crossword puzzles.

I found it difficult to understand the most revered philosopher of the day, Ludwig Wittgenstein, which I feared was partly because I found I was not as good at philosophy as I had hoped. A poll of professional philosophers in 1998 rated Wittgenstein as the most important philosopher of all time after Plato, Aristotle, Nietzsche and Kant, and ahead of Descartes and Hume. In Cambridge, where he held a chair, he was worshipped by passionate acolytes, who even copied his dress and mannerisms. He inspired poetry and novels; in one he features as a desert mystic who lived on bread, rainwater and silence.[†] However, some years later I was delighted to discover what I had not realised at the time, that two philosophers I greatly admire were highly critical of the linguistic school and were very anti-Wittgenstein. Bertrand Russell held that the new ideas he promoted were dragging Cambridge philosophy (and presumably Oxford philosophy, too) down a cul-de-sac of tedium and triviality, and described Wittgenstein's later work, *Philosophical Investigations*, which spellbound my Greats contemporaries, as 'completely unintelligible'. Karl Popper inveighed against the Wittgenstein view that there were no philosophical problems, only linguistic puzzles. In a television interview he told Bryan Magee, another contemporary of mine:

> I have spectacles and I am cleaning them now. But spectacles have a *function*, and they only function, when you put them on, to look through them *at the world*. It is the same with language. That is to say, one should not waste one's life in spectacle-cleaning or in talking about language.[‡]

Bryan, who has remained a friend of mine since Oxford days, had an impressively varied career: president of the Union at Oxford, a presenter of an arts programme on television, a Labour then SDP Member of Parliament, then a philosophy don at Oxford, a presenter of a remarkable TV series of interviews of contemporary philosophers and the author of books on politics, Wagner and philosophy, including a brilliant little book on Karl Popper.

However, even if current fashion seemed to cramp its scope,

[†]   Edmunds, D. and Eidinow, J., *Wittgenstein's Poker* (London: Faber, 2001), p. 24.
[‡]   Magee, B., *Modern British Philosophy* (London: Secker and Warburg, 1971), p. 138.

any study of philosophy will raise the big issues that have fascinated and troubled mankind: happiness, for instance. It is argued, not unreasonably, that GDP is an unsatisfactory criterion of national success and that an index of happiness or wellbeing should be substituted. But how far can happiness be the objective of political action? Life, liberty and the pursuit of happiness? What is happiness? What about the aim of utilitarianism, the greatest happiness of the greatest number? Is the least misery for the smallest number not a more realistic objective? At least we know what misery is. Would you rather be Socrates dissatisfied or a pig satisfied? (To read the Socratic dialogues was in itself an education.) One of those I know who is most satisfied with life is our cat, judged by the amount of time he spends purring. The Epicureans thought a philosopher could be happy on the rack (a claim most philosophers might not wish to test). St Augustine identified some 289 versions of happiness and in the eighteenth century it was the subject of over fifty treatises.[†] And even if happiness is not the same as pleasure, can happiness be successfully pursued directly, or can it only be achieved as a by-product of less selfish objectives? Henry David Thoreau observed that 'happiness is like a butterfly: the more you chase it, the more it will elude you, but if you turn your attention to other things, it will come and sit softly on your shoulder'.

The eternal verities and the wisdom of the ages cannot be avoided in any philosophical syllabus and their discussion is a most valuable part of a liberal education. Indeed, Greats was once defined as an education that teaches you to despise the wealth it prevents you from earning. While it did not actually

---

†   See Bruckner, P., *Perpetual Euphoria: On the Duty to Be Happy*, translated by Stephen Rendall (Princeton: Princeton University Press, 2011).

condemn Greats graduates to a life of ascetic poverty, it did help
to give a sense of perspective and discourage the chasing after
false gods. It represented a rather different view of the purpose
of higher education than the Browne Review of October 2010,
which opined:

> Higher education matters because it drives innovation and
> economic transformation. Higher education helps to produce
> economic growth, which in turn contributes to national prosper-
> ity... On graduating graduates are more likely to be employed,
> more likely to enjoy higher wages and better job satisfaction, and
> more likely to move from one job to the next.[†]

On reflection what now surprises and dismays me is that there
was one aspect of civilisation that nearly all of my friends ignored,
namely science. Science and medical students tended to play a
less active part in extracurricular activities because they could
not afford to be dilettantes. They had to spend a lot of time on
experiments in laboratories. I knew only one scientist well during
my time at Oxford – and married her. Today science policy and
promoting an understanding of how science works and what it
contributes to a civilised society are among my main interests.
But this neglect of science was typical of the gap between the
two cultures that so concerned C. P. Snow. It explains why so few
influential civil servants and politicians or producers in television
or the media generally (with the honourable exception of the
specialist science correspondents) know anything about science.
That is why the government takes no steps to discourage the

[†] 'Securing a Sustainable Future for Higher Education', The Browne Review,
    October 2010.

NHS from funding homeopathy, why the Department of Health has several times asserted that its policy is neutral as between evidence-based medicine and alternative medicine (in effect between sense and nonsense) and why much government policy is not evidence-based. Science is not just useful in making us more prosperous and healthy, but is one of the pillars of civilisation, in the words of Karl Popper, 'one of the greatest spiritual adventures man has yet known'. As the enemy of ignorance and superstition, of dogma and of autocracy that does not allow criticism, it is one of the cornerstones of democracy and human rights. I develop this theme more fully in Chapter 10, about the stage in my career when science became my principal interest.

Of course, reading Greats was not the only way to develop a measured view of life. None of my friends or acquaintances was particularly interested in earning lots of money. They wanted to join the BBC, become academics, civil servants, journalists, teachers, politicians or barristers (not then as remunerative a career as it can be now) or write, act, produce plays, do research or become doctors. I knew no one who wanted to be a banker and earn big bonuses or become an accountant, and few were willing to soil their hands, as we then saw it, in the world of commerce.

My own interests became more and more political. One of the debates I attended in the Oxford Union was on a motion 'That this house would rather be a dustman than a don'. It was meant to be a light-hearted debate. In the Union, wit was more valued than wisdom. The motion was proposed by someone I barely knew called Michael Croft (later director of the National Youth Theatre), whose speech was not a success because it was deadly serious. He attacked the arid irrelevance of much academic life and ended with a passionate plea: 'Be anything but a don, be a dustman.' To me it was an inspiring speech. It was the irrelevance of linguistic philosophy to the practical problems of the world that made me concentrate on politics.

I started off with mild Marxist tendencies, as a hangover from school, and at first divided my time between the socialist club, which was effectively dominated by Communists[†] and the Labour club, which had broken away from the socialist club. My sympathies soon moved firmly towards the Labour club. I joined the Labour Party and when in 1948, towards the end of my first year at Oxford, the coup in Czechoslovakia established a Communist regime and ousted President Beneš, I was finally cured of the Marxist virus. After that I regarded myself as a social democrat rather than a socialist and joined ranks with those who wanted to make the Labour Party a party of conscience and reform rather than ideological socialism. Several Labour club members became friends and later parliamentary colleagues, such as Shirley Catlin, who became Shirley Williams after she married Bernard Williams and who succeeded me in due course as chair (I was elected chairman in 1949), and Bill Rodgers.

The Labour club led to the most important meeting of my life. In the general election of 1950, one of my Labour friends, Michael, son of prominent feminist and Labour Cabinet minister Dr Edith Summerskill, led a party of undergraduates to canvass for his mother in Fulham. The group included Gerald Kaufman (later a Labour minister) and a school friend of Michael's sister Shirley, one Janice Hennessey. I had briefly met her once, when

---

†   Their chairman, a student with a strong demotic accent, was called Monty Johnston. I learned that he was actually a scion of the aristocracy with the surname Montague-Johnston.

she was accompanied by a friend of mine, on the stairs at the Oxford Union and had noticed what an extremely attractive girl she was. I made sure she and I canvassed together, except for a short break while I took a bus to Conservative headquarters to buy a portrait of Winston Churchill for my mother, one of his greatest fans. On the return journey to Oxford we sat together in the back of the coach and then had dinner in a popular Oxford restaurant, the Taj Mahal. My luck was in. During dinner one of our party was asked what he read. He said geography. The questioner said, 'Geography? You might as well read zoology.' In all innocence I asked, 'What's wrong with zoology?' 'Thank you,' said Janice. 'I'm a zoologist.' It all happened on St Valentine's Day and was love at second sight. A few years later we married and lived happily ever after. Meeting Janice not only enhanced the joys of life at Oxford, but also played a vital role in the last and most unexpected part of my career. It was her enthusiasm for science that led me to take up the public understanding of science as an issue and to found the charity Sense About Science some forty years later (see Chapter 10).

The main focus of my political education, however, was the Oxford Union rather than the Labour club. In its debates I took my first faltering steps in public speaking – at the start I was so nervous about any impromptu public expression that I would even learn questions, let alone speeches, off by heart. I also, I regret to say, appear to have made at least one early short speech that was an extreme example of the kind of precious absurdity for which the Union was sometimes notorious. My philosopher friend John Lucas recently told me he had made a note of me once citing the Greek sage Parmenides and declaring, 'That that is, is. For what is "that" but "that"? And what is "is" but

"is"? Therefore that that is, is.' In arguments with my friends,
particularly Robin Day and Keith Kyle, I also like to believe
that my political views gradually became less naive. Both were
formidably talented.

Keith was not only regarded by his tutors as an outstandingly
good historian, but was the most natural speaker of his Oxford
generation, effortlessly eloquent, humorous and forceful. I never
saw him use a single note. He started as a Liberal, joined the
Conservatives after leaving Oxford but resigned over Suez, then
joined Labour, then the SDP and then Labour again – as Robin
observed, the only party he never joined was the Communist
Party. In fact, his views were consistently centre or somewhat
left of centre and it was his misfortune that the two main parties
veered from time to time across his steady course. He became
an outstanding journalist, voted best foreign correspondent
when he was the *Economist* representative in Washington, won
several TV awards and acquired an encyclopaedic knowledge
of different parts of the world. He nearly wrote books about
many of them, but was always distracted by a new assignment.
I suspect that never in the history of publishing have so many
publishers paid so many advances for so many books that were
never written – no less than ten in all. His friends wondered if he
would ever write even one, until finally his book *Suez* appeared,
a magisterial account of the war of 1956 which won the highest
acclaim.[†] Later he also wrote a book about Kenyan independence and a fascinating autobiography.

One of Keith's most singular qualities, which deeply worried
him and both frustrated and delighted his friends, was his

---

†   Kyle, K., *Suez* (London: Weidenfeld and Nicolson, 1991).

absent-mindedness. Two particular examples illustrate why he was right to worry. The first was when he was the American correspondent of *The Economist*. When he came home on leave, he would stay with Robin Day and for some reason, not very clearly explained, would ask Robin to pay his monthly salary cheque into Robin's account so that Robin could supply him with cash. When this had happened a couple of times, Robin not unreasonably complained and told Keith that everyone had a bank account and he should really open one of his own. Keith then explained that he did in fact have a bank account, but could not remember where it was. Robin made Keith conduct a search of all the places he had lived in and they eventually found that Keith had no less than four bank accounts, all with significant deposits. The second example was told me by Bryan Magee. Bryan, who had not seen Keith for several years, met him on the tarmac of an airport in America, staring at the ground. He hailed Keith like a long-lost friend and asked him what he was now doing. Keith did not look up but replied, 'Bryan, I am trying to work out where I am and where I am supposed to be going.' He was many hundreds of miles from his target destination.

Keith stood three times as a Labour candidate, but never for a winnable seat. He was known to the public as a television journalist and left no mark on politics, but I believe, with others who knew him, that he was the best Foreign Secretary we never had, provided his civil servants looked after him.

Robin Day was the most impressive president of the Union of my time, all the more impressive because he added weight to wit. As an undergraduate he weighed over seventeen stone. He spent much of his life losing weight with a huge effort and then slipping back with no effort at all. Fortunately he never regained his undergraduate size. If ever there was a big personality, his was it. He was almost bound to become famous, which in due course he did as the Grand Inquisitor of television.

His impact on political television journalism was immense. Before the Day era, interviews with leading politicians were profoundly deferential. Robin, who had spent a short period at the Bar before he turned to television, rigorously cross-examined his interviewees, not rudely and with constant interruptions, a style many modern interviewers adopt to show how tough they are, but with a deep knowledge of the issues of the day that enabled him to probe the weak spots in their position most effectively. He generally respected and liked politicians, again unlike his modern equivalents, who often assume they are untrustworthy. As a famous editor of the *Sunday Times* once advised his journalists, 'Always start your interview of a politician with the question at the back of your mind: Why is that bastard lying to me?' In fact Robin had a great love of Parliament and its history – not that he could always hide his irritation when a politician did not answer the question and went off on a different track to say what they planned to say. He once told me that the next time he interviewed Mrs Thatcher he would ask her: 'Prime Minister, what is your answer to my next question?'[†]

He was often impossible, with enough faults to ruin ten good men: a male chauvinist, often rude to people he didn't rate, and indeed sometimes he seemed only interested in the rich and famous (old friends excepted). On the other hand he could take infinite pains to help friends, to whom he revealed himself as a man of great warmth and generosity, and he was surprisingly

---

†   He never did but told several other people of his intention – one of them the television journalist Michael Cockerell.

humble about his success, which was not restricted to television appearances. He was the driving force behind the introduction of the lottery and one of the earliest and most persuasive advocates for televising Parliament. He strongly supported letting the cameras in not just to benefit television but because it would benefit Parliament. Despite his pre-eminence as a television interviewer, he often spoke of his career as a failure, mainly because above all he would have loved to have been an MP.

He did in fact once stand, rather improbably in the light of his later very conservative views, as a Liberal candidate for Hereford in 1959. As he put it in one of his two autobiographies, *Day by Day* and *Grand Inquisitor*:

> 1959 was a year of great significance in British politics. It was the year in which Margaret Thatcher succeeded in entering Parliament. 1959 was also the year in which I failed to enter Parliament. Such are the quirks of the popular will by which the destiny of great nations is decided.

He loved making speeches (and published a volume of them). In fact it could be hard to stop him. He appointed himself as best man at my and Janice's wedding, which we planned to make very informal, and insisted on making a speech although we never asked him to. It was a wonderfully witty speech, as it turned out. Some of his speeches were brilliant, always carefully prepared and rehearsed, although he had the quickest impromptu wit of anyone I knew. If he had been a Member of Parliament, he would have been one of the few whom MPs would flock into the chamber to hear. In showbiz, too, he would have excelled. As he wrote: 'For years I've been asking the BBC to let me have an orchestra, so I could dance like Bruce Forsyth down the studio steps to conduct a stirring item – on the exchange rate mechanism ... or the common agricultural policy.'

Despite its striving for cleverness and wit, the Oxford Union was an exciting environment for anyone interested in public life. Many of my contemporaries there became MPs or prominent figures in the arts or journalism. The biggest star when I first arrived was Kenneth Tynan, who published *He that Plays the King*, a much-acclaimed book about the stage, within a year of leaving Oxford. He soon became widely acknowledged as the leading theatre critic of the day, first on the *Observer*, then the *New Yorker*. Many were the friendships he sacrificed for the sake of a striking phrase, as with his description of an actress who played Cleopatra 'like Lady Bracknell cruelly starved of cucumber sandwiches'. At Oxford he was the archetypal aesthete, his hair unfashionably long and he dressed in purple trousers. When he was listed as a main speaker in light-hearted debates the Union was packed. One of his memorable triumphs was in a debate that 'this house wants it both ways'. He opposed it on the grounds that it implied there were only two ways of having it, whereas he said, 'I personally know of at least thirty-seven different ways, not including the one on the grand piano.'[†] The only time he made a serious speech was in a debate on whether the fascist party should be outlawed. Ironically, given his later ultra left-wing views, he spoke passionately in defence of fascism and the need to protect art from the culture of the mob. It seems a pity that the theatrical contribution by which he made his greatest mark was the nudist play *Oh Calcutta*, mainly noteworthy for its capacity to shock.

---

†   Quoted in Day, Sir R., *Grand Inquisitor: Memoirs* (London: Weidenfeld and Nicolson, 1989), p. 29.

Many undergraduate politicians later became MPs after changing their political allegiance. Peter Blaker, then a Liberal, became a Conservative MP and junior minister. Peter Tapsell was selected as the Labour representative on the biennial Union debating tour of the US, which I had been on two years earlier. Later he became a Conservative MP and later still Father of the House of Commons. Others included Peter Francis Hannibal Emery, a leading Conservative at Oxford who, after an unsuccessful attempt to win Lincoln in 1955, became a long-serving MP for Honiton. He was a somewhat bizarre figure in the Union, most elegantly dressed, moustachioed, his oratory notable for its very upper-class accent and frequent malapropisms. Robin Day called him 'the immaculate misconception'. Towards the end of my time in the Union, a young Michael Heseltine appeared who became president not because he was a good debater, which at that time he was not, but because he was a good waiter, so I was subsequently told. On becoming treasurer he rescued the shaky finances of the Union by improving the service in the dining room. He would personally show every diner to their table and thus became known to far more voters than his rivals. As MP and minister he was later one of the best speakers in the House of Commons, one of the dominant figures of Mrs Thatcher's Tory government and finally her nemesis.

One big advantage of the Union was that its reputation attracted leading parliamentarians to its political debates, generally on a motion 'that this house has no confidence in the government'. Among them R. A. Butler, Herbert Morrison and Hugh Dalton, all famous politicians in their day, did not greatly impress. An unknown junior Minister of Agriculture, one George Brown, later Foreign Secretary, was brilliant. Two, who sparkled as much as any visitors and left me with vivid memories of their double act, were the rogue Tory Bob Boothby and the Labour maverick Dick Crossman. At the end of one debate, Boothby rose and proclaimed in his deep, gravelly, whisky-sodden voice, 'I have an overwhelming sense of having won the argument.' Up got Crossman in his light, rather mocking style: 'Ah yes. But won it for whom? Won it for him? Or won it for me?' Crossman was a favourite for many Labour club members like me because he paid you the compliment of taking your arguments seriously, however juvenile, and destroying them mercilessly if they deserved it.

Although the Union had a reputation as the nursery of Prime Ministers, no ex-president or holder of any Union office in my time or since has been Prime Minister. Blair and Cameron went to Oxford, but were non-political and did not speak in the Union. Mrs Thatcher (then Margaret Roberts) was chair of the Conservative association in my first term but, as a reminder of how bigoted it still was less than seventy years ago, at the time women were barred from Union membership and this exclusion was assumed to be the natural order of things. When Michael Summerskill (who was instrumental in introducing me to Janice) proposed a motion that women should be allowed to join, it was considered a brave thing to do but the motion was defeated over-whelmingly. It was also held against him that he had taken the surname of his mother as a tribute to her lifelong feminism. It was not until January 1963 that the necessary two-thirds major-ity was obtained to admit women and even then attempts were made, mainly by irredentist life members, to blackball all women applicants. But they failed and the Union finally entered the modern world. I wonder how long it will be before we look back with similar astonishment at the discrimination against women that we still tolerate today, for example in their remuneration for similar work.

In my last year at Oxford I stood for the presidency against my Carthusian contemporary, William Rees-Mogg, who was also at Balliol, and Jeremy Thorpe, from Trinity College, Balliol's traditional rival. Jeremy was later an impressive leader of the Liberal Party from 1967 until 1976, when he had to resign after being charged with the murder of his lover, a former male model, Norman Scott, a charge of which he was acquitted. Jeremy was a brilliant speaker, a wonderfully funny mimic, a gifted violinist and the most unscrupulous of undergraduate politicians. Though canvassing was prohibited in the Union, he canvassed extensively. When he stood for the presidency of the university Liberal club, where canvassing was also prohibited, he persuaded one of his friends to canvass for his principal opponent who would then be disqualified if he won. In the event Jeremy won easily. All his machinations were carried out in a spirit of great ebullience, with no attempt at concealment. Just before the Union's presidential election in which he was standing against two Balliol men, someone asked the question: 'Is it true that the member from Trinity (i.e. Thorpe) is the best fiddler in the house?' His instant riposte: 'I will fiddle till Balliol burns.' Jeremy narrowly beat me and William came third. It was a disappointment (though shared, I later learned, by Harold Macmillan and Roy Jenkins, two other candidates who were narrowly defeated in their bids for the presidency). However, I decided not to stand again in order to concentrate on getting a good degree and in the next term William was elected. At the end of the summer, much to Jeremy's chagrin, it was William and I who were selected for the biennial debating tour of America organised by the International Institute for Education, following in the steps of Tony Benn, Sir Edward Boyle, later the most progressive Conservative Cabinet minister ever, and Robin Day. Jeremy, though much the best debater, was not considered 'a fit and proper person' by the selection committee.

For an exhilarating three months at the end of 1951, William and I performed as a duet in fifty-three colleges and universities in the USA, debating socialised medicine, the return of Churchill as Prime Minister, whether the sun had set on the British Commonwealth and whether the Communist Party should be outlawed. (Our answer: no). Except on Churchill we were on the same side. Our tour ended in the Massachusetts state penitentiary. We were told beforehand that this was an unusual prison, regarded by some as a country club where you had to have political influence to get in, and that inside were some of the ablest politicians in Boston – and others ought to be there, too. It was a great occasion, with posters plastered all over the prison showing a timorous professor with a mortar board on one side and a convict in a striped suit on the other, wielding a huge hammer with which he was about to silence the arguments of his opponent. After some of the debates on our tour, judges had evaluated the performances of the two teams and ruled who won. (They often applied a curious points system, based on logic, style, humour, presentation, persuasiveness, argumentation and gesture.) This was the only debate on our tour when they ruled we lost. One of our opponents was the most impressive speaker we had faced. He was a lawyer who could not resist signing someone else's name on a cheque.

Far removed from the atmosphere of the Union, with its officers attired in coat tails and white ties and its somewhat pretentious imitation of the formalities of the House of Commons, was my experience on a building site in Headington, near Oxford. During some summer vacations I would look for a job to earn money. In 1949, after my second year, I worked for four weeks as a cement and concrete mixer, earning a basic five pounds a week, plus a lot extra for overtime. That was then a very good wage. It was a glorious summer and I loved the job. I joined the Transport and General Workers' Union (TGWU) and for a while lived in a completely different world. As I cycled up to Headington in my working clothes or had fatty bacon, eggs and sausages in a transport café for breakfast or drank tea in the canteen, fellow workers would greet me, joke and pull my leg. It didn't matter that I was an 'undergrad', especially when they found out I was an enthusiastic member of the Labour Party. I spent two happy Friday evenings with my new friends in a pub, drinking whisky and chasers (pints of bitter) and ending up far from sober when I got back to my room in Balliol. One mate, Wee Jock, who became a particular friend, almost tempted me to stay and pursue a career in the TGWU. For four weeks I was an honorary member of the 'working class' and caught a brief glimpse of the feeling of the class solidarity that Richard Hoggart memorably described in *The Uses of Literacy*.[†]

After this very British, very privileged education, I am occasionally asked, 'Do you still feel Dutch?' I greatly admire the Netherlands as a well-run and civilised society. Its virtues are many and impressive: a long history of tolerance, although this

---

[†] In Lincoln I once mentioned my time as a building labourer and the news was passed on to a local journalist. When I was promoted to Minister of State at the Treasury in 1968, the *Lincolnshire Echo* congratulated me on my giddy rise from building site to the most powerful department of state.

is currently somewhat stretched by Muslim immigration; its contribution to the arts; and its social achievements. Holland has a high standard of living and education and is a much less unequal society than Britain with much better provision for its pensioners, disabled citizens and the unemployed. It shows much more compassion for the old by having legalised euthanasia with effective safeguards against abuse of the vulnerable. (Euthanasia is supported by over 85 per cent of Dutch doctors as well as the population as a whole.) It scores high in international comparisons of happiness, for what they are worth. I still speak fluent Dutch, if a very old-fashioned Dutch, the equivalent of the English spoken in old Pathé Pictorial newsreels. When I speak my quaint Dutch in shops in Holland, they look at me strangely as if I am a visitor from another planet or someone caught in a time warp. But admiration for the Netherlands does not answer the Tebbit question, 'Who do you cheer for in a test match?', or as one of my Dutch relatives asked me, 'Who do you support when England play Holland in the world cup?'

Football inspires the most passionate loyalties to club and country. While I like watching football, I feel no strong tribal loyalties and tend to support whichever team plays the more attractive football. In the 2010 world cup final between Holland and Spain, I supported Spain because the Dutch team, uncharacteristically, committed foul after foul and played disgracefully. I once failed to give a proper answer during one of my periodic lectures to American students about the differences between British and American politics, when I quoted an oft-cited comment to an American journalist by Alastair Campbell: 'We don't do God.' (That was before the issue of gay marriage came up in Parliament and before the right wing of the Conservative Party began to look more and more like the American Tea Party.) I then added that we do have our religion: football. Whereas American candidates for office all seem obliged to state which church they attend, most British politicians (even the women) declare on their election literature which football club they support. One student asked me, 'Which club do you support?' 'None,' I replied. 'So you are an atheist?'

National identity is, however, an intriguing issue, especially to right-wing parties obsessed with immigration. Europhobes often express the fear that closer ties with the European Union will make Britons lose their identity, though it won't of course change the French or the Germans or other beastly foreigners. I suppose if anything I feel British, but also a European and a cosmopolitan. But what is it to be 'British' or 'English' for that matter? Public opinion has changed. In 2001 an Ipsos MORI poll found, encouragingly, that 86 per cent of Britons disagreed with the statement that to be truly British you have to be white. In fact, the British and English are, like most nations, a mongrel breed and, it seems, always have been. At the time of the Norman conquest the English character 'was already, at this early stage, a robust mixture of Mediterranean, Celtic, Saxon, Roman, Jute, Angle, Danish and Norwegian'.[†]

To quote Daniel Defoe:

> Thus from a mixture of all kinds began
> That Het'rogenous thing, an Englishman…
> A true born Englishman's a Contradiction
> In Speech an Irony, in fact a Fiction.[‡]

[†] Winder, R., *Bloody Foreigners: The Story of Immigration to Britain* (London: Abacus, 2011), p. 28.

[‡] Quoted in Winder, *Bloody Foreigners*, p. 11.

Since the Norman conquest there have been many waves of different immigrants. First they came mainly from Flanders, Biscay, Genoa and Venice. There were a significant number of Jews, who were expelled at the end of the thirteenth century, later readmitted by Cromwell; then came Huguenots and German Protestants fleeing from Catholic persecution, the Dutch who accompanied William of Orange, more Germans who came over with the Hanoverians and of course there was the massive immigration of Irish in the nineteenth century, particularly after the potato famine. By 1861 there were over 600,000 Irish-born people in Britain and 5 per cent of the population of London was Irish and an even greater percentage in Manchester, Bradford, Paisley, Dundee and, above all, Liverpool.[†] Then came the post-war immigrations from the Commonwealth and different parts of Europe. They have all made Britain what it is today.

What could be a more British institution than the BBC, which can lay some claim to be the greatest British cultural invention of the twentieth century? Many of the most notable contributions to its post-war cultural influence were made by Jewish refugees from the Second World War. One became one of my dearest friends, Stephen Hearst, born Hirshtritt, who escaped from Austria before the war and came to England because he had watched Arsenal play in Vienna, which made him a lifelong Arsenal fan. He was responsible for some of the BBC's outstanding intellectual offerings such as *Civilisation* presented by Kenneth Clark, *The Glory that was Greece*, *The Grandeur that was Rome* and Alastair Cooke's *America*. You could never mention a good book on almost any subject that he had not read or a good film or

---

†   Winder, *Bloody Foreigners*, p. 11.

play that he had not seen. One of his friends arranged to meet him for dinner after not seeing him for years. Before he could sit down Stephen hailed him, 'Have you read the new biography of Wittgenstein?'

At a moving posthumous tribute to Stephen staged by the BBC, I learned how many of those responsible for the high cultural standards of the BBC were central European Jews. Many of them, including Stephen – all Hitler's bitterest enemies – were temporarily interned as 'enemy aliens' early in the war in an extraordinary display of ignorance and insensitivity by the Home Office. At least the discomforts of internment were partly offset by the distinction of their fellow internees. At one stage Stephen was in a tent next to three members of the Amadeus quartet and he was briefly in Reading jail, he recalled, with half of the future Arts Council.

I would not argue that any reference to national characteristics is meaningless. But even then the characteristics we select are gener-ally chosen on a very subjective basis. Winder quotes John Betjeman: 'For me England stands for the Church of England ... Women's Institutes, modest village inns ... creeper-clad wardens's cottages, rusty croquet hoops on rectory lawns, swinging inn-signs...' etc. Winder observes that the important words are 'for me'.

For me, a number of cultural differences between the British and the Dutch stand out. The Dutch value privacy less than the British do. They are much more sociable and are more likely to do things, like going on holiday, in groups. When during vaca-tions from Oxford I befriended a number of Leiden students, I learned that after a period of 'greening' (as also undergone in American fraternities) which involved humiliating freshmen in unpleasant initiation ceremonies, students would divide into 'year clubs' and would be expected to spend most of their time at university with fellow year club members. I gathered that if a year club member isolated himself from his colleagues for a while, perhaps to read intensively or just to be alone, this would be considered anti-social. Curtains are not drawn in the windows in Dutch streets because, it seems, everyone has a right to see the inside of people's homes. I value privacy very highly. The Dutch tend to be straightforward, despise hypocrisy and like to think that what you see is what you get, all admirable qualities, although their directness can sometimes lead to rudeness. I have come to value the traditional English understatement and a certain reserve, accompanied by an element of surprise when hidden talents, interests or virtues are almost reluctantly revealed. The Dutch are much tidier and orderly. I remember an article by a Frenchman in an English paper about English fashion (not my normal reading) explaining why English designers were internationally so successful. It said, in effect: we, the French, dress very well and generally follow fashion. You dress very badly, but anything goes and the result of this chaos is a creativity we often lack. Similarly, by comparison with the Dutch, English life is more disorderly, but can have the advantage of generating an attractive eccentricity.

I came across a good example of the Dutch preference for the direct rather than the tactful or diplomatic approach when in 1979 I was part of a small international committee appointed by Roy Jenkins, then President of the European Commission, to review the workings of the commission itself and recommend reforms. There were five of us, but the Italian member was a senator in the process of being re-elected and seldom turned up. A very nice German trade unionist contributed very little and three of us did the real work: a very impressive Frenchman, Paul Delouvrier, Head of Électricité de France and formerly Governor of Algiers, me and a splendid Dutch chairman, Dirk Spierenburg, a former ambassador to the European Community.[†] We heard evidence from all the commissioners, including one of the two German ones, Guido Brunner, who told us that in the commission all was for the best in the best of all possible worlds. At the end of his evidence Spierenburg said, 'Thank you for giving evidence, Herr Brunner. Of course you can't expect us to believe a word. Everyone knows the Commission is in a mess. Excuse me for being tactless, but eight years as ambassador in Brussels would make anyone tactless.' That was not true. He was blunt and tactless because he was Dutch.

Many people have found difficulties in being nationally or ethnically stereotyped. Tony Judt in his deathbed essays *Memory Chalet* (Heinemann, 2010) discusses what it means to be Jewish if you are not religious and disapprove of the Israeli government. He concluded he was a non-Jewish Jew. Jonathan Miller in *Beyond the Fringe* observed that he was not really a Jew, just Jew-ish.

My Dutch origins have never been the slightest handicap when people knew or found out I was born Dutch, not even in politics. When I was up for selection as a parliamentary candidate before the management committee of the Lincoln Labour Party in 1962, I told them about my Dutch origins and added that I thought they were irrelevant because I was an internationalist. They still selected me. Because the occasion was an important by-election, I also mentioned my foreign birth to Percy Clark,

† At the same time another commission had been appointed to look at the future of the European institutions as a whole. They were known as 'Les Trois Sages' while we were known as 'Les Petits Sages'.

the Labour Party's National Head of Public Relations. (This by-election was in 1962 and is not to be confused with the more notorious 1973 by-election in which I fought as an independent – see Chapter 7). He was much relieved to find I was born a Dutchman as Lincolnshire had a lot of historical ties with the Dutch. After I defeated Labour (as well as the Conservatives) in my second by-election, one traditionalist Labour MP, Joe Ashton, complained that the party should have made a big issue of the fact that I was really a Dutchman (and also that I owned a catamaran!). His comments were ignored, or condemned. He had earlier predicted that Labour would win.[†]

I suppose it might be partly because of my Dutch background and peripatetic youth that I am pro-EU and an internationalist, but then many of my friends who are British born and bred have similar views. In fact since, according to Defoe, an Englishman – and the same can clearly be said of a Briton – is such a 'heterogeneous thing', I have decided that perhaps after all I am a true Brit. Of course one cannot ignore the influence of birth and early upbringing but I believe that my education at Charterhouse and especially Oxford were a greater influence on my values and attitudes to life than my tribal origins.

[†]   As a very much 'Old Labour' politician, he once told me there could never be a woman Prime Minister because all the important decisions were made in smoke-filled rooms, which were no place for women.

CHAPTER 3

THE LAW

Halfway through my time at Oxford, I decided that after finals I would read for the Bar. I liked arguing, the law and justice are an important part of politics and I envisaged that, in time, after establishing myself at the Bar, I would try to take up politics seriously. I practised as a barrister for eleven years, twelve including my year of pupillage, though as a pupil I earned virtually nothing from the law. The first years were years of famine; they later became years of relative feast.

After returning from the Union debating tour of America in 1952, I had to learn enough law to pass the Bar exams so I started a correspondence course. At the same time I looked for temporary jobs to combine with my studies. The first was teaching Latin at Belmont Mill Hill Junior School, a job that also provided me with accommodation. It was a lovely summer and I played a lot of cricket, went to lots of parties given by Oxford friends who now worked in London, thoroughly enjoyed teaching the boys – and learned very little law. While there I was awarded two law scholarships on the basis of my Oxford degree: an Eldon scholarship from Oxford and a Harmsworth scholarship from the Middle Temple, which eased my financial problems. Each paid £200 a year for three years.

After one term as a teacher, I decided I must find a less distract-
ing occupation and took up residence in cheap digs in London,
working for a year for Securicor as a night guard in a firm in
Hammersmith, Froys, that sold hearths, baths and lavatories,
and later guarding a chemical works in London's Limehouse.[†]
This time I did pursue my studies and did so full time for the last
six months before the exam, living on my scholarship income.

In January 1954 I passed my exams and was called to the Bar.
I was then awarded a Blackstone scholarship, which paid my
pupil fees, but my only legal earnings during pupillage were the
occasional two guinea briefs to take notes at inquests or defend
someone on a charge of careless driving. After pupillage, briefs
still came in very slowly. Nevertheless, despite protestations from
my clerk (and misgivings from my parents) Janice and I were
married in 1955. We found a tiny rent-controlled flat above the
bookshops in the Charing Cross Road owned by Improved
Industrial Dwellings, for which we paid rent of a guinea a week.
It had a very small bedroom, kitchen, living room and toilet but
no bathroom. We washed in the kitchen or went to public baths
nearby and, when invited to dinner by friends, we would ask
if we could come early and first have a bath. We lived on my
scholarships and a grant of £300 a year awarded to Janice by
the medical research council to study for a PhD at the London
School of Tropical Medicine and Hygiene. Our first luxury
was a refrigerator, when our very first Sunday roast went bad
in a heatwave; our second was a radio. We also both walked to

---

†   Many years later, in 1971 when I was an MP, I was approached about joining
     the board of Securicor (now part of G4S). I refused, because the company
     wanted me to represent their interests in Parliament, but they were intrigued
     to learn I had once been one of their guards.

work, when it was not raining, and collected the three-penny bits thus saved on bus fares. Later we spent them on another luxury: two beautiful Chinese watercolours that we bought for £5 in a Communist bookshop opposite the British Museum.

I gradually supplemented our meagre income in a number of ways. I lectured on law on Saturday mornings to detainees in an army glass house in Colchester. Rather than boring them about the duties of the good citizen, as I was supposed to do, I provided them with some light relief by recounting details of some of the more gory criminal cases. Some evenings I lectured on international affairs to a Workers' Educational Association class. This was an unusual way for young barristers to supplement their income, but by chance it later helped me to be selected as a parliamentary candidate (see Chapter 4). I also wrote and delivered talks for BBC radio, mainly in the form of a 'Letter from London' on the European Service. One was a light-hearted description of my WEA class, to illustrate how penniless young barristers kept alive in their early days at the Bar. A solicitor from a firm in Gravesend called Church, Bruce and Hawkes, happened to hear the talk and was moved to send me a brief in the local county court. They became one of my best early clients. For a few years I was a regular performer in the Gravesend county court and won all but one of the cases they sent me, which was, alas, not true of my practice generally.

The Bar and the Bench have changed since I practised, mostly for the better. I gather those who qualify nowadays may have difficulty finding chambers but, when they do, they are paid a basic salary as pupils from the earnings of other members of their chambers. In my day the Bar was a very conservative institution, in every sense. A special dress code, black coat, pin-striped trousers, bowler hat and umbrella, was de rigueur. I refused to wear a bowler. Every evening as I left my first chambers, the clerk would say, 'Goodnight, sir. Got your briefcase, your umbrella and your hat? Oh no, of course, you don't wear a hat.'

My chambers specialised partly in commercial law, mainly shipping law, and partly in tax. Tax did not attract me and I hoped to base my legal career on commercial and mainly shipping law. There was little small-scale work for a young barrister, who might well take four or even more years to establish a practice. I thought I might try to get some work during the lean years by joining one of the 'circuits' into which the bar's criminal practices were divided. Because I knew a solicitor in Oxford I applied to the Oxford circuit, hoping he might send me some work. This meant an interview with a senior QC whom I had to convince that I was the right sort of chap. He asked me two questions: which school and which college did I go to? 'Charterhouse and Balliol.' 'Well,' he said, 'I don't think there is anything I can tell you about the standards of the circuit which a good school and a good college won't have taught you.' I was in. I paid one fruitless visit to the Oxford circuit court, did not fancy the criminal law and never visited the circuit again.

Another example of legal conservatism concerned Gerald Gardiner, the most distinguished QC of his day. He was a gentle and humane man, utterly without self-importance, who later became an outstanding Lord Chancellor in Harold Wilson's first Labour administration. Before his appointment, law reform traditionally proceeded at a very stately pace, if at all. When the Labour MP Leo Abse introduced some modest reforms of the divorce laws, he apologised to the House of Commons for introducing a Bill recommended by a Royal Commission report 'on which the dust has been allowed to settle for a mere twenty-five years', whereas Lord Gardiner introduced a host of law reform Bills based on recommendations from the Law Commission, often within six months or less of their publication. He was the most progressive Lord Chancellor one could hope for – except when it came to reform of the legal profession.

A rather unconventional and talented young woman barrister called Nemone Lethbridge met an ex-prisoner called O'Connor who had been convicted of a murder that he almost certainly did not commit. (Someone else confessed to the murder on his deathbed but died before he could swear an affidavit that would have led to a review of O'Connor's case.) They fell in love and married secretly but, when the marriage became public, she was expelled from her chambers. Subsequently, sometime between 1962 and 1964, at a party I attended after I had been elected to Parliament but before Labour became the government, she met Gerald Gardiner. He listened so sympathetically to her tale of woe that her hopes were raised and she asked if she could possibly join his chambers. He replied that regrettably his chambers did not take women.

Political prejudice was rife. However, in retrospect it was political prejudice that saved me from a very dull and much more conventional career. In 1958, because I had little work, I did some 'devilling' (preparatory work) for a barrister, a most able man called Henry Brandon, later a Lord of Appeal, in another set of chambers specialising in shipping law. He liked my work and invited me to join his chambers, which had much more work than mine. I was delighted, but told him that perhaps he should know that I had just been adopted as a Labour candidate for Parliament in Putney. Very apologetically, he explained that while he himself could not care less, the head of chambers, Roland Adams QC, would never admit someone who was a member of the Labour Party, let alone a Labour candidate.

What would have happened if I had been accepted? Many barristers who started with political ambitions found the demands of a successful practice overwhelming and abandoned their hopes for a political career. I would probably have spent my professional life interpreting charter parties and bills of lading or having to argue which of two large companies had been the least businesslike in its correspondence.

Another example of the Bar's resistance to change was the reform of jury trials. In 1966, when I was appointed Parliamentary Under-Secretary at the Home Office, one of the first questions the Home Secretary, Roy Jenkins, asked me was whether we should introduce majority verdicts for juries. The judges and the police, he said, were in favour, because in several very important recent cases well-heeled criminals had managed to bribe or threaten one or two jurors and secure a hung jury. However the Bar was bitterly opposed. As majority verdicts in Scotland and in magistrates's courts did not appear to cause glaring miscarriages of justice, I strongly supported reform and majority verdicts were duly introduced. The Bar announced that the sky would fall, that this would be the end of justice as we knew it.

Many years later, during the late 1970s and early 1980s, I used to chair a radio programme on Radio 4 called *You the Jury*, in which a proposition was tried before a jury. Two advocates briefly stated their case, called two witnesses, who put their case and were then cross-examined, and the jury voted. One programme was about the merits of trial by jury. The champion of jury trials was the then chairman of the Criminal Bar, Richard

Du Cann. He won easily. Afterwards I asked him what he and the Bar generally thought about the introduction of majority verdicts: 'Best thing that ever happened.'

After five frustrating years I decided either to change my career to one in television or find new chambers. I had started to do some part-time work in television, chairing a book programme called *Bookstand* and presenting an educational programme on current affairs for schools. Stephen Hearst was the producer of *Bookstand* and the scriptwriter who adapted excerpts from books for dramatic presentation was Dennis Potter, later one of our best television playwrights. Stephen insisted that the programme should not be one for the elite and become a sort of literary *Brains Trust*. We were beginning to appeal to a wider audience when after a year *Bookstand* was scrapped because the BBC high-ups felt it was not highbrow enough, a strange criticism of a programme produced by the arch-highbrow Hearst.

It seemed that a career in television beckoned. But it so happened that a set of chambers headed by Dingle Foot QC, an ex-Liberal turned Labour MP and brother of Michael Foot, was looking for a new tenant. The chambers specialised in Commonwealth law, a much more interesting field than commercial law. My Labour sympathies would be an advantage instead of a handicap so I applied and was accepted. In my new chambers my practice flourished almost overnight.

I had once heard Dingle Foot speak at an Oxford meeting when I was an undergraduate and he was a Liberal MP. All I recall was that he described the Liberal party as 'the Third Programme of British politics' (the predecessor of Radio 3). As a QC, Dingle Foot had represented nearly every African nationalist leader imprisoned by the British in colonial days, and after independence he regularly appeared for opposition leaders imprisoned by his former clients. I was Dingle's junior on many of his cases, mostly appeals in London before the Privy Council, the ultimate appeal court in the Commonwealth in those days, but occasionally cases tried in Africa. Dingle was eloquent, passionate about liberty, completely uninterested in social or economic issues, impersonal, absent-minded and an alcoholic. In many African countries he was a celebrity, because many political battles were fought out in the courts and Dingle was the star performer. One of the cases in which I was his junior was tried in Lagos, where he would be hailed in the street with a cry of 'Hey, there's Dingle Foot', and a crowd would gather as if he was a pop star or famous footballer. He hated change and always stayed in the same, often rather scruffy hotels. The manager would meet him on his arrival and say, 'Welcome back Mr Foot. Your pyjamas are already on your bed and your shoes are still in the cupboard.'

During one of several visits to Lagos, he invited some visiting African politicians to dinner, greatly to my benefit because Dingle, as often happened, drank a lot and went to sleep and I was left to entertain them. I became very friendly with an ANC representative whose name, alas, I no longer remember, but he was one of those people you instantly recognise as a soulmate. He was originally a sports journalist and turned out to be far more interested in sport than politics. I asked him about a famous former Oxford cricket and rugby blue and South African test cricketer, Clive van Ryneveld, then a South African Member of Parliament for Helen Suzman's United Party, which later became the Progressive Party. What was he like as a politician? He didn't think much of him, but then his eyes lit up and he described with great animation how he had seen him flight his leg breaks, or jinx his way through the rugby field.

During dinner we got talking to a friendly waiter who invited us to visit him and his friends in one of the Lagos compounds where he lived. We accepted and, as honoured guests, had the time of our lives. Our host's friends, a group of young Nigerians from every humble walk of life, waiters and shop girls and workers on building sites, engaged in animated, heated political argument about the different parties in Nigeria and their prospects. Politics was all they wanted to talk about. This was in 1961 just after independence, some time before the Biafran war, when Nigeria's democracy flourished under the benign premiership of Sir Abubakar Tafawa Balewa and Nigeria was seen as the most promising of the newly independent countries in Africa. We danced to 'Ghana music', then much in fashion, and when I revealed that I was a supporter of the Labour leader, Hugh Gaitskell, whom they all knew about, they did a little shuffle dance chanting in unison: 'Gaitskell – Labour Party, Gaitskell – Labour Party' (with the emphasis on the last syllable). It was the highlight of my visits to Nigeria.

Dingle told many anecdotes about his African experiences. One of the best was about the time in Kenya when he defended some of the leading Mau Mau suspects. One day his instructing solicitor invited him into the enclosure of the Nairobi racecourse and on the way in an African whispered to him the name of a horse. His host showed him the race card and recommended a particular horse. Dingle declined and backed the horse the African recommended. It won. In the second race his host, with some hesitation, suggested another horse, but Dingle saw that

a horse was running called Ipswich, the town where his wife
was born and which he later represented as MP. So he backed
Ipswich, which also won. For the third race his host made no
recommendation and by now other punters, who had resented
this defender of terrorists in their midst, waited with bated
breath to see which horse Dingle would back this time. There
was a horse called Trial and Error, an eminently suitable choice,
he thought, for the business on which he was engaged. Trial
and Error won. The verdict of the white settlers was that the
man might be a dangerous Communist but, by God, he knew
his horseflesh.

Dingle could be indefensibly casual in preparing a big case
for which he was paid a large fee. But if there was an *in forma
pauperis* (unpaid) appeal to the Privy Council on behalf of some
tribesman from Borneo convicted of murder, he would spare
no effort. I would look at the case and tell him I could find
no possible grounds on which we could succeed. He would
reply that we had to find something as the man had been
condemned to death. And he would find some plausible argument, after working all night without drinking, and argue it
brilliantly, even though we usually failed in the end. Those sorts
of cases would be some of the most upsetting experiences of
life at the Bar.

Someone once told me that, at the beginning of a drinks
party he attended, he had talked to one of the most fascinating
and delightful people he had ever met. Towards the end of the
party he had encountered one of the most boring and rudest
people he had ever met. They were both Dingle Foot. In fact,
Dingle was never intentionally rude – he would merely forget
whom he had talked to earlier and in time alcohol would take

its toll. He died in 1978, choking on a sandwich in the famous Mandarin Hotel in Hong Kong. It so happened that Janice and I were staying in that hotel that same day on a visit to China, but we did not know he was there, too, or hear the news until after we returned home.

Of the cases in which I was involved in my new chambers, I remember two with particular pleasure.

One was an important constitutional case.[†] Exasperated by the autocratic behaviour of Mrs Bandaranaike, the Prime Minister of Ceylon (now Sri Lanka), prominent members of the Ceylonese establishment – senior policemen, lawyers, former test cricketers among them – sought to overthrow the government and start a coup by arresting a key minister. The plot misfired and the conspirators were themselves arrested. The government majority in the legislature then passed a law which created a new offence – conspiracy to arrest a minister – for which the penalty was death and confiscation of all the defendants' property (a provision without precedent) and it also provided that the trial of the named defendants would be without a jury, and that when the trial was over the law would cease to have effect. The defendants were duly convicted. Noel Gratiaen, a former Attorney-General of Ceylon who was a member of our chambers, and I were briefed for their appeal to the Privy Council. The only possible ground for appeal was not on the facts, which could not be disputed, but that the law under which they had been convicted was invalid.

However, under Commonwealth constitutional law at the time a sovereign Parliament was supreme and its laws could

---

† *Liyanage and others v. The Queen* [1965] UKPC 1.

not be challenged if the proper procedure was followed. This law had been passed under the proper procedures. There was no doctrine of natural law we could appeal to. Nothing under Roman-Dutch law, sometimes applicable in Ceylon, could help. In the end the argument that prevailed was based on the separation of powers between the executive, the legislature and the judiciary in the written Ceylon constitution. The act of the Ceylonese Parliament under which our clients were convicted applied only to named individuals, imposed penalties on them and on no one else, by a mode of trial that applied only to them. It was therefore not a law, we argued, because laws are general, but was a judicial act, and was therefore *ultra vires*. Under the constitution, only the judiciary, not the legislature, had the power to decide particular cases. We had a very sympathetic hearing from a court determined to find in our favour if they could, and we won. As far as I am aware (and I am no longer up to date in legal developments) it must be one of the few cases of a law duly passed by a Commonwealth Parliament being declared illegal. I might add that among the Ceylonese community in London there were many friends and relatives of the accused, and Noel Gratiaen and I were widely and generously feted after our victory.

The other case also involved high politics, in both senses. I had become friendly with David Astor, a shy, wonderful man of high principle and a champion of liberal causes, who was editor of *The Observer* from 1948 until 1975. Sometime in the mid-1960s he asked if I would advise the Maharaja of Sikkim, who had recently succeeded to the throne, on his relations with the Indian government. Sikkim was then a kingdom, nestling in the heart of the Himalayas. The Maharaja was unhappy with the treaty between Sikkim and India signed in 1950 after Indian independence, which made Sikkim an Indian protectorate, and he wanted pro bono legal advice as to whether there might be grounds for revoking the treaty. I duly met the Maharaja and his sister and wife at a flat in Ambrosden Avenue in London. His full title was Muwong Padma Bhushan Sri Panch Chempo Palden Thondup Namgyal, Maharaja Chogyal [king] of Sikkim, formally addressed as 'Chogyal'; his sister was Princess Pema and his wife was called Hope. The Chogyal had married Hope Cooke in 1963, a 22-year-old American socialite who was a graduate of Sarah Lawrence College, a highly rated progressive college in Bronxville, New York. The marriage had brought worldwide media attention to Sikkim.

What I vividly remember was the discussion at our second meeting when I gave him my legal Opinion, the gist of which was, as far as I recall, that there was no explicit time limit in the treaty, but its terms implied that it could be ended with due notice. I made a comment that the politics might be difficult. This he confirmed, saying that the Indians would bribe the assembly to reject any such initiative. At this stage the two ladies intervened, egging him on. 'But can't we pay them more?' they whispered, the traditional way in which women apparently addressed the Chogyal. Their message was: 'Be a man Charles.' He replied that the Indians could always pay even more.

They decided to study my Opinion and take it back to Sikkim. But what if they were searched by the Indian customs? Here Princess Pema intervened. 'I will print your Opinion on rice paper and eat it if the customs search me.' Never having had any of my written work eaten, I was disappointed to learn later that it never was.

In the end the Chogyal took no action. In 1975 the people of

Sikkim voted in a referendum for union with India, by a majority of 97 per cent to 3 per cent, and he was deposed. He was divorced from Hope in 1980 and died in America in 1982. I have two mementos from our meeting: a beautiful engraved silver spoon he gave me and a fulsome letter of congratulation he wrote me on my by-election victory as an independent in Lincoln in 1973, news of which had somehow reached the Himalayas. He had also invited Janice and me to visit him in his palace in Gangtok and I often wish we had.

In 1966 I had to leave the Bar because I was appointed a minister. I left it with no regrets, partly because in the first phase of my legal career I had had too little work, while in the second I had too much. My experience was very different from that of my contemporaries. In the early days, a group of friends used to lunch at a communal table in the Middle Temple and discuss politics, plays and films we had seen, and books we had read. Then those whose practice began to flourish would mainly discuss their cases. Eventually they would buy a house in the country or suburbs and talk about their roses. I was gradually left behind.

Later on, when my practice took off, not only was legal work increasingly time-consuming, but in 1962 I had become an MP. I had to work harder than I vowed I would ever do again. I would often have to get up at 4 a.m. to read briefs and prepare my cases. On Friday evenings I would collapse into my seat in the train to my constituency, which provided me with two and a half hours of peace and sleep. Sometimes, like Dingle Foot, but for a different reason, I would fall asleep in the middle of supper while entertaining friends.

In 1965, eleven years after being called to the Bar, I applied for silk and became a very young Queen's Counsel. The application has to be approved by a committee of senior judges, but I was in an advantageous position because my practice had involved regular appearances before the Privy Council on which the Law Lords sat, and two of them were my sponsors. In fact I applied much earlier than I would have done if my aim had still been a legal career, because taking silk is likely, at least for a time, to reduce a barrister's workload (and therefore income). Owing to an odd rule at the Bar, a Queen's Counsel could only appear in court with a junior, who prepared the early stages of the case and who was paid two-thirds of the fee paid to the QC. Hence QCs were expensive and were only briefed in major cases. New QCs often had a difficult time. I practised as one for less than a year until I was made a minister and the pressure of legal work duly decreased, but it was still close to intolerable.

My dual career had another disadvantage: it did not allow time to be an effective MP. It is a common complaint about the present House of Commons that MPs nowadays are all professional politicians, with little experience of life outside politics. There is much in this criticism, but there are also good arguments against an MP pursuing a second career once elected. Effective MPs specialise, consult experts and learn from events in other countries. I did go on some foreign visits, but had to refuse many others because of legal commitments. Apart from the law, my main interests were Britain's relationship with the European Community and defence. However my law practice limited the number of major debates on these subjects that I could take part in and I was a less effective MP than I might have been.

Another reason for welcoming a change of occupation was that I had some reservations about spending my life as a barrister. There is much to be said in favour of the legal profession: it makes an essential contribution to democracy and to a civilised society. The rule of law is a cornerstone of both. Something about a legal training makes lawyers show some respect for human rights in the most unexpected places. Even at the height of Stalin's tyranny, some Soviet lawyers argued that the accused should have some inkling of the charges against them and have the right to be represented. Joel Joffe's account of the Rivonia trial of Nelson Mandela and his colleagues in South Africa describes how the judge, Mr Justice de Wet, as confirmed a racist supporter of the regime as one could find at a time when apartheid was at its worst, occasionally paid some attention to evidence and even sometimes ruled in favour of a point made on behalf of the defendants.[†] As an aside, de Wet is Afrikaans (or Dutch) for 'the law', so the judge was somewhat inappropriately named. (At the time of writing, the surname of the last Lord Chief Justice in England is Judge.)

I regard today's judiciary as a generally humane and enlightened body. When politicians express outrage that unelected judges can exercise discretion and decide issues which politicians feel should be the prerogative of Parliament, I would rather place my trust in judges, who have generally become more liberal over the years, while in their attitudes to crime politicians have become more reactionary. When I was a Home Office minister from 1966 to 1968 and Roy Jenkins was Home Secretary, we made every effort to stop reactionary judges sending people to jail who need not be there. We passed one major criminal justice act which introduced suspended sentences; we created a parole

---

[†] Joffe, J., *The State vs. Nelson Mandela* (Oxford: One World, 2007).

board and initiated a number of other measures to reduce the numbers of people held in jail. We were deeply concerned that the prison population was then about 55,000. When Michael Howard was Home Secretary in 1993 he announced that 'prison works' and under the Conservatives the number of prisoners duly rose. The same happened during the Labour governments of 1997 to 2010. They introduced a stream of Criminal Justice Acts that created over 500 new criminal offences and provided for longer sentences, some of them mandatory. Politicians have allowed the tabloids, not evidence, to dictate their policies and have pandered to the public's demand for prison sentences instead of arguing the case against it. As a result, the prison population is now approaching 90,000, by far the highest per head of any EU country. Sending people to prison is also very expensive. In the US it has been noted that it costs more to send someone to jail than to Yale. In Britain a place in an institute for young offenders costs more than a place at Eton.

At one time, the coalition government of 2010 promised a new regime by appointing the liberal-minded Ken Clarke as Lord Chancellor and Secretary of State for Justice. Clarke produced a Green Paper, with full Cabinet support, that aimed to reduce the prison population by over 3,000. However, at the first whiff of grapeshot from the tabloid press, the Prime Minister David Cameron surrendered, abandoned the core of the Green Paper, which he had himself approved, and turned his back on the man whom the tabloids described as 'the paedophile's pal'.

Many barristers find their career wholly satisfying and make the world a better place, championing civil rights, defending liberty, improving constitutional law and doing many other kinds of valuable legal work. Moreover society would not function properly if commercial lawyers did not slave away on their complex briefs, and justice would suffer if criminal lawyers were not prepared to defend those who seem, and may well be, guilty. At the Bar the system requires you not to pick and choose your briefs. This is a defensible rule because otherwise less reputable clients, who still deserve to have their case properly argued, would be represented by less reputable barristers. I should add that when I became a member of the House of Lords I was immensely impressed by the contributions on legal, civil rights and constitutional issues by peers who had been former judges or were leading practitioners at the Bar. They are, almost without exception, eloquent, lucid and liberal-minded.

Nevertheless I personally did not find the law a wholly satisfying career when 50 per cent of the time most practitioners are likely to be on the side that ought to win and 50 per cent on the side that ought to lose. Barristers in the heat of litigation easily persuade themselves that theirs is the case with right on its side. In fact the more successful you are, the more likely it is that you will be briefed by those with money, who pay higher fees, and who would not necessarily be clients you would like to work for.

Furthermore, there is something wrong with our legal system when to fight a civil case you have to be a plutocrat or a pauper or resort to the 'no win, no fee' procedure that has led to widespread injustice and dissatisfaction. Expenditure on legal aid has soared, yet the conditions to qualify for aid have become ever more restrictive. Every attempt to reduce costs seems to fail because lawyers have defeated any proposal that they perceive threatens their interests or even slightly detracts from what they regard as our Rolls-Royce system, however costly and time-consuming. I suspect reform will continue to be frustrated while

most lawyers are paid on the taxi-meter principle, by the time
they spend in court or in preparation, providing an often irresistible, if unconscious, temptation to make work more complicated
and long-drawn out. This is the reason why litigation costs can
be out of all proportion to the value of the dispute, and not infre-
quently exceed it several times over. Lawyers are not, of course,
unique in equating public good with their own interests or in
their reluctance to accept change in a system in which they were
brought up. But they have been particularly effective advocates
of their own case. To quote from Simon Jenkins in *The Guardian*:

> A former Lord Chancellor, Lord Havers, said that he only once
> voted against his party. It was on a matter so serious, so immoral,
> so damaging to the national interest that he had 'no option'.
> That matter was the attempt by the Thatcher government to
> end the barristers' monopoly in the high court... He fought and
> was successful.

One further reason why I welcomed a change of career was that
sometimes the intricacies of the law can be boring. The arena
of politics and government appealed to me more. So when I
had to leave the temple for Whitehall because I was appointed a
minister, and could concentrate on one career not two, moreover
with a chance of influencing the governance of the nation, my
heart leapt with joy.

CHAPTER 4

THE ROAD TO WESTMINSTER

Looking for a seat and becoming an MP can be a long-drawn-out and frustrating quest. One friend, Neville Sandelson, stood unsuccessfully as a Labour candidate in five general elections and two by-elections from 1950 onwards, until he was finally elected in a by-election in 1971. By that time, he once told me, his views had become Conservative.† Betty Boothroyd, the former Speaker and now Baroness Boothroyd, contested two by-elections, her first in 1957, and two general elections, finally breaking and entering in 1973. Some are lucky, like Tony Blair who was adopted at the age of thirty for a safe Labour seat at the last minute before the 1983 election. I, too, was lucky, selected as a candidate in the 1959 general election and then elected MP for Lincoln in 1962 at the age of thirty-three, without ever actively looking for a seat.

It all started one morning in November 1958 with a chance meeting in Fleet Street with my friend Bill Rodgers from Oxford University Labour Club days, who was then secretary of the Fabian society. Bill told me that Putney, an interesting constituency, had started the process of selection. One of the wards was

---

† He joined the SDP in 1981, lost his seat in 1983 and then rejoined the Labour Party in 1996.

holding a panel discussion for four would-be candidates in two days' time and, as one of them had dropped out, he had been asked to suggest a last-minute replacement. Was I interested? I had been a reasonably active party member, mainly as one of the organisers of an informal group of graduates called 'The Group'[†] that met regularly to discuss policy, often at my flat. I accepted the challenge.

The panel proceedings went well. Foreign affairs was the issue of the moment – Harold Macmillan had just sent British troops into Jordan to protect King Hussain against Nasser – and one of my recent lectures to the Workers' Educational Association had been an analysis of the conflicts in the Middle East. So I was temporarily well-informed. Nominated by the ward, then short-listed for the full selection conference, I was lucky again. As was usual in the Labour Party, left and right were at war. The favourite in Putney was a passionate left-winger, a young woman called Anne Clark[‡] who had just become a London county councillor for Wandsworth. Unbeknown to me, the party agent and other local Gaitskellites had identified me as the best bet for keeping Anne Clark out. They prepared two or three difficult questions to be put to the candidates, including one as to whether Britain should join the Common Market, which in 1958 hardly anyone in Britain had heard about, let alone thought about what our policy should be. My views were clear: strongly in favour of our active membership, seeing a European union as the most constructive and hopeful world development since the war. A

---

†   See a monograph by Michael Summerskill and Brian Brivati, *The Group: 1954–60 – A Time of Hope*.

‡   She later married another left-winger and became MP for Chatham as Anne Kerr.

group of nations had decided to bury past differences, acting not as nationalist rivals but together for the common good. It also seemed to me that in the future, Britain's influence in the world would be most effectively exercised as part of the European Community. As the agent hoped, Anne Clark floundered and, quite unexpectedly, I was selected.

I did not win. Putney was then a safe Conservative seat and, in the 1959 general election, the Conservatives led by Harold Macmillan inconsiderately increased their majority to 107 seats. But against the national trend I reduced the Conservative majority from some 7,000 to 5,000, a result which appeared much better than it was because new council estates had brought in a lot of new, largely Labour, voters.

As I was deeply involved in the struggle for the soul of the Labour Party, it is worth recalling what divided the party in those days. It was originally as much a personal conflict, Gaitskell versus Bevan, as an ideological one, and duly became a battle between two very different views about domestic and foreign policy. Hugh Gaitskell had been elected to Parliament in 1945 and gradually established himself as the dominant figure of the 1945 intake, through his ability, application and the loyalty he won from colleagues. He was not the first of that intake to join the Attlee Cabinet: Harold Wilson was appointed President of the Board of Trade in 1947 aged thirty-one – the youngest member of the Cabinet in the twentieth century. However Gaitskell demonstrated his exceptional qualities as Minister of Fuel and Power and succeeded Sir Stafford Cripps as Chancellor of the Exchequer after Cripps became fatally ill in 1950.

At first there was no particular animosity between Gaitskell and Bevan, leaders of the right and left of the party, certainly not on

Gaitskell's part who understood the respect Bevan commanded in the Labour movement as the architect of the National Health Service. He wrote in his diary: 'He is so much the best debater; so much the best speaker on the front bench, indeed in the House, that he can always raise his prestige by his performance.' They enjoyed congenial dinners after arguments in Cabinet committees. Bevan stayed cool: 'He's nothing, nothing, nothing,' he once told Strachey.[†] When Gaitskell was appointed Chancellor, Bevan resented the fact. He had hoped to succeed Cripps and also felt that Gaitskell was disqualified for the party leadership as an alien invader from a distant class. In fact, the trade unions and their leaders, especially the miners, were among Gaitskell's strongest supporters. In 1954, when Bevan and Gaitskell both competed to become party treasurer, Bevan asked Sam Watson, leader of the Durham miners, 'How can you support a schoolboy from Winchester against a man born in the back streets of Tredegar?'

In 1951, personal animosity became a conflict of policy during Gaitskell's chancellorship. North Korea had invaded South Korea and there were widespread fears that this invasion was the start of a general military aggression by the Soviet bloc. Gaitskell, a strong supporter of the Western alliance, produced a draconian Budget to pay for a major rearmament programme, including tax increases and charges for teeth and spectacles. Bevan and his supporters opposed the heavy increases in taxation and the extra defence expenditure but also regarded charges for NHS services as a breach of the sacrosanct principle of a free health service. Bevan threatened to resign.

[†]   Brivati, B., *Hugh Gaitskell* (London: Richard Cohen, 1996), p. 116. Brivati's biography is one of two excellent accounts of Gaitskell; the other most impressive is by Philip Williams (London: Cape, 1979).

In fact, several of Gaitskell's colleagues, including Attlee, urged him to compromise and Bevan appealed to Hugh Dalton, Gaitskell's close friend: 'If it is such a small thing why not give way? The compensation for giving way would be me. Is that a very small thing?'[†] But Gaitskell, always a stubborn man, also thought a principle was at stake: halting the seemingly irresistible rise in the costs of the NHS for which Bevan seemed to want a blank cheque. In the end Gaitskell won Attlee's approval, the charges were included in the Budget and Bevan resigned, followed by Harold Wilson, who had also hoped to be Chancellor and thought himself better qualified than Gaitskell, and John Freeman, later High Commissioner in India and then Ambassador in Washington in the first Wilson government. That was the birth of the Bevanites.

The personal conflict became ever bitterer. As a Gaitskellite, but not personally involved at the time, I was disturbed by the apparent intolerance shown by Bevan's opponents. In 1955 his reckless and vitriolic attacks on the leadership, including Attlee and various trade union leaders, led to the whip being withdrawn from him. He must have been a difficult colleague. Dick Crossman, for a while the organiser of that group and himself an occasional rebel, observed in his diaries that Bevan himself was never really a Bevanite. No team player, he would make tactless speeches, exasperating his allies. On a deck littered with stray cannonballs, it would seem that he was the loose cannon. In 1955, when Gaitskell defeated Bevan for the leadership, they initiated peace talks and Bevan joined the shadow Cabinet. In 1957 he became shadow Foreign Secretary. Famously, Bevanites

---

†   Brivati, *Hugh Gaitskell*, p. 118. (In fact the yield from the charge was relatively low.)

would later be outraged when, with unilateral nuclear disarmament having become the Left's principal foreign policy issue, he warned against going 'naked into the conference chamber'. When his former friends protested, he described their reaction as 'an emotional spasm'. In fact, after Bevan's truce with Gaitskell in 1955, they could hardly be Bevanites and regrouped as VFS, Victory for Socialism.

To those who shared Gaitskell's general views, Gaitskell became an increasingly inspiring leader, an idealist, but not an ideologue, passionate but realistic, and a politician of exceptional integrity and principle. As Roy Jenkins wrote, 'He was a standing contradiction to the view that only those with cold hearts and twisted tongues can succeed in politics.'[†] For many years after Gaitskell's death in 1963, many of the social democrats in the party still thought of themselves as Gaitskellites.

The faults were there, too. In his stand for principle, he could be stubborn and unnecessarily uncompromising (as over the teeth and spectacle charges). Sometimes he seemed to court confrontation. A Communist policy of infiltration into the party existed, but in a famous speech at Stalybridge in 1952, pointing to the bitterly divisive conference that year at Morecambe, he went over the top. The conference was, as Michael Foot described it, 'rowdy, convulsive, vulgar, splenetic; threatening at times to collapse into an irretrievable brawl.'[‡] But for Gaitskell:

> a most disturbing feature of the conference was the number of speeches and resolutions that were Communist inspired ... I was

---

[†]   Jenkins, R., 'The Only Politician I Loved', *The Guardian*, 11 January 2003.

[‡]   Foot, M., *Aneurin Bevan: A Biography* (London: MacGibbon & Kee, 1962), vol. 2, p. 376.

told by some well-informed correspondents that about one-sixth of the constituency delegates appeared to be Communist or Communist controlled. This figure may well have been too high, but if it should be one in ten or even one in twenty, it is a most shocking state of affairs.[†]

These comments laid him wide open to an effective riposte in *Tribune*:

Twinkle, twinkle, little Hugh.
Oh I wonder how you knew.
Who was red and who was not?
Mass Observation on the spot?

Outside the dangerous gas zone of Parliament, I did not share the Gaitskellites's bitter dislike and mistrust of Bevan, whom I never met. Despite his obvious vanity, his erratic conduct and taste for rather antiquarian notions of socialism, he was still fascinating and charismatic, rather a romantic figure. He was an ex-miner from the Welsh valleys with wide interests, learning, intelligence and wit, and a superlative speaker. Class mattered a great deal to Bevan. When he married fellow Labour MP Jennie Lee, she had to overcome a major obstacle – that her father had been a foreman!

The Tories, not altogether surprisingly, held it against him that he once described them as 'vermin'. But some of the most eminent politicians have used extreme language against their opponents. Disraeli compared the Whigs to swine 'guzzling and grunting in a bed of mire'.

---

†   Brivati, *Hugh Gaitskell*, p. 176.

Bevan had an exceptional feeling for words. An occasional stutter delayed the crucial word, making triumphant delivery explode. Some denounced him as a demagogue, but far from demagoguery, the impact came from argument and teasing, devastating ridicule. Edward Boyle, a profoundly intelligent and compassionate man, and the most progressive Conservative I ever came across, told me that as a Conservative candidate during a general election, he heard Bevan at a public meeting and nearly resigned his candidacy to vote Labour.

The memory of two speeches I heard lingers vividly. The first was in 1956 at a mass protest rally in Trafalgar Square about the British invasion of Suez. 'We are not at war. Mr Eden has assured us: we are not at war [a word slowly drawn out]. We are in a state of [pause] armed conflict,' with the word 'armed' long-drawn-out and ending the last syllable of 'conflict' on a high note. Later in the same speech: 'Mr Selwyn Lloyd, the Foreign Secretary, says we have invaded Suez to pave the way for the United Nations ... [again, long pause] ... like a b...burglar, who says he is there to train the police.'

The second was a speech made just before cancer killed him, winding up the acrimonious debate at the Blackpool Labour Party conference of 1959, a post mortem on that year's general election defeat. Gaitskell had opened with a speech proposing that Labour should abandon Clause IV of its constitution, which committed the party to the common ownership of the means of production, distribution and exchange. This outraged Barbara Castle, party chairman and a fiery left-winger, who quoted a speech by Bevan. Gaitskell had also quoted Bevan. Winding up amid the debris Bevan became the conciliator:

I used to be taught as a boy ... one of Euclid's deductions: if two things are equal to a third thing, they are equal to each other. Yesterday Barbara quoted from a speech that I made some years ago ... Hugh Gaitskell did the same thing. So Barbara and Hugh both quoted me. If Euclid's deduction is correct, they are both equal to me and therefore must be equal to each other. So we have a kind of trinity – I am not going to lay myself open to a charge of blasphemy by trying to describe our different roles.

It was wonderful stuff. Yet the same speech also confirmed his outdated view of socialism, because he strongly defended the need for more public ownership:

The challenge is going to come from Russia. The challenge is not ... going to come from the United States ... from Western Germany, nor from France. The challenge is going to come from those nations who ... are at long-last being able to reap the material fruits of economic planning and public ownership.

Labour's heated debate about public ownership, which unexpectedly led to my election to Parliament, gradually emerged as one of the two main divisive issues after Labour's defeat in the 1955 election, the other being nuclear disarmament.

In four elections after 1945, Labour had listed with open-minded abandon any number of industries as targets for nationalisation. The Left now argued with increasing stridency that capitalism was incompatible with Labour's objective of a classless society, which could only be achieved by common ownership as declared in Clause IV. The clause was the Ark of the Covenant, which, together with strict import and exchange controls, would protect a socialist Britain from the chill blasts of international capitalism. This inevitably led the Left in due course to oppose British membership of the European Community – UKIP-ers before their time! Equally dear to their hearts was the class struggle in which Labour should be identified with the working class, or as Tony Benn liked to describe them 'working people' (implying that professional people do not work).

In foreign policy the Left argued that Britain should follow a third way, holding a balance between the Soviet Union and the United States. They were neutralists rather than pro-Soviet, but frequently treated the Soviet Union more tolerantly than the United States. The Left also passionately argued that we should abandon nuclear weapons, as an example to other nuclear powers.

By contrast, the Right, or as I preferred to regard them, the social democrats, accepted the mixed economy. We believed in greater economic and social equality and put community values before the free play of market forces. We aimed to diminish class distinctions, but did not regard Labour as a class party. We also backed reforms of our social laws, as on homosexuality and abortion, which were duly enacted by the next Labour government, introducing the permissive society as some critics saw it or, as I would call it, the more civilised society. In foreign affairs, social democrats supported the Atlantic alliance, opposed unilateral nuclear disarmament and largely favoured accession to the European Community. Most of the party walked serenely between Bevanite left and social democratic right. It was generally loyal to the leadership and its attitude could probably be summed up by murmuring what Herbert Morrison had snapped, 'Socialism is what a Labour government does.'

The philosophy of the Social Democrats, or 'revisionists' as they were also called, was expounded by Tony Crosland in his book *The Future of Socialism* published in 1956, which inspired many of my generation when it was published and remains a most impressive work. I would rank it as one of the most important intellectual contributions to British social democracy. The book was not only outstanding for the rigour of its argument but displayed a profound knowledge of sociological and psychological literature, as well as of economics in which Crosland had already made his reputation as an Oxford don. It was a genuine attempt to base conclusions on objective analysis of the best available evidence, rather than on dogma, prejudice or conventional wisdom. It rejected the ideological approach. Socialism is often described by its advocates as a crusade or a pilgrimage. Both can end up dogmatic. Practicality must be the permanent corrective. At an early stage in my political career I avoided the use of the term 'socialism' but, after I had left the Labour Party, I was once taken to task for calling myself a social democrat during a TV discussion with Eric Heffer, a prominent, likeable left-wing Labour MP. 'Dick,' he said. 'I forgive you your desertion of the party. I now understand that you are not a socialist. But I do resent your calling yourself a social democrat, because the original social democrats, like Rosa Luxemburg, were out-and-out Marxists.' True, but the meaning of the description has changed over time.

Crosland did not use the term 'socialism' in an ideological sense. Capitalism had changed. Marx's pauperisation of the working class had been disproved by events. The experience of nationalisation had been mixed and had not delivered the benefits expected: improvements in industrial relations, and productivity and greater equality. He contrasted the success of the private company that built the Fawley oil refinery near Southampton, which achieved excellent industrial relations and full union cooperation, with the poor industrial relations in the publicly owned mines and railways. He did not reject public ownership, but believed each case should be argued on practical not ideological grounds. There were better ways to social and economic equality and prosperity, for example through education and fairer taxation.

Crosland was too optimistic about planning as the path to economic growth and not all his analysis or prescriptions stand up. The nature of capitalism has changed in the last fifty years to a much freer market economy. Social problems have changed, too. At that time globalisation and climate change did not dominate public debate. The industrial scene was innocent of private equity, seeking where it might downsize. Yet much of the book is still relevant and I still accept most of its political philosophy today. We need a new Crosland to re-examine the role of social democracy.

Crosland's appeal was enhanced by personal charisma. Tall and good-looking, he had great charm, though he could also be unforgivably rude and his boredom threshold was low. During one television discussion about the alleged incompatibility of environmentalism and economic growth, an idea he ridiculed, he fell asleep. Someone later described it as 'the famous Crosland sleep-in'. Part of his appeal for me was that he was not driven by ambition to be party leader. I think he recognised that an uncompromising intellectual lacks popular appeal. In fact his deep seriousness was matched by an attractive insouciance, cheerfully causing offence, making enemies and harming his career in the most politically incorrect manner imaginable.

I became personally more actively involved in the Left/Right conflict soon after the 1959 conference. Gaitskell had by general consent fought an excellent campaign and had greatly increased his public standing. After much soul-searching, he concluded that one of the reasons for defeat was Labour's doctrinaire commitment to Clause IV. He suggested that it should be replaced by a more modern statement of industrial policy. Most of his friends advised against this on two grounds: that he would fail to get it through the party; and that it didn't matter. In government, Labour would act, and would be seen to act, pragmatically.

My thoughts wandered to the Thirty-nine Articles of the Church of England. Most did not believe in them. Most thought it would be useful to the Church to bring them up to date. But woe betide the wrath of fundamentalists if anyone trod on sacred ground.

Characteristically Gaitskell persisted, proclaiming the need to replace Clause IV in his speech to the party conference. The reaction was violent: it was as if the Archbishop of Canterbury had proposed that the Church of England should renounce God. Little groups formed on the fringes of the hall and talked of treason. Several telling speeches were made in Gaitskell's defence. The most effective was by Denis Healey. He turned on Michael Foot, who had made a violent attack on Gaitskell (and had been heavily defeated in Plymouth). 'The speeches that win the biggest cheers at this conference are not the speeches that win votes in Plymouth.' The most brilliant, in favour of a more modern approach to politics, was by Shirley Williams, who was hailed as the coming star of the younger generation. The most unpopular was mine: I was loudly booed – an unusual conference achievement.

None of Gaitskell's supporters had directly echoed his call for the abolition of Clause IV, except me. As a convinced Croslandite, I believed that Labour could only hope to be a successful party by officially and explicitly renouncing ideological socialism based on public ownership, as the German SPD had just done at Bad Godesberg earlier that year. Somewhat naively I got to the platform to declare that Gaitskell was right, that Labour's commitment to widespread nationalisation was an unpopular embarrassment. I did win some praise: *The Economist* approved, mentioning that some of the younger ex-candidates shared Gaitskell's views on nationalisation, and added, 'but it was symptomatic that when a single one of them, Dick Taverne, who had fought Putney, spoke up in support of his leader's views (and added sensible observations about ending class warfare within the party) this was considered an exceptionally courageous thing to do.' My speech also won me one very influential fan and proved to be a key event in my political career.

Gaitskell lost the battle. Clause IV remained the text inscribed on the party card for forty years. Tony Blair returned to the issue in 1996, when he too proposed the abolition of Clause IV. Most of his colleagues tried to dissuade him with much the same arguments of 1959: Clause IV was irrelevant and, in any case, he would lose (as the press also predicted). Blair persisted and won. He never lacked courage and his victory improved Labour's image: it could no longer be argued that Labour stood for fundamentalist socialism. The changing of Clause IV was seen by political commentators as the defining moment at which Old Labour became New Labour. Labour's 'Clause IV Moment' has subsequently become a metaphor for any need or perceived need for a fundamental recasting of a political party's principles or attitudes. It was one of those cases when politicians will kowtow (in the company of political journalists) to a vocal minority in the mistaken view of its authority and popularity. Sometimes, when you are told it is no use swimming against the tide, it has already turned in your favour.

After the conference, Gaitskell faced a second crisis, over unilateral nuclear disarmament. Many of the unions, including the two biggest, adopted resolutions sponsored by the Campaign for Nuclear Disarmament (CND), now also advancing among constituency activists. Unilateral disarmament would, it seemed, be voted official Labour policy at the next conference in 1960. Sometime in early 1960, Bill Rodgers and I on our way to a Fabian conference discussed the 'state of the party'. Did we really want to belong to a party dedicated to large-scale nationalisation at home and neutralism abroad?

We decided that something should be done and that we should try to rally moderates in the same mood. We were not alone. Meetings were held by a London and Oxford group of party members. Bill and I organised a letter in support of Gaitskell's leadership signed by thirteen candidates in the recent election. It dispelled the inspissated gloom and got the idea talked about, including in the newspapers. And it showed up the fearful, timorous conduct of MPs. We were the voice of (relative) youth. The oldest of us was thirty-nine, the youngest (Ivor Richard) twenty-seven. Nine of us (including Bill, Shirley Williams, Ivor Richard and I) subsequently became MPs, six of us ministers.

We also decided to draw up a manifesto. Since Gaitskell was determined to fight the neutralists and put his leadership on the line, then our future was linked to his. And neutralism was a better pitch than nationalisation. At the 1960 conference in

Scarborough, CND duly won the vote. But the loser's speech won the argument and got into history. In defeat, Gaitskell made such a magnificent, rousing and defiant speech, 'to fight and fight and fight again to bring back sanity and honesty and dignity', it stuck in the mind. Defeat felt more like victory. He had fired the enthusiasm of the moderates. Moderates of any kind do not cheer wildly. It isn't done. But they cheered and cheered this speech.

Immediately afterwards, the signatories of our earlier letter published our manifesto, which attracted support from all over Britain. Its opening paragraph read:

> We are long-standing members of the Labour Party who are convinced that our movement cannot afford another Scarborough. Rank-and-file opinion must now assert itself in support of Hugh Gaitskell and of those Labour MPs – the great majority – who are determined to resist and then reverse the present disastrous trend towards unilateralism and neutralism.

The Campaign for Democratic Socialism (CDS) was launched. CDS was a grass-roots movement. We had little faith in the parliamentary party which we regarded as pusillanimous, obsessed with unity and compromise. Organisationally, CDS was an unusual phenomenon, a group working together in an atmosphere of harmony and trust. Throughout its history, there would not be a single damaging leak to the media. We had three principal aims: to rally the moderates and support them in their constituencies and unions; to reverse the vote for unilateralism at the next conference; and to get new Gaitskellite candidates adopted.

And we did. We were successful beyond our expectations. At

the conference, the majority in favour of unilateralism was over-turned by three to one. Two people who played key roles in our success were Tony Crosland and Bill Rodgers. Crosland oddly enough was our apparatchik, not just our intellectual guru, who drove the executive committee. Drinks before any meeting were banned by this non-teetotaller because, he said, people would talk too much. The pressure he put on everyone was unrelenting, likewise his contempt for the appeasers who sought to avoid the bitter confrontation with CND.

Bill Rodgers proved himself as CDS's brilliant organiser. Bill and I are almost exactly the same age – he is ten days younger – and my closest friend in politics for over sixty years, although he has always been a more dedicated and successful politician than me. We became MPs in 1962 within a month of each other and both served in the Treasury under Roy Jenkins in Wilson's first government. In Wilson's second administration, Bill was appointed to the Cabinet as Transport Secretary in 1976 and was one of the Gang of Four who founded the SDP in 1981. He has played a key role at critical moments and, though he never achieved the public prominence of the other three members, Roy Jenkins, David Owen and Shirley Williams, colleagues have always recognised his political judgement and integrity. Roy Jenkins described him as 'his single most important politi-cal associate of the younger generation'. When Bill's views and mine differ, I worry that I may be wrong.

I was treasurer of CDS but played a relatively minor part, because the real fundraising was done by Jack Diamond, an MP and accountant with good connections to Labour sympa-thisers and Gaitskell supporters in the City. The Left's rumour that we were financed by the CIA was untrue. As the treasurer

I am sure I would have known. My most important contribution was to turn down a promise of big money, to the dismay of my colleagues. It came from a rich, pro-Gaitskell parliamentary candidate. I decided to make careful inquiries and concluded that he could not be trusted, had a shady past, would not deliver what he promised and, if we took his money, would insist on running the whole show. His name was Robert Maxwell. Subsequently Maxwell was elected as the Labour MP for Buckingham from 1964 to 1970, but his main claim to fame was his business activities. He built up a major publishing house, Pergamon Press. In 1971, a Board of Trade inquiry found that 'he is not in our opinion a person who can be relied on to exercise proper stewardship of a publicly quoted company'. This did not prevent him successfully extending his business activities, which included buying the *Daily Mirror* for £113 million. When his huge business empire fell on hard times in 1991, it emerged that he had stolen hundreds of millions of pounds from his own companies' pension funds. There was no way out for him and he was found dead, floating in the Atlantic Ocean off the Canary Islands, having fallen overboard from his huge yacht, the *Lady Ghislaine*.

The success of CDS had one unexpected result. A by-election was announced in Lincoln at the end of 1961, when the pro-Gaitskell Labour MP Geoffrey de Freitas was appointed High Commissioner in Ghana. It was viewed as a particularly important by-election as there had been a resurgence of support for Labour after the conference defeat of the Left and it was thought this would be a good test of public opinion. Gaitskell, whom I had barely met, and members of his inner circle, including his principal aide John Harris, later a close friend of mine, discussed whom to put forward as a suitable candidate.

Apparently Gaitskell asked, 'What about that young man who made that speech about Clause IV at Blackpool? Isn't he also active in CDS?' They decided I was a suitable horse for the course. Although my practice at the Bar was finally prospering, I was happy to put politics before the law, met the local agent and two local CDS stalwarts and scrambled a nomination.

The pro-Gaitskell wing had a small majority on the Lincoln party executive committee, which they used ruthlessly (and in my view unwisely) to exclude left-wingers from the shortlist. The shortlist, in the end, consisted of three Gaitskellites: Arthur Bottomley, a former Minister for Overseas Trade who had lost his seat; Neil McDermott, an able and experienced barrister, later Financial Secretary to the Treasury; and me. Before the vote, a group of left-wingers led by Leo Beckett, the chairman of the largest ward and later chairman of the local party, walked out in protest at the composition of the shortlist. I was selected despite the other two shortlisted candidates having many more nominations than me.†

A week or so after I had been selected, Beckett's left-wing group staged a successful coup for control of the party executive and the management committee, which was due for re-election. I was present at a meeting of a key ward choosing the new management committee and clearly the voting had been fixed. One group all received thirteen votes each; in the other, three. The thirteen were all members of Leo Beckett's left-wing group. The three were former right-wing members of the old management committee, including a past chairman. Similar results followed in other wards. Thus, before I became an MP in March

---

† Leo subsequently married Margaret Jackson, later MP for Lincoln, who as Margaret Beckett eventually became Secretary of State at DEFRA and then, briefly in Blair's terminal days, Foreign Secretary.

1962 and for the next ten years, my local party was dominated
by a left-wing faction, supporting extensive nationalisation and
unilateral nuclear disarmament and passionately opposed to the
European Community.

On the whole, despite our fundamental differences, I got on
quite well personally with most of the left-wingers – until near
the end – and I had a particular liking for Leo Beckett. Local
political troubles were still some years away. We were all united in
wanting a Labour government and the good result we achieved
in Lincoln in 1962 was an important step.

The by-election campaign was well organised. I remember it
mainly for three things. First, a stunt organised by John Harris,
Labour's publicity chief. Seven telegenic daughters of prominent Labour figures came canvassing for me: Julia Gaitskell, Pat
Brown (daughter of George Brown), Margaret Callaghan, Ann
Gordon Walker (daughter of Labour's foreign affairs spokesman), Frankie de Freitas (daughter of Geoffrey, the retiring MP
for Lincoln), Judith Pakenham and Susan Walston (daughters of
prominent Labour peers). Immediately dubbed 'the Daughters
of the Revolution', pictures appeared prominently on the
front of most newspapers of them canvassing in the snow
(throughout the by-election the weather was bitterly cold).

The second was my visit to the theological college Bishop
Grosseteste, which would, I feared, present me as a non-believer
with a quandary. I was accompanied by Richard Winterbottom,
MP for Sheffield Brightside, a steel-making city. He specialised
in deeply embarrassing loudspeaker appeals as we toured the
constituency in the party van. A mother with a baby would be
hailed: 'You there, that mother with your baby daughter in your
arms, think of her future. Vote Dick Taverne.'

In fact the theological students were as humorous and intelligent an audience as I could have hoped for. I said truthfully that I felt like a lion in a den of Daniels, but the atmosphere could not have been more stimulating. Then Richard asked to speak. He announced ponderously, 'I am proud to represent the constituency of Sheffield Brightside' – my heart sank – 'and I can boast', he went on, delighting several dozen vicars to be, 'that more throats are cut by knives made from steel in Sheffield Brightside than from any other constituency in the country.'

The third was the Conservative campaign slogan. My opponent was a charming and able QC, perhaps a little unsuited to the rough and tumble of a by-election. His name was Percy Grieve and the slogan plastered all over Lincoln was 'Grieve for Lincoln'.

During the first year after my successful election, two distressing events occurred. At the 1962 conference, Gaitskell rejected the terms on which Macmillan sought to join the European Community, mainly because he was not satisfied that they met the needs of the Commonwealth. He delighted the Left and appalled his supporters. As his wife observed, 'All the wrong people are cheering.' Then, a few months later, he suddenly died.

We were all shell-shocked and we also had to choose a new leader. Before it became public knowledge that Gaitskell was seriously ill, my brother-in-law, who was a medical student at the hospital where Gaitskell was being treated, had warned me that his condition was very serious indeed. I rang Bill Rodgers and in a gloomy discussion of his possible successor we agreed that we should not rule out Wilson.

After some preliminary discussions, a group of Gaitskellites met at Tony Crosland's flat. Among those I remember as being present were Tony Crosland, Jennifer Jenkins (Roy's wife who was representing her husband while he was in America), Douglas Jay, George Thomson (later Commonwealth secretary), Jack Diamond (later Chief Secretary of the Treasury), and Desmond Donnelly, a former Bevanite who had very publicly denounced Bevan and was now close to George Brown. Also present were John Harris, the party's PR chief and head of election strategy, Austen Albu, a much-respected MP, Bill Rodgers and me.

John Harris stressed how important it was that everyone should be frank and that nobody should leak. (We later found out that Donnelly reported every word to George Brown.) Harris himself would have to work with whoever was chosen. As a fairly new MP, I offered no view and listened to those with far more experience than I. They ruled Wilson out unanimously – 'he will not put a foot wrong before the election, but will ultimately run the party into the ground.' George Brown was deemed in many ways a brilliant mind with great persuasive powers, but unreliable. Some argued his occasional drunkenness should disqualify him. John Harris said that from his experience drink was only a symptom of Brown's basically neurotic personality. Crosland, Jay and Thomson backed Callaghan. Albu revealed that when Callaghan, very much a layman in economics, had been appointed shadow Chancellor, he attended economic tutorials at Oxford and would start by asking intelligent and pertinent questions. But when an issue was examined in greater depth and became more complex, his eyes would glaze over and he would ask, 'Forget about the details, what is the political angle?' The general view was that, deep down, Callaghan was shallow.

In the end, we decided to vote for Brown, except Crosland, Jay and Thomson, who stuck with Callaghan. As Bill later observed, 'It was decided: better George drunk than Harold sober.'

Were we right? In retrospect I think not. Brown was brilliant – also erratic, often drunk. But Gaitskellites could not forgive Wilson for standing against Gaitskell as a 'unity candidate' after the 'fight and fight again' speech. Wilson proved an election winner; not a good Prime Minister nor as bad as I had feared. He had several major achievements to his credit: keeping us out of Vietnam, helping Roy Jenkins get tough decisions as Chancellor through Cabinet and eventually keeping Britain in Europe when his party wanted us out.

Many years later, I learned from Dick Crossman's diaries that, after his election as leader, Wilson discussed with Crossman whom he should appoint as his Parliamentary Private Secretary – often a quick route to high office. Crossman suggested he should appoint one of the bright young Gaitskellites and recommended me. 'But what reason have you to think he is trustworthy?' asked Wilson. 'Oh, no reason at all. But what makes you think he is untrustworthy?' Wilson replied: 'I don't give people jobs if I don't know if they are trustworthy.'

Crossman championed my promotion again in 1969. I had worked with him as Financial Secretary to the Treasury on his imaginative plan for a national superannuation scheme, part of the Labour manifesto in 1970. When the pensions minister, Stephen Swingler, died, Crossman recommended me as his replacement. Wilson ruled it out completely. 'He is a silken, treacherous member of the CDS group.' (CDS had actually been disbanded after Labour's victory in 1964.) Roy Hattersley was also considered, but Crossman defended me. 'Hattersley is no more loyal to Roy Jenkins than he is to you. He is just an able

young man on the way up and I think Dick Taverne has rather
more loyalty and decency about him.' Neither of us got the job. I
never knew that Crossman was so well disposed towards me and
Wilson so bitterly hostile.

CHAPTER 5

TRIBUNE OF THE PEOPLE

I doubt if any new MP does not feel a thrill to be elected as a member of one of the oldest democratic assemblies in the world, one which gradually evolved into a form of government that has avoided the revolutions, dictatorships, autocracies, civil wars – except one – and other upheavals that have afflicted so many countries in Europe and elsewhere. Taking part in the democratic process in Parliament is a great honour.

I made my maiden speech within two weeks of my election. The timing was ideal because there was a Bill before the House on a constitutional issue in which I had already been legally involved and which, somewhat ironically in the light of later events, enabled Tony Benn to play a major, though not exactly beneficial, role in the history of the Labour Party during the next thirty years. The Bill allowed hereditary peers to renounce their peerages.

In 1960, Anthony Wedgwood Benn, as he was then known, the MP for Bristol, was disqualified from continuing to be an MP because his father, Viscount Stansgate, had died and he succeeded to the title. According to the law at the time, this automatically made him a member of the House of Lords and so prevented him from sitting in the House of Commons.

Tony Benn loved the House of Commons and was determined
to fight his disqualification. In 1950 he had been elected at the
age of twenty-five and because of his eloquence, charm and wit
he was widely regarded as one of the brightest young hopes of
the Labour Party. First, he defiantly stood again in Bristol in the
by-election caused by his disqualification and was triumphantly
re-elected, only to be disqualified again by an election court. He
then took his case to the Committee of Privileges of the House
of Commons claiming that peers were only disqualified from
the House of Commons if they accepted the writ of summons
to the Lords, which he had refused to do. He asked Dingle Foot
and me to represent him, which we did pro bono. At Balliol I
had been a close friend of Tony Benn's younger brother David
(sometimes known as Little Benn). As a result my wife Janice and
I occasionally had dinner in the Stansgate household and went
to Tony's parties, where we became friends.

Some fifty years earlier the same case had been argued by the
famous Lord Curzon, who had hoped to be Prime Minister and
feared he would be deprived of the prize when he inherited his
father's title.[†] The research I did showed that his argument was
historically correct. Peers in the thirteenth and fourteenth centuries frequently chose to attend the House of Commons rather
than the House of Lords without losing their title. However,
Curzon's case was rejected in favour of the law as laid down by
a seventeenth-century judge, the formidable Sir Edward Coke,
that peers were disqualified by their noble blood. The historian
Horace Round, in a splendid tirade against lawyers' reliance on

---

†   He was generally regarded as someone not unaware of his own importance,
hence the doggerel: 'My name is George Nathaniel Curzon. I am a most
superior perzon.'

authority rather than evidence, condemned the preference for Coke's edicts rather than the facts of history.

> Fiction is not converted into fact because it happens to proceed from the mouth of a learned judge ... What the historian seeks to know is, not whether a lawyer was 'great', 'eminent' or 'learned', but what authority he had for his statement and whether he was right in his facts.[†]

But the courts ruled that Coke was a supreme authority. Therefore, damn the evidence, he must be right and Curzon lost.

I argued that the House of Commons Committee was not bound by precedents and was free to take a historical rather than a legal view. I cited the cases of the Peers who had sat in the Commons after inheriting their title and were allowed to do so as long as they had not accepted the writ of summons to the Lords. The committee would have none of it and its chairman, Sir Reginald Manningham-Buller, later Lord Chancellor, cavalierly dismissed my argument. He was commonly known as Sir Bullying-Manner.[‡] Benn next took his case to the courts, where he argued his cause in person with great eloquence. That too failed. But he had aroused widespread public sympathy for his attack on a clearly absurd and outdated law, and in 1962 the Leader of the House, Iain McLeod, introduced the Peerages Renunciation Bill that, *inter alia*, allowed Tony Benn to resume his parliamentary career. The theme of my maiden speech was that

---

[†] Round, H., *Studies in Peerage and Family History* (London: A. Constable, 1901), vol. 1, p. 144.

[‡] His daughter, Eliza Manningham-Buller, ex-head of MI5, now sits in the Lords and is a much-admired and eloquent advocate of liberal causes.

the Bill would not only do justice in Benn's case, but would abolish an absurd anachronism in our constitution. A man could not alienate a title of honour, ruled a judge in a 1907 case, following the infamous ruling of Sir Edward Coke, because 'it is a personal dignity which descends to his posterity and is fixed in the blood'. This, I said, was a doctrine of pure tribalism – though I added, lest I should seem unduly disrespectful to their Lordships in my maiden speech, that it was quite the most dignified and elegant form of tribalism there could possibly be.

After this speech, on top of my earlier legal efforts, I acquired a temporary halo in the Benn household. Later in 1972 my halo was exchanged for a pair of horns when I resigned from the Labour Party and announced that I would stand as an independent Democratic Labour candidate in a by-election. Tony Benn then dramatically denounced me as an enemy of the Labour movement.

Why did we fall out? There is no doubt about Tony Benn's extraordinary gifts and public appeal. His fight to retain his seat in the Commons was a personal triumph. He has a sparkling personality, and he combines eloquence, wit, charisma and good manners. But I would add that he also had another unusual gift: despite later achieving high office in a number of senior departments, as Secretary of State for Technology, then Industry and then Energy, he managed to remain uncorrupted by the slightest taint of realism. Even when we were on good terms, when I was a callow party member somewhat in awe of this brilliant young MP, long before he became a populist left-winger, I thought that there was an element of eccentricity about his views. This sense of discomfort was confirmed some years later in 1963, after I had also become an MP, when I sat beside him in a bus on the way to Königswinter for an annual conference of British and German politicians and journalists. He told me that one of the first and most important things a new Labour government should do when it came to power, in order to create a new progressive mood in the country, was to design new postage stamps – not, I thought, everyone's top priority. In the event, when Labour won in 1964 he became Postmaster General and, I am told, proposed that the Queen's picture should be replaced on postage stamps by a Spitfire. When he mentioned this to Her Majesty, he thought she approved, or at least accepted it. But it turned out that protestations went out from Buckingham Palace the moment he left. The Queen's picture was saved.

After Labour's defeat in 1970, Tony Benn lurched to the far left and our views clashed. He played a leading part in making Labour unelectable for well over a decade.

I found that 1962 was a good time to enter Parliament – a time of 'glad confident morning', when the bitterness of left/right struggles seemed to have subsided and there was a real prospect that Labour would soon come to power. At the end of my first year, two events shook Harold Macmillan's government and seemed to improve Labour's chances: de Gaulle's veto of Britain's bid to join the European Community, which had been the centrepiece of Macmillan's strategy, and, from the tragic to the absurd, a scandal involving an attractive girl, a Russian diplomat and the Minister of War, John Profumo. While the Profumo affair, which broke in early 1963, did not greatly enhance the reputation of Parliament as a serious forum for national debate, I must admit I enjoyed a seat in the stalls at an absorbing drama.

The talk of the town was that Profumo had had an affair with Christine Keeler, who had also been the mistress of the naval attaché at the Soviet embassy. The brouhaha stirred up by the media forced Profumo to make a personal statement to the House of Commons. He denied the affair. It turned out that this was a lie and he had to resign. There were three views of the incident. One was that of the Labour MP Reggie Paget, who observed, 'I understand that the Secretary of War has had a close acquaintanceship with an exceedingly pretty girl. I regard that as a matter for congratulations.' The second was the view of Lord Hailsham, who passionately repeated three times on television: 'It is a moral question.' Paget responded to Lord Hailsham, who was not exactly a slim athletic figure, with a memorable piece of invective: 'When self-indulgence has reduced a man to the physical shape of Lord Hailsham, continence merely shows a keen sense of the ridiculous.' The third view was that of the official Labour opposition, which claimed from a high moral plane that they were not interested in the prurient details but in the security of the realm. How could we be sure vital secrets were not leaked in the bedroom? It was an unattractive display of opportunism disguised as patriotism. However, commentators seemed to agree that the government was severely damaged by the affair, although I noted that at a subsequent by-election in Stratford in August 1963 the Conservatives actually did slightly less badly than in previous by-elections, and post-Profumo polls showed them to be slightly less unpopular than before.

In 1963, the Prime Minister, Harold Macmillan decided to resign, either because of the Profumo scandal or his belief that he was seriously ill.† He was succeeded by the fourteenth Earl of Home, who renounced his peerage under the new act to qualify for the Commons. He entered as Sir Alec Douglas-Home after

---

†   He recovered to flourish, for most of the rest of his life as Chancellor of Oxford, well into his nineties.

a by-election. Although he was an able man, he was a much less formidable tactical adversary for Wilson and suffered from the disadvantage of his ancestry, which seemed out of keeping with the prevalent mood of a desire for change. As a Labour back-bencher I admired Macmillan – except for his original support for the ill-fated Suez venture – and in retrospect my admiration has grown. He was one of the very few British statesmen since the Second World War to show vision. After Suez he recognised the changed context for Britain's role in the world, first by accelerating the transition from Empire to Commonwealth, signalled by his 'Wind of Change' speech in Africa in 1960, then by his acknowledgement in 1961 that Britain's future influence, as well as its prosperity, depended on our membership of the European Community. Unfortunately his application to join the Community was vetoed by de Gaulle. Our position would have been immensely stronger if we had joined at the start in 1957, as I hoped at the time. Then our reputation in Europe was high. We would have been joint leaders with the Germans and the French and we could have negotiated a much more favourable agricultural and fisheries policy settlement than that we inherited when we finally joined on the 1 January 1973.

When I entered Parliament, my impression of my fellow MPs was generally favourable. They were unrecognisable from the bunch of self-serving, out-of-touch nonentities nowadays regularly caricatured in some of the tabloid press. I should add that the Conservative Party of the 1960s and 1970s was very different from the party at the time of writing, whose most vociferous members are groups of little Englander, anti-immigrant campaigners, whose social attitudes are not a million miles removed from the views of the American Tea Party.

I found MPs were not 'only out for themselves'. In my experience most enter public life to try and make the world a better
place. No one with any sense or ability goes into Parliament for
the money. It is true that a complicated system of reimbursing
expenses recently tempted some MPs to make extravagant and,
in a few cases, fraudulent claims. But most to blame was the
system. Over the years a series of independent tribunals have
recommended substantial increases in salary, but successive
governments have been too pusillanimous and too scared of the
tabloids to accept them. The rot started long ago when I was
still an MP. A tribunal reported that MPs should have a substantial rise in pay, which should in future be linked to a particular
grade in the civil service. The Prime Minister, Harold Wilson,
rejected the tribunal's report because he felt this would be very
unpopular. However, disgruntled MPs were reassured by the
Chief Whip: 'Don't worry. We'll make it up in your expenses.' In
the early 1970s, Norman Miscampbell – a very honourable and
likeable Conservative MP who was a near neighbour of ours
– told me he drove up to his constituency in Blackpool two or
three times a week because he was paid £120 a trip as a tax-free
mileage allowance, a substantial addition to his parliamentary
salary. When expenses become a serious part of remuneration, corruption creeps in. But most MPs I knew were honest
and would not abuse expenses, and many of them, as political
correspondents will readily confirm, are also good company and
highly intelligent.

Further, contrary to popular belief, I did not find that MPs
are out of touch and do not know what life is like or what ordinary people think. It is true that gradually MPs themselves have
become less representative of different sections of the population.

Nowadays an unduly large proportion of parliamentary candidates have been members of PR companies or think tanks, or are former special political advisers. But to me one of the advantages of being an MP was that it gave me an experience of life equalled by few other professions. Nearly every MP knows what is going on in his or her constituency – such as what the schools are like, what parents think and what the main problems of the teachers are. Part of my constituency life was visiting local factories and talking to the unions and to management, learning about people's problems with their pensions, the state of their council house and the cost of their council rent, what it was like to live on welfare, the shortcomings or virtues of the local hospitals and schools and so on. All human life flows into an MP's surgery. As for what people think, you are certainly made aware of it during elections. In theory, canvassing on the doorstep gives the candidate a chance to explain policy and some people do want to know, though most learn about policy from television, party leaflets, perhaps even the press – or could not care less. But in my experience most people who want to talk on the doorstep want to tell you what they think, especially, if they are *Sun* or *Daily Mail* readers deeply worried about crime and immigration. They leave you in no doubt about their own views and there is little you can do to change them. Interestingly, while the public has a low opinion of politicians in general, most make an exception of their own MP because almost all MPs are conscientious about their constituency duties.

Among my own most satisfying activities as a backbencher was acting as one of a panel of MPs on behalf of the anti-apartheid movement, helping refugees from South Africa (several of them Communists) on their arrival into Britain in the days of

apartheid. One of those I helped was Joel Joffe (not a Communist),
the lawyer who acted for Nelson Mandela in the Rivonia trial
and who arrived without a passport and almost penniless at
Heathrow in the middle of the night. He later became a friend
and colleague in the House of Lords. I do not remember the
occasion, but he mentioned my assistance in his maiden speech.
Some MPs feel that to represent one's constituents provides sufficient job satisfaction in itself. Indeed getting someone a disability
pension they have been denied, stopping some deserving asylum
seeker being deported, preventing a development that would
deface the countryside, these are the kind of achievements of
which assiduous MPs can rightly be proud, though in my experience the successes were relatively few.

Another myth about MPs is that they will do anything for
votes. In fact, most MPs often stand up for principles, however
unpopular. Votes on the death penalty are a good example. Polls
show public opinion wants it restored, yet motions to restore
it are overwhelmingly defeated because MPs defy public opinion, since the evidence shows that capital punishment does not
lessen the number of murders, while there are also strong objections of principle to state killing. My near neighbour Norman
Miscampbell was particularly courageous. After Superintendent
Gerry Richardson was murdered in Blackpool, Miscampbell's
constituency, his widow won huge support for a campaign to
restore the death penalty for the murder of a policeman. Despite
the strong feelings of his constituents, Norman swam against a
strong tide and refused to sign the petition. Surprisingly, at the
next general election his vote increased by more than that of
the other Blackpool Conservative MP, my old Oxford friend
Peter Blaker, who had (reluctantly) supported the petition. At

the count, Peter Blaker said to Norman Miscampbell: 'Norman, it must be your views on capital punishment that make you so popular.' In fact Norman was an immensely popular MP anyway. Labour candidates in Blackpool were warned by their agent: 'Not one word against Norman. He is loved here.' He must also have been almost unique among MPs in refusing the knighthood that is routinely offered to long-serving Conservative MPs.

An MP has exceptional opportunities to learn about foreign affairs through official or unofficial visits. I met politicians, journalists and diplomats in Germany, Holland, France, Sweden, Belgium and the United States, many of them exceptionally attractive and interesting people. Some visits were to exotic parts of the world. Soon after I was elected I paid a visit to the Yemen and Aden at a time when they were still separate. I was part of an official all-party delegation in 1962 to find out about a revolution in the Yemen that had recently taken place, ending a thousand years of rule by the Imams. It was an unusual experience. We travelled together with the new revolutionary leaders to places that they had not visited themselves. Huge crowds came out to greet the leaders who were accompanied by our rather strange group of British MPs. There were speeches from the new leaders and star schoolboys would be paraded before us to recite long passages of the Koran. The most useful member of our party was an eccentric Conservative MP, William Yates, an Arabist who was reputed to conduct his election campaigns in his constituency, the Wrekin, wearing Arab headdress. He translated the speeches and helped communication during the most elaborate, endless feast, served as a special gesture of hospitality at the end of our visit, that I have ever had the misfortune to partake in.

Soon after our return, a bomb exploded in Aden. A group of trade unionists and the general secretary of the Aden TUC accused of complicity in the attack were arrested and detained in some remote part of the Aden Protectorate. Two other Labour MPs and I were approached by Aden socialists who asked us to investigate reports that the trade unionists had been tortured. We flew out at their expense. The High Commissioner, Sir Kennedy Trevaskis, happily allowed us to visit the trade unionists in prison, whose main complaint, we found, apart from having been confined in a very small space on the night of their arrest, was that they had to eat the local food, which was very different from their more sophisticated Aden diet. Had they been tortured? No, but Al Asnag, their leader, had been, and he was now detained in a place unknown. I asked the High Commissioner, with whom I had already had long talks about the local political situation, if I could visit Al Asnag. Sir Kennedy was most cooperative and said his deputy would accompany me, as he was due to visit Al Asnag to take him some books about the Portuguese in the Arabian Peninsula in the sixteenth century. Al Asnag turned out to be an impressive man, highly articulate and erudite, and politically, it seemed, the very model of a responsible trade union leader. Did he have any complaints about his treatment? Well, he suffered from an ulcer and the food was far too rich for his health.

At a press conference before we went home we reported that we had not found any evidence of torture and I confirmed that Al Asnag was being well-treated. However I added a comment that in my view the plans of the Conservative government for a South Arabian federation were ill-conceived and would not work. I felt rather embarrassed that we had refuted the allegations of those who had financed our visit but they were delighted! They had never really believed, they said, the allegations of torture, but how wonderful that I denounced the plans for a federation, which they passionately opposed. I followed up our visit by reading what there was to be read about the Yemen[†] and I was for a while the main Yemen expert in the House of Commons, which was not a hugely useful expertise.

As a member of the Western European Union Defence Committee,[‡] I visited Brussels, Paris and Washington. After a visit to the State Department in Washington to discuss a strange proposal for a multilateral force to be composed of merchant ships with an international crew that were to carry nuclear missiles, I had a private lunch with Senator William Fulbright, a leading expert on defence and a highly influential chairman of the Senate's Foreign Relations Committee.[§] He asked me what I had learned at the State Department and then complained that they were more forthcoming to British MPs than to members of the Senate!

One of my most interesting meetings was in 1965 with an official in NATO's information department in Paris. Together with a committee colleague and friend, Ron Brown MP, younger brother of George Brown, I was leaving a party when we met a fascinating German lady called Inga Haag, who suggested we should have dinner. We met again from time to time over the

---

[†] Harold Ingram's *The Yemen: Imams, Rulers and Revolution* (London: John Murray, 1963) was much the best source.

[‡] It had been set up after Eden committed Britain to maintain a British presence in Europe as part of NATO.

[§] The House of Representatives has a committee on 'foreign affairs', but the Senate's committee is about 'foreign relations' as most senators are reckoned too ancient for foreign affairs.

years and, by dribs and drabs, I gradually found out more about her life, which was unusually eventful.

It turned out she had been a spy. Her father, who was a Prussian liberal-minded banker, and her family were violently anti-Hitler. Before the war, she had been sent to school in England and briefly attended the LSE, where she studied under Harold Laski. When war was imminent her parents were tempted to let her stay, but decided she should come back to Berlin and asked her to take a job as a secretary in the Wehrmacht. She protested that she could not type, but was told that that was irrelevant. She would be there for her political views and to report to her political friends. One of them was Adam von Trott, a relative, who was later hanged for the anti-Hitler bomb plot in 1944. At some stage she was told it would be wise to move from Berlin and she was sent to Paris, where she and another anti-Hitler Wehrmacht employee spent much of their time tearing up denunciations of Jews (most of which came from the French) and sometimes arranging false passports for them. Then she married a like-minded German officer and spent the rest of the war in Hungary.

After the war she got a job with NATO. The history of one of her colleagues was even more dramatic than her own. She was a French Jewish woman and Inga asked what happened to her during the war. She said she was at first hidden by a French family but one day there was a knock on the door and a German officer appeared. 'You,' he said, pointing at her, 'out.' After tearful farewells she followed the officer ready to submit to her fate. When they were outside, he said to her, 'You have been denounced. I am taking you to a safe house,' where indeed she survived the war. She never found out his name, what happened to him or anything about him.

Inga eventually received the Cross of the Order of Merit from the German government for her wartime exploits. She died in 2010 at the age of ninety-one.

I had one other encounter with a spy and a counter-spy. Sometimes contacts with foreign embassies led to friendships, but inevitably they proved temporary. One strange friendship was with a member of the Soviet embassy called Mogalevchik. Soon after I became an MP he invited me to lunch. I accepted, as I thought it might be interesting; I assumed that any Soviet diplomat who cultivated Labour MPs would be a member of the KGB. I asked him about his other Labour contacts and was not surprised that they were mainly left-wing MPs. I suggested he should ignore the views of left-wingers who were well disposed towards the Soviet Union, especially their views about the likely stance of a future Labour government. They would tell him what he wanted to hear. Instead he should tell his masters that Labour in power would be no less pro-American and anti-Soviet than the Conservatives. I think he enjoyed the lunch as much as I did and I suspect he found my comment refreshing and useful. Anyway, sometime later he invited me again and said that he had a lunch allowance from the embassy; that most of his lunches were very boring; and would I like to join him occasionally in exploring some of the better restaurants in London, which we did.

I learned later that KGB employees were allowed some latitude and did not always act and talk like strict party apparatchiks. That was certainly true of Mogalevchik. He proved a most entertaining companion, full of good stories. For example, shortly after the Chinese had denounced the Soviet Union for being too accommodating to the West, he had been at an international

conference and found himself next to an American delegate in
the gents. His companion greeted him: 'Hail fellow imperialist.'
Most of the time we did not discuss politics and I kept away from
possible security issues, which was not difficult as he had wide
interests and was a passionate cinemagoer. So was his charming
young wife, another ex-foreign service employee whom, he told
me, he had met in Berlin. Unfortunately she spoke no English.
He would see a film first, rush out to tell her the plot and then
she could know what the film was about at the next showing. As
a Christmas present he gave our three-year-old daughter a book
which she still has, called *The Old Genie Hottabych.*

I felt I had to discontinue contact with him in 1964 when I
became PPS to Denis Healey, the new Secretary of State for
Defence, and I have no idea what happened to him. But I suspect
he much enjoyed his stay in London. He was later the subject of
a curious encounter I had with a man from MI5. When I was
appointed Parliamentary Under-Secretary at the Home Office
in 1966, an ex-Rhodesian policeman vetted me for security clear-
ance. At the end I asked him what he knew about Mogalevchik,
who I had assumed was employed by the KGB. Nothing. Even
though I told him he was the embassy contact with the Labour
Party, I was assured he was definitely not KGB. A week or so
later my Private Secretary rang me to say that someone who
could not give his name wanted to see me urgently and I should
see him. My door was opened slowly and the man from MI5
looked behind it apprehensively to ensure we were alone. 'We
have just found out Mogalevchik is a KGB man!' He asked me
to tell him everything I knew about him, where he served before
and what I knew about his wife. What I could tell him, I regret
to say, did not change the course of the Cold War.

Gradually I found that life as a backbencher had its limitations. My main personal ambition was to contribute to national and international – not local – politics. Many constituency duties are less than sparkling occasions, attending dinners, opening bazaars, being seen. 'He is always there, you know' is one of the greatest compliments an MP can earn, irrespective of what he is there for. I spent a lot of time 'being seen', not particularly profitably in terms of the good I did, except in electoral terms. A local opinion poll taken at the time of my by-election in 1973 found that 82 per cent of the Lincoln electorate thought I was a good MP and 2 per cent thought I was a bad one.

Soon after being elected in 1962 I found that the mother of Parliaments, often claimed to be the most admired assembly in the world, displayed some less than perfect examples of democracy in practice. MPs do not always know what they are voting on. My first vote was on the Finance Bill of 1962. I asked what the vote was about. This was regarded as a somewhat eccentric enquiry, though excusable from an innocent newcomer, and I was simply directed to the correct lobby. I obediently followed my Labour colleagues but, once there, persisted with my enquiry. The first person I approached said he had no idea, but referred me to a financial expert. The 'expert' thought it might be about the Schedule A tax, a property tax that was abolished that year. A third intervened to say that was nonsense: Schedule A had been voted on the previous day. He thought we were voting on a purchase tax on furniture. Finally a real expert intervened who had actually taken part in the debate and revealed that the vote on furniture would take place later and that this was a vote on a tax on kiddies' sweets, which was the most controversial item of that year's Finance Bill.

Unless a bill is about an issue they know and care about, MPs vote as the whips tell them. The charge is frequently made in debate: 'But when you were in government (or in opposition as the case may be) you voted in favour of the measure you are now opposing (or vice versa).' But a vote may give no indication of an MP's views. In fact MPs sometimes even speak in favour of a measure yet, for reasons of party loyalty, then vote against it. The rule at Westminster was laid down by Disraeli: 'Damn your principles. Stick to your party.' And whatever you do, do not vote with the Conservatives if you are Labour, or with Labour if you are a Conservative. MPs have recently shown more signs of independence and now vote against the whip or abstain more often than before on matters they know and really care about. Labour MPs rebelled over Iraq in 2003 and control orders to deal with suspected terrorists, and Tory MPs have recently almost routinely rebelled over policy on Europe. But in general in my day voting against the party or even abstaining on a three-line whip was strictly taboo.

During my time at Westminster that taboo was only seriously broken once in a major rebellion. On 28 October 1971, on the historically important decision that Britain should join the European Community, sixty-nine Labour MPs voted in favour, against a three-line whip and in support of the Conservative government. But their rebellion produced a violent reaction. Roy Jenkins, who led the revolt, was screamed at by Labour loyalists and called 'a fascist bastard'. In an interview in 1995, over twenty years later, Barbara Castle said she could still never forgive the Jenkinsites for their 'party treachery' in 'putting Europe first' and she proudly recalled describing 'the pro-market fanatics as sanctimonious, middle-class hypocrites'.[†] A European

---

[†]   Young, H., *This Blessed Plot* (London: Macmillan, 1998), p. 260.

Communities Bill that made the decision effective in law followed soon after the vote in principle. Without it we could not have become members. Naturally the Bill was opposed by Labour's anti-Europeans but, for the rather disreputable reason of peace and party unity, it was agreed at a meeting of the pro-Europeans that they would also oppose the Bill. Several of them made strong speeches in favour of it but voted against. Since a number of Tory anti-Europeans also opposed the Bill, it was touch-and-go at its third reading whether it would be passed, reversing the effect of the vote on membership of the EEC. I told my friends I would abstain. Bill Rodgers, David Owen and others of my pro-European colleagues strongly pressed me to vote with the party (from which I had not yet resigned) because it was well-known that I was threatened with deselection by activists in my local party. I abstained nevertheless, but agreed to do so quietly and not make a speech. Even abstention was considered a reckless act by pro-Europeans, and treachery by the antis.

In retrospect, I regret I was not more principled and courageous. I should have voted boldly for the Bill. I should have spoken out to denounce the extraordinary spectacle of MPs speaking one way and voting another. But at the time, I too felt inhibited by Westminster convention.

Of course Europe is a special issue, like the Corn Laws in the nineteenth century and Imperial Preference in the early twentieth, one that arouses such passionate feelings that it breaks up parties. In the 1970s and 1980s, it was the Labour Party that was so anti-European that only anti-European candidates were likely to be adopted at selection conferences. Europe was the biggest single cause of the birth of the SDP. By the 1990s roles were reversed: Labour became broadly pro-European and it is among

Conservatives that ideological aversion to the EU now seems to overrule all other considerations, such as party unity or even electoral consequences.

Apart from Europe, there are other occasions when a debate and the subsequent vote may influence a historic decision – for example whether Britain should go to war in Iraq. These can show the House of Commons at its best and individual speeches may even have some influence. However, I found much of my time spent in the Commons frustrating and even boring. You hang around waiting for votes. You are endlessly busy attending meetings but without any useful result. On those occasions when I put my name down to take part in a debate on a major issue, I would sit in the chamber for hours waiting to make my own uniquely important contribution – if I was called at all, because there are too many MPs and in major debates only some would be called. If you did speak, your speech seldom made any impact. At most, in those days, it might rate a few lines in the broadsheets. Since then, press reporting of speeches has ceased altogether, except for parliamentary sketches. But at least aficionados can nowadays watch proceedings on the parliamentary channel on television. In time I found speeches became the perfect cure for insomnia and ever since leaving the Commons I have a Pavlovian reaction that makes me struggle desperately to stay awake during almost any speech anywhere.

The biggest change for the better since my day has been the rising importance of select committees, which do have influence and attract widespread publicity, as they did over phone hacking, Plebgate, the mismanagement of banks, security leaks and a range of other issues that make headlines. They have greatly increased the powers of Parliament as a check on the executive and as a watchdog over other manifestations of misconduct in public life. Nevertheless, I believe there are many MPs who begin to wonder after a while whether their life as a backbench Member of Parliament is altogether satisfying.

In the late 1970s one of the guests on the BBC Radio 4 programme *You the Jury* was John Pardoe, the Liberal MP for North Cornwall, who over a drink after the broadcast raised the question, 'Why do MPs fight so hard to stay in Parliament despite all the frustrations of parliamentary life? In my case,' he said, 'the sole reason is that I can't stand the thought of the other buggers winning.' Many MPs fight on long after they realise that they are unlikely to make a significant contribution to the government of the nation. They stay on, either because they do not know what else to do, or because of that dog-in-the-manger attitude expressed by John Pardoe. Anyway, what alternative occupation could many of them find, since nowadays most are professional politicians? Even if MPs come from another profession, such as the law or teaching, constituencies now demand full-time commitment to their parliamentary duties, allowing no easy way back if they lose or resign their seats. John Pardoe himself had many talents that he could have exploited outside Parliament, and did so when he lost his seat in 1979. At Cambridge he was active in the amateur theatre club Footlights – one critic of its 1955 revue panned Jonathan Miller while predicting a bold comic future for Pardoe.

One of the strongest attractions of Parliament is the chance to become a minister and bring about changes in the law or public policy that you have always talked about but never been able to influence. Many are the able MPs, however, who never become ministers. John Mackintosh, for instance, was a very

able academic and a brilliant speaker, possibly the most talented
Labour MP of his generation. He died in 1978 at the age of
forty-eight. He displeased both the Labour Prime Ministers
of his day: Wilson who regarded him as too disloyal and
Callaghan who thought him too clever. If it had not been for
Roy Jenkins's influence, I too might have been disqualified by
Wilson's strong hostility. Waiting for office may also turn out to
be a very long and disappointing wait, depending not only on
the goodwill of the party leader, but on which party is in power
and for how long. Furthermore, there is no doubt that hope of
preferment does not encourage independence and dissent.

Some, splendidly, do not care. Bob Marshall-Andrews who was
a Labour MP from 1997 until 2010 seems to have greatly enjoyed
his time in Parliament, yet clearly demonstrated that he had no
ambitions for office, or if he had could hardly be accused of
ingratiating himself with his leader. When Tony Blair was at the
height of his popularity, he once told the BBC *Today* programme
that Blair was 'the worst Prime Minister for a century and a
half'. When carpeted by the Chief Whip, he apologised: 'On
reflection I have come to the conclusion that I was wrong ... I
think it is necessary to go back to Wellington before we can find a
Prime Minister who has treated his people with more contempt
and deceit.'[†] He fought many a battle for civil rights, several of
them with some success, against the oppressive anti-terrorist
legislation of the last Labour government.

In another case, rebellion rather perversely led to promotion.
It happened to the young David Owen. I have never been an
unqualified admirer of Owen, and we differed profoundly about

---

[†]   Marshall-Andrews, B., *Off Message: The Complete Antidote to Political Humbug*
      (London: Profile Books, 2011), p. 30.

the relations between the SDP and the Liberals after the SDP was launched, but I have always rather liked his bloody-mindedness. No one can accuse him of being a glad-hander desperately eager to please. In September 1967, three young backbenchers, John Mackintosh, David Marquand and David Owen, wrote a pamphlet titled 'Change Gear', which criticised the policies of Wilson's government. As Owen records in *David Owen Personally Speaking*:

This pamphlet got a lot of favourable publicity, a great deal of it from Norah Beloff in the *Observer*. It was put about, apparently from No. 10, that there was more to the Marquand, Mackintosh and Owen relationship with Miss Beloff than supplying information. It was a scurrilous campaign; Norah was a much respected political columnist, older than any of us and totally professional in her approach to politics. I was very angry about this, not so much about the innuendos – which were comic, really – but that they were coming directly from No. 10. In the spring of '68, I met Harold Wilson in a House of Commons lift. I thought this was not an opportunity to be missed and said in effect: 'now, look here, these stories that keep coming out about us three being involved with Norah Beloff: they're absolutely bloody nonsense, and you know they are. Yet I gather they're being put out with your agreement from No. 10 Downing Street. I'm not having it. If you believe this stuff, you should say it to our face.' Harold Wilson mumbled away – I can't remember what he said – the lift doors opened and he stepped out, and walked away hurriedly. I thought that conversation had finished any promotion prospects I might ever have.[†]

---

† Owen, D., *David Owen: Personally Speaking to Kenneth Harris* (London: Pan Books, 1988), pp. 41–2.

Soon afterwards, impressed, it seems, by Owen's talents, not least as a troublesome rebel, Wilson gave Owen a job. I believe that the main reason why Owen still commands public respect is because the public values his independence of mind. He is also no tribalist and judges proposals or opinions irrespective of their party source.

I was lucky, because in 1966 I was appointed a junior minister under Roy Jenkins, first at the Home Office and then in 1968 at the Treasury, and my life as a minister in those departments was deeply satisfying. In a number of ways I believe I did make a difference and, on top of that, it was a hugely enjoyable time. If my sole experience of Parliament had been as a loyal foot-soldier on the backbenches I would not have regarded my twelve-and-a-half years as an MP as a wholly satisfying part of my career. Furthermore, my parliamentary career itself became unusually dramatic and exhilarating when I defied party convention and stood against both major parties as an independent and won.

CHAPTER 6

POWER

When Labour won a disappointing, wafer-thin majority of six in the election of October 1964 I took my first step on the ministerial ladder by becoming Parliamentary Private Secretary to Denis Healey, the new Secretary of State for Defence. However, being a PPS (except PPS to the Prime Minister or party leader) is something of a non-job. You are the eyes and ears of the minister in the House and must be able to explain to your colleagues what he or she is trying to do. The main advantage is that you learn something about the way your minister works and gain an inside view of his or her department. Denis was a good minister to be attached to: outstandingly intelligent, hugely knowledgeable about international affairs and a polymath, with interests ranging from literature, philosophy and the arts to photography. He was witty and utterly lacking in self-importance or pomposity and was probably the best Secretary for Defence there has been since the war, not least because his own wartime experience made him sceptical about much of the professional advice he received.

One of his idiosyncrasies was to be more impressed by the written than the spoken word. He was not a good listener. As mentioned in the last chapter, in the mid-1960s the Americans promoted a somewhat eccentric scheme for a multilateral defence force (MLF) consisting of merchant ships to be armed with nuclear missiles and crews of mixed NATO nationalities. I told Denis there was no support for this idea and that it could not work. He did not disagree but seemed to dismiss my comments as irrelevant. I then put exactly the same comments in a written submission. He responded with enthusiasm, praising me for the excellence of my analysis, with which he said he completely agreed. In fact the scheme won little support and was duly dropped.

I had one clash with him over policy. Before my appointment I had been asked to give a lecture on Aden by the Royal United Services Institution, a body highly respected on defence issues. After my visit to the Yemen I had written an article in *The Observer*, titled 'Storm Clouds over Aden', arguing that the proposed South Arabian Federation would fail and that the longer term prospects for our naval base in Aden were doubtful. I asked Denis if he had any objections. 'None at all,' he said, 'provided you don't say anything I disagree with.' I told him what I planned to say, in line with the article. He said I was completely wrong and must refuse to speak, which I did. In due course we abandoned our base in Aden.

I liked him a lot, but never got to know him really well. He was a political loner, not interested in cultivating his fellow MPs, probably because he valued his private and family life too much, a view with which I wholly sympathise. The parliamentary party contained groups of Jenkinsites, Wilson followers, Croslandites, the Victory for Socialism group – but no Healey-ites. Those who became his PPS after me ended up much closer to Roy Jenkins than to Denis. However he introduced me to some extremely interesting people. I met several of the top brass of the services, who told me that whereas the Tories had been condescending, assuming that they were rather stupid, Denis treated them as intelligent equals. Inside and outside the ministry he was regarded as a successful Secretary of State, a commendation bestowed on few of his successors at Defence. He was also unique in holding the same post for the whole period of Wilson's first government.

Most rewardingly, he made me his deputy on the executive committee of the Bilderberg Conferences, in which he played a leading part. These were annual meetings of leading politicians, economists, businessmen and journalists of the Western world (a sort of smaller, more select political Davos – the annual jaunt of the world's great and the good) that were then presided over by Prince Bernhard of the Netherlands. They would discuss two major topics, one economic and the other about the future of the Western alliance. Bilderberg was often referred to as a sinister international conspiracy, since the media were excluded. They were excluded, not unreasonably, because it was thought that exchanges at such a high level would not be frank if they were reported. I attended four of these meetings at exotic locations: at Villa D'Este on Lake Como, Mont Tremblant in Canada, Saltsjöbaden near Stockholm and, somewhat less grandly, at Cambridge. When it was Britain's turn to be host, sponsors for grand mansions or castles were in short supply but someone imaginatively suggested St John's College, Cambridge, where the international dignitaries were housed in humble student lodgings. Austerity was more than compensated for by having our meetings and meals in its historic hall with portraits of Wordsworth and other eminent alumni on the walls. The participants loved it.

At the meeting in 1968 at Mont Tremblant (a Canadian skiing resort), I had the strange experience of sharing a chalet with Enoch Powell MP, very shortly after he had made his notorious speech about seeing the Tiber foaming with blood if we did not put a stop to immigration. Several of the participants at the conference had been discussing whether they could bear to shake hands with him when they met him. I thought I should be polite and talk to him when he arrived at our chalet. I found he was on a high, seemingly intoxicated by his new status as popular hero. Dockers had marched through the streets of London chanting 'don't knock Enoch'. He told me he had formerly regarded the arrival of a friendly Post Office van as an uneventful occasion but now each van would disgorge a vast flood of fan mail, more than he could cope with. His only regret, he later declared, was that he ought to have quoted the phrase in the original Latin. I have looked it up and it was part of Virgil's account of the ominous ravings of a prophetess who foretold horrid wars: '*et Thybrim multo spumantem sanguine cerno.*'[†] I suspect that quoting the Latin original might have sparked off a rather less explosive popular reaction. Enoch Powell was a dedicated classical scholar, appointed Professor of Greek at Sydney University at the age of twenty-six and was at the time the youngest professor in the then British Empire. He was one of the last British politicians to quote Latin in the House of Commons, which was not an unknown occurrence in pre-Second World War days. Then Conservative MPs would pretend they understood, even if they did not; Labour MPs would pretend they did not, even if they did.

For my own amusement, I once wrote a letter to *The Times*

[†]   'And I see the river Tiber foaming with much blood.' *The Aeneid*, book Six, line 87.

in Latin, which surprisingly they published. In 1981, at the time
of the founding of the SDP, I quoted some Virgil that seemed
appropriate as an appeal to all former Gaitskellites to join the
new party. In Book Two of the *Aeneid*, at the time of the fall of
Troy the ghost of Hector appears to Aeneas in a dream and
urges him to leave and found a new country:

> *Hostis habet muros. Ruit alta a culmine Troja*
> *Sat patriae Priamoque datum. Si Pergama dextra*
> *Defendi possent, etiam his defensa fuissent.*

Literally, this said: 'The enemy has captured the walls and
mighty Troy now lies in ruins. You have done what you could
for King and Country. If anyone's valour could have saved Troy,
mine would have done so.' I roughly translated it as a speech
by the ghost of Gaitskell to his old friends who had not yet
joined the SDP:

> The Left have taken control of the party.
> Old Labour is finished.
> If I could not save Labour, who could?
> Your only hope is to found a new party.

A journalist friend of mine, Terry Lancaster, wrote a comment
in the *Daily Mirror* about what an elitist lot the prominent SDP
people were. Why, one of them even wrote a letter to *The Times*
most of which was in Latin! Beside his comment there was a
cartoon of me with the subtitle: 'Latin lover'.

After Labour's disappointing result in 1964, the election that
followed in March 1966 was a triumph for Harold Wilson,

who won a majority of ninety-eight. This time I became a real minister. To my delight I was appointed to one of the ideal jobs in government: Parliamentary Under-Secretary at the Home Office, where Roy Jenkins was Home Secretary. It promised and proved to be ideal because law reform had been one of my special interests as a barrister, Roy Jenkins was a friend and the rising star of the government, and major legal and social reforms were on the agenda. As it turned out, the twenty months that followed, before Roy went to the Treasury, were the most intensive period of reform in the history of the Home Office.

The reforms included the legalisation of abortion in defined circumstances and of homosexual conduct in private between consenting adults; the abolition of flogging in prisons and of theatre censorship; the introduction of a parole system, suspended sentences, majority verdicts in jury trials; the reform of race relations; and major reform of the gaming laws. Roy reorganised the police service, reducing the number of separate forces from 117 to 49; supplied them with walkie-talkies on a scale they never expected; and introduced new blood into the Metropolitan Police, beginning a process of recruiting ethnic minorities that had been completely neglected and is still disappointing in the progress made.

Ben Pimlott summed up the Jenkins reforms in his biography of Wilson as consolidating a mood of change in British society, which promoted more civilised social values and benefited millions. They were the most important changes of the Wilson administration.[†]

I should add that Roy's success in social reform was matched

---

†   Pimlott, B., *Harold Wilson* (London: HarperCollins, 1992), p. 487.

by his success with the police. When Roy Jenkins left the Home
Office he not only received the accolade of liberal reformers but
also what I believe was unprecedented: a special presentation
by the Police Federation for his support of the police. A senior
superintendent buttonholed me at a party to say how much the
police regretted his departure. 'Before Roy's time,' he said, 'we
were vainly pushing Home Secretaries as hard as we could to
modernise the service and improve our equipment. Then along
came this man and we had to run to keep up with the pace of
his reforms.'

What contribution did I, as a junior minister, make to this
remarkable record? My experience was very different from
that of Chris Mullin, who regretted that during his five years as
junior minister between 1999 and 2003 he had achieved nothing
that made any difference.[†] Many years later at a special lunch
for Roy Jenkins and some of his friends given by the Master of
Balliol, Anthony Kenny, Roy described me as his favourite junior
minister.[‡] I greatly benefited from the fact that Roy believed in
delegation. If he trusted you, he left you in charge of your area
of responsibility.

Within a few weeks of my appointment I was thrown in at
the deep end: to chair a conference about a proposed treaty on
extradition between Commonwealth countries. It was not an
easy conference because many Commonwealth countries had
special problems of their own. Ours presented the most difficult
of all, the right not to extradite those convicted of murder in

---

[†]   Mullin, C., *A View From the Foothills* (London: Profile Books, 2009).
[‡]   It was a curious lunch, attended among others by the novelist Anthony
       Powell, who sat next to Janice. He recorded it in his diaries and described her
       as 'quite pretty, but I suspect a bit of a handful', as if she was a somewhat
       troublesome filly.

Britain to a country where they would be subject to the death penalty that Britain had recently abolished. I was asked, 'Do you really want to become the haven for the worst criminals in the Commonwealth?' I was helped by three factors.

The first was that several of the Ministers of Justice and Attorneys-General representing their country had at one time been members of Dingle Foot's chambers, my own chambers, where many promising barristers from the Commonwealth had experienced some of their early practice in the law. They could not have been more friendly. Secondly, there was an extraordinary atmosphere of general goodwill and a determination to reach agreement, particularly among the newer Commonwealth states. Thirdly, this general support was bolstered by the behaviour of the one exception, an Attorney-General from one small West African country who raised constant objections and seemed throughout to be under the influence of either alcohol or drugs. Whatever he opposed the others would support. (I learned he had once been prosecuted for some offence by another of the Attorneys-General present, when they had both been barristers in the same home state.) In the end our deliberations were successfully concluded and resulted in the Fugitive Offenders Act of 1967.

Another task I was given was to introduce a scheme for the accelerated promotion of graduates in the police, later known as the Taverne scheme. At the time there were very few graduates in the police and little to attract them to a police career. According to the Home Office Permanent Secretary at the time, Sir Philip Allen, later Lord Allen of Abbeydale, the scheme proved a success, but it was hard work persuading the police to accept it. They had bitter memories of a previous scheme, to create a service-type officer class in the Metropolitan Police through a special course at Hendon Police College, which was widely regarded as introducing a form of elitism alien to the democratic traditions of the force. I did a lot of work with the police and got on particularly well with the Police Federation. When I ceased to be a minister after Labour's defeat in 1970, they invited me to be their parliamentary adviser, a reasonably well-paid post. I said I would be happy to advise them on particular issues if they needed help, but could not accept their offer as I had to be free to express my own views when they differed from theirs. For example, their rank and file favoured the return of capital punishment, which I strongly opposed.

I also played some part in the social reform laws passed between 1966 and 1968. Abortion and homosexual law reform were regarded as issues of conscience, not a matter for government. The best hope of changing the law was sponsorship by an MP who had won a high place in the ballot for a Private Member's Bill. (Only a very few Private Members' Bills have any chance of enough parliamentary time to go successfully through all the necessary legislative stages.) In 1966, the most promising winner was a young Scottish Liberal MP, David Steel. Roy asked me to persuade him to sponsor homosexual law reform but David said, regretfully, as a son of the manse that was impossible. However he did agree to take on the formidable task of piloting a bill through the House of Commons to reform abortion law, which he did with great skill and courage (and with invaluable support from the Home Office). As for decriminalising homosexual acts between consenting adults, Roy persuaded the Cabinet to take the most unusual step of giving time to a Ten Minute Rule Bill sponsored by the MP Leo Abse. They did

so somewhat reluctantly because this procedure had not been
adopted before. Again, credit for taking the Bill through its various stages belonged to Leo Abse, but the Home Office gave vital
technical help. There is no doubt that without Roy's powerful
support neither reform would have been achieved. Looking
back on the decriminalisation of homosexuality, it was a good
example of how leadership by government can help to change
public opinion by changing the law. In 1967 the change was
deeply controversial, especially in Conservative circles. In 2013
gay marriage was approved by overwhelming majorities in both
Houses of Parliament, with a majority in the Lords of 390 to 148
which included a large number of Conservative peers.

One issue left entirely to me to manage was the reform of our
gaming laws. I was first asked to introduce the Bill at the end
of 1967 to give effect to the Royal Commission of 1951. This
commission seemed to pay excessive regard to the views of the
churches, with an underlying tone of moral disapproval of all
gaming, and was often referred to as 'the vicar's charter'. One
of its central proposals was to forbid casinos to keep the zero in
roulette. Representations from gambling friends as well as from
legitimate casinos convinced me, for rather complicated mathematical reasons, that this would inevitably lead to the bankruptcy
of the bank and would make legal gaming impossible. Much
gaming had already gone underground. The police warned us
that the Mafia were sniffing around several major cities including London, Manchester and Newcastle, and if the Mafia got
a foothold, there would be grave results on crime in Britain.
Witnesses would be bribed or terrorised and would never testify
against the Mafia. Furthermore, rigid legal regulation would be
ineffective since sophisticated gamblers would always find a way

round it. Some, I was told by experienced gaming friends, could make a pack of cards stand up and sing the national anthem.

On my advice, the new Bill abandoned the recommendations of the Royal Commission and allowed legal gaming to be profitably conducted under the strict controls of a powerful Gaming Board, with arbitrary powers, modelled in some respects on those of the Jockey Club, which would be unacceptable in other legal contexts. In the committee stages of the Gaming Bill, Conservative opposition members, many of whom had far more experience of gambling than Home Office civil servants or Labour MPs, helped to create a board with draconian powers of control over casinos, bingo clubs and gaming machines. The underlying approach was practical: accepting that there would be gambling but ensuring that it was properly controlled. Subsequently, a Royal Commission set up in 1974 to review our handiwork declared that the act we fathered was working well and gave it a completely clean bill of health.

One of the valuable lessons I learned from Roy was not to be overwhelmed by minor matters and to avoid working too hard. He had spells of acute crisis when he could not avoid working long hours, but generally by good organisation he kept his desk clear and found time to think, to read (not only official papers) and to talk, preferably over a good dinner and a good bottle of claret. Roy was blessed with an almost Johnsonian memory which meant that he never had to reread papers or books. He also had the ability to see quickly the essential points of any document or presentation. My own experience of colleagues in government was that those who complained that they were overwhelmed with work were the least effective ministers.

One of the duties of junior ministers is to answer letters

written by MPs on behalf of their constituents. A flood of letters seemed to take up nearly all the time of many of my colleagues. I greatly reduced this burden by telling my civil service private secretary that I would sign most letters without reading them, except for checking the odd one to ensure that letters were written in a readable style. However, I insisted that I had to see any letter that might be important or politically sensitive. I remember no occasion when this injunction was ignored.

I also made sure that when I had to make an important decision or attend an important departmental conference, I first had time to think, read and discuss the views of others. When a parole board was about to be established for the first time, Roy arranged a conference to decide whether it should be a Home Office board or an independent one. The official recommendation was to keep it in the Home Office. Roy said he had originally favoured an independent board but was impressed by the apparently unanimous view of the department, backed by powerful arguments, to keep it internal. He asked my views. I had postponed all other business the previous day, and spent it finding out what the Home Office arguments were and discussing pros and cons with my very able private secretary, Syd Norris, and some outside experts. I was well prepared with counter-arguments and in the event my case for an independent board won the day.

Another lesson I learned from Roy was the importance of making the right appointments. He said appointments were the most important decisions he took. Looking back on my own career, two of the most important decisions I made were my choice of John Kay as Director of IFS (see Chapter 8) and of Tracey Brown as Director of Sense About Science (see Chapter 10).

I did not stay long at the Home Office after Jenkins swapped jobs with Jim Callaghan, who became the new Home Secretary, because a few months later in March 1968 he persuaded Wilson to appoint me Minister of State at the Treasury, and in 1969 as Financial Secretary, a job I held until the Labour Party's defeat in 1970. I therefore had four years, as his junior minister and a friend and colleague, to observe why Roy came to be widely acknowledged as by far the most successful minister of the first Wilson government, not only at the Home Office but also at the Treasury.

From the moment he entered the Cabinet he became its most influential member. As Chancellor his standing rose even higher than it had been at the Home Office. In 1968 Dick Crossman described him in his diaries as 'the dominant force', in 1970 as 'omnipotent'. I believe he was one of the two outstanding figures of British politics since the war – only Margaret Thatcher, I would reluctantly concede, had greater impact. He was unique in combining three rare qualities: mastery of the House of Commons; a major and lasting influence on events and on our society; and great distinction as a writer and historian. No one else in the last century except Churchill combined these three qualities, though of course in oratory and achievement Churchill was incomparable.

What was the reason for his success and why was he such a pleasure to work with? First, in debate he dominated the House of Commons, despite a rather poor delivery and a voice that lacked resonance. He could not say his 'r's, which became 'w's, hence his nickname 'Woy Jenkins', but these handicaps proved irrelevant. His greatest triumph came early on in his Home Office days, on an issue that seemed likely to cause him greatest embarrassment. In October 1966, when Labour morale was at a very low ebb, despite the recent election victory, a spy called George Blake escaped from Wormwood Scrubs where he was serving a 42-year prison sentence. He had been responsible for the death of a number of British agents. There was a national uproar and the Conservatives, led by two of their most eloquent House of Commons performers, Quintin Hogg and Enoch Powell, put down a censure motion. Roy wound up the debate and in his reply, a speech that several commentators described as the most outstanding parliamentary occasion of the time, he launched a devastating attack on the Conservatives for moving a censure motion. It was a Conservative Home Secretary who had decided to commit Blake to Wormwood Scrubs and another who had kept him there, without extra security precautions, even after a prisoner had reported that an escape plot was being hatched. At the end of his speech the Labour benches were cheering wildly and waving their order papers. It was such a boost to party morale that one of them remarked: 'Can we not arrange for a spy to escape every week?'

Jenkins scored many other parliamentary triumphs, as Chancellor as well as Home Secretary, though none to match the Blake debate. For example, after the fiasco of the 1967 devaluation that led to his appointment as Chancellor, his first Budget speech in 1968 lasted two hours and twenty-seven minutes, as he recorded – he loved numerical exactitude. It imposed tax rises and expenditure cuts unprecedented in their severity. But the speech was so carefully prepared, so powerfully argued and felicitously phrased, and so persuasive that at its end Labour benchers cheered him to the echo. In his frequent arguments with the shadow Chancellor, Iain Macleod, perhaps the most able member of the Conservative front bench, Roy invariably came out on top. The Conservative magazine *The Spectator* (which Macleod had once edited) described their confrontations as a contest between Macleod's cobra and Roy's Rikki-Tikki-Tavi.

Not only were Jenkins's speeches meticulously prepared but, like Churchill, he had an exceptional gift for impromptu repartee. I remember one speech when Enoch Powell made what appeared to be a particularly effective interruption. Roy paused, thought, and looked at the ceiling. The pause lasted so long that the Labour benches began to stir uncomfortably, feeling that perhaps for once he had been put off his stride. Then he answered: 'The Right Honourable gentleman's logic is as always impeccable, but as he always starts from false premises, he is bound to come to a wrong conclusion.' In a way, that summed up Enoch Powell's whole career.

It mattered, because a telling interruption can demolish a speech. Simon Hoggart once told me, when we travelled back from some television discussion after I had left Parliament, that it once happened to Roy Hattersley. He had waxed eloquent about some U-turn in Conservative policy and asked dramatically, 'Can anyone imagine a more signal example of the triumph of expediency over principle?' Norman St John-Stevas interrupted him: 'Has the Right Honourable gentleman considered his own career?' Apparently the whole House, Labour benches as well as Conservatives, dissolved in laughter and Hattersley was barely able to continue his speech. (In due course, Hattersley recovered and the incident was forgotten.)

I remember another occasion when Jenkins was asked on television what he thought of Neil Kinnock, who had recently become Labour leader. Roy observed without any hesitation: 'He is an amiable young man with no very settled opinions, except for a strong but ineffective desire to be Prime Minister.' At a later stage of Kinnock's career, in the light of his brave stand against the Militant tendency and his vital role in bringing the Labour Party back to sanity after its erratic Bennite phase, I think Roy's judgement would have been very different.

Wit and a felicitous choice of phrase were part of both Jenkins's oratory and his writing. One of my favourite examples of the latter occurs in his magisterial biography of Gladstone in which he describes Gladstone's unfortunate failure to keep the Marquess of Hartington onside on the issue of Irish Home Rule. Shared classical knowledge, he wrote, was important in Gladstone's personal relations. All his close personal friends 'could confidently and happily exchange Latin and Greek quotations with him', but 'Hartington preferred quadrupeds to hexameters'.[†]

Roy's judgement impressed me even before I knew him well. The group of Oxbridge graduates we had formed, known as 'The Group', (see Chapter 4) to discuss politics would ask interesting Labour MPs to talk to us after a dinner. It was then that I met Roy for the first time, towards the end of 1958. We asked him about the likely composition of the next Labour government, which the polls forecast was almost inevitable. I vividly remember his answer: 'Why do you assume we will win? Our party is deeply divided over defence. Macmillan has established his authority in the Commons and the Conservative Party, and his stature in the country is rising. [He duly became 'Super Mac'.] An economic boom is under way.' Later, after Labour's

---

[†] Edward Pearce, that erudite journalist and biographer, told me that Hartington was known as 'Harty-tarty' for reasons too enjoyable to need clarification.

dispiriting defeat in 1959 and the violent row at the subsequent party conference, commentators predicted an indefinite period of Conservative rule. Jenkins wrote an article in *The Spectator* to the effect that, while prospects for Labour did not look good, we should remember that in 1902, with the Liberals deeply divided in the aftermath of the Boer war, there seemed no cloud on the horizon for Salisbury's government. Four years later the Conservative government suffered the biggest defeat in modern British history. Roy's extensive knowledge of history helped to give his judgements a sense of perspective that meant he changed his mind on major issues less often than any other politician I can think of.

Good judgement as well as political clout was crucial in the Treasury, where the task he faced was as formidable as any faced by any Chancellor since the Second World War, until the crash of 2008. In one of his favourite meteorological metaphors he compared his experience at the Home Office, where 'sudden storms blew up out of a clear sky and vanished almost as suddenly as they arose', with his time at the Treasury, which was one of 'a long Arctic winter slowly lightening into spring'.

Not only did he have to persuade the Cabinet that the measures he took were right but had to persuade the party and the country, which he did. In 1964 when a Labour government was elected after thirteen years of Conservative rule, it was committed to an ambitious programme of public spending based on a highly optimistic assumption of a much higher rate of economic growth than its Conservative predecessors had been able to achieve. Within weeks of coming to power Labour's plans were wrecked by a balance of payments crisis, which continued until near the middle of 1969.

Today it is hard to envisage how completely the balance of payments dominated economic policy at the time. Those were the days of the post-war Bretton Woods Agreement that required the maintenance of currencies within narrow limits round a fixed exchange rate, unless consent was obtained from the International Monetary Fund to a formal devaluation.

Early devaluation would almost certainly have eased Britain's problem, but was ruled out by Wilson for political reasons. Instead, a succession of restrictive emergency measures slowed down economic growth but failed to improve the balance of payments or restore confidence in the pound. All the time public expenditure grew unrestrained. In November 1967, Wilson and the Chancellor, James Callaghan, lost their costly and hopeless battle to save the parity of the pound and sterling was devalued by 14 per cent. Not only Callaghan's but Wilson's reputation was shattered and his loss of standing was aggravated by an ill-judged broadcast in which he reassured the public that devaluation did not 'mean that the pound in the pocket is worth 14 per cent less now than it was'. The statement was technically correct but the tone of the broadcast was, according to Barbara Castle, 'too complacent by half', or as his biographer, Ben Pimlott put it, 'If there was a suitable tone for such an occasion, it was prob-ably Dunkirk spirit. Instead, Wilson seemed to be announcing El Alamein, or Trafalgar.'[†]

So when Roy Jenkins became Chancellor in November 1967 the state of the British economy and the fortunes of the Labour government could not have been more dire. Not only was the balance of payments in deep deficit, but the Bank of England's

---

[†]   Pimlott, *Harold Wilson*, p. 483.

reserves were so low that there was every possibility that we would be forced into a further devaluation or into floating the pound, which in the circumstances would probably have been calamitous. However, as the man to deal with the crisis, Roy's reputation after his outstanding success as Home Secretary could not have been higher. His appointment was met by general acclaim and by what Roy himself described as 'hyperbolic editorial comment' in the *Sunday Times*, which said that the whole future of the British economy and of the Labour Party, and even of British democracy, depended on his success in the Treasury.

In fact his appointment was far from inevitable. Callaghan, whose relations with Roy were not good – according to Pimlott he once denounced Roy when he was Home Secretary to Wilson as 'an ambitious, conspiring opportunist' – lobbied strongly for Crosland, who was considered by many to be an obvious choice because he was a professional economist which Roy was not. Roy had a first-class Oxford degree in philosophy, politics and economics, but that did not make him an economist. However, Wilson recognised the importance of Roy's high standing in the parliamentary party and had greater trust in his judgement. He also got on better with Roy than with Crosland. Roy found the Prime Minister amiable and personally considerate, as most people did. On at least two occasions they had pleasurable conversations about trains. As an undergraduate Wilson had won the Gladstone Memorial Prize with a long dissertation on 'The State and the Railways in Victorian Britain' and Roy, with his eclectic tastes, his passion for numerical detail and his own fascination with the railway system, was happy discussing timetables. They must have been interesting conversations.

The lightening of the Arctic winter into spring took a very

long and stressful time. His first two years in the Treasury seemed an unending struggle to prevent a collapse of sterling and a further devaluation. The monthly trade figures were watched as closely as a patient's heartbeat after a severe heart attack. Most of the time the heartbeat was irregular, and the patient's condition was aggravated by uncertainties in the currency markets at the time. Indeed I vividly remember a conference that Roy went to in Bonn in November 1968 that failed to produce any help from Germany, France or the United States to stabilise the markets. We thought Armageddon was upon us this time. I had to address a large and important City audience and raised loud and prolonged laughter by comparing the task of having to make an amusing after-dinner speech to giving a lecture on the funnier side of the bubonic plague.

However, sterling survived, the trade figures started to improve and the sun rose slowly – but, as Roy observed, oh how slowly. By mid-1969 the monthly balance was mainly favourable. By the end of Roy's chancellorship the dollar and gold reserves had been strengthened dramatically, the balance of payments was in steady surplus, there was a solid budget surplus as well, we had enjoyed two and a half years of economic growth at 3–4 per cent annually and inflation was not appreciably higher than in the United States, which had not devalued, and France, which had devalued by less. It was a formidable success story. But it had been won at a price. Seldom can a Chancellor have inflicted greater pain during his tenure. However, as one of his few critics, Edmund Dell, wrote: 'Never has pain been inflicted with greater elegance.'[†] Dell, who was eventually President of the Board of

---

† Dell, E., *The Chancellors: A History of the Chancellors of the Exchequer, 1945–90* (London: HarperCollins, 1996).

Trade in 1978, was about the only one to criticise Roy's 1968
Budget for not being tough enough. In rather refreshing contrast
to all other Labour ministers of his time, Dell out-hawked every
hawk and was always inclined to believe that either spending
should be cut back further or taxes raised even higher.

Despite the stress, I found the Treasury a happy place to work
in. Roy's team was handpicked, people he trusted and respected
and whose company he enjoyed. Indeed Iain Macleod described
the Treasury team as 'the most formidable team in the government', adding for good measure, 'the only formidable team in the
government'. The most important member was Jack Diamond,
the Chief Secretary, who held the post throughout the period
from 1964 to 1970. Harold Lever was Financial Secretary and
I was the most junior, as Minister of State, and, without false
modesty, the least influential. In October 1969, Harold Lever was
promoted to Paymaster General, I became Financial Secretary
and Bill Rodgers was brought in as Minister of State.

Jack Diamond was a man of the utmost integrity, a charming
but relentless dedicated scourge of spending departments, once
he had Roy's support as a powerful Chancellor, and a miserly
guardian of the public revenues. By contrast, Harold Lever was
an unusual socialist who had made millions speculating on the
Stock Exchange, a skilful gambler and bridge player, a brilliant
dilettante with instincts the exact opposite of Jack Diamond's.
We had to overrule him constantly because he opposed just about
every proposed cut in public spending and rise in taxation and,
at a time of income restraint, favoured giving everybody whatever pay increase they asked for. He also argued that the more
we borrowed, the stronger our international bargaining position
would be, because big debtors caused everyone big problems.

However, he was exceptionally imaginative and effective in dealing with the IMF and the moguls of international finance, which
more than made up for his domestic heterodoxies. He was also
the wittiest speaker in Parliament.

I remember an all-night debate on the committee stage of
the 1968 Finance Bill when Harold Lever and I were in charge.
At 6 a.m. we had both nodded off. A Conservative, John Hall,
MP for High Wycombe, asked not unreasonably which minister
was dealing with the particular clause being debated so that at
least one of them could wake up. It was Harold's clause. He
woke from deep sleep and instantly answered, 'The Honourable
gentleman is no more justified in inferring from the fact that our
eyes are closed that we are asleep than we would be in inferring
from the fact that his eyes are open that he is awake.'

On one rare and memorable occasion, during a conference
with Roy Jenkins on a rather important decision about tax, it was
Jack Diamond, a much quieter, much less extrovert character,
who turned the tables on Harold. A proposal was made that tax
relief should no longer be allowed on overdrafts. In my view the
proposal was right because it would block a widely used method of
tax avoidance and reduce consumption. Roy's formidable Private
Secretary, David Dowler, was against it for personal reasons.
Harold was against it because it would increase tax burdens. Some
Treasury civil servants had economic objections. As Jack and I and
other civil servants were known to be in favour, David Dowler carefully arranged the meeting to discuss it with Roy for a time when
neither Jack nor I could attend, and in our absence the proposal
was rejected. We protested and Roy was persuaded to have a
rerun. Harold led the opposition and started an argument about
the hardship it would cause: 'Take poor Charlie, a man of modest

means on an income of £10,000 a year. [Harold's examples were often about 'the average man' on an income of £10,000, which is the equivalent of some £100,000 today.] Poor Charlie who has invested in a row of back-to-back houses in Manchester—' Jack Diamond interrupted, 'Correction, Harold. Not poor Charlie, proper Charlie.' Harold did not recover and we won.

The top civil servants in the Treasury also played an important part, chief among them the Permanent Secretary Sir Douglas Allen, later Lord Croham, a most able and congenial man, who described Roy as 'the finest Chancellor I ever worked with'. The Treasury civil servants had never felt at ease with James Callaghan and had little regard for his judgement. In the words of Sir Douglas Wass, who was relatively junior at the time but later also became Permanent Secretary, when Roy Jenkins arrived there was a change from 'a Byzantine, unpredictable system to an open and logical one'. Roy was a good listener and although he liked to keep meetings small, he listened to the views of more junior officials as well as those of the top mandarins and would positively encourage dissent. He was not particularly interested in the way the Treasury was run, which he was happy to leave to the Permanent Secretary, just as he left the details of implementing cuts in expenditure to Jack Diamond. One criticism that can be made is that he was not interested in tax reform, which was badly needed. But overall the respect in which he (and Jack Diamond) were held in the department was demonstrated when after the change of government in 1970 the four top mandarins, Sir Douglas Allen, Sir Frank Figgures, Sir Donald Macdougall (chief economist) and Sam Goldman, unusually gave a farewell dinner for Roy and Jack in the Cabinet room of the Reform Club.

My own contribution at the Treasury was much more limited than in the Home Office. In the Treasury the Chancellor is dominant and other ministers' tasks are mainly to carry out his decisions, persuading spending departments to accept cuts or pursue alternative policies, arguing the details of a Finance Bill in committee, meeting delegations and so on. The Chief Secretary, to whom the management of the purse strings is delegated as the Chancellor's deputy, has considerable discretion in controlling the spending departments. Other ministers can occasionally influence the Chancellor's decisions, as Jack Diamond and I did on taxing overdrafts. But there are few cases when one of them has as much influence as Nigel Lawson exercised as Financial Secretary in Mrs Thatcher's first administration, by virtue of his intellectual power. She promoted him to Secretary of State for Energy and then to Chancellor in 1983 when Geoffrey Howe became Foreign Secretary.

I tried once to introduce a major new tax, an annual wealth tax. A leading economist brought into the Treasury from outside, Nicky Kaldor, was in favour.[†] I had always thought that a wealth tax was a better way to tax the rich than very high marginal income tax rates. Roy encouraged me to explore the idea and I held a meeting at which Nicky argued the case in favour and senior mandarins from the Inland Revenue argued the case against, on the grounds of its great administrative complexity. As Nicky, a very fair-minded man, admitted, the Revenue won hands down. Many imaginative proposals for reform from Nicky were defeated on similar grounds. In fact it seemed that the

---

†   Nicky was a round-shaped, ultra-benign Hungarian. There was also another not at all benign Hungarian economist in the Ministry of Power, Tommy Balogh. The two were known as Buddha and Pest.

Inland Revenue's experts could prove that almost any major tax reform was administratively impossible. In that particular case I think the Inland Revenue was right.

Ireland did introduce a wealth tax. On one of our summer sailing holidays Janice and I were anchored in the harbour of Schull in West Cork, where our friends Anthony and Katya Lester had a cottage.[†] They took us to a party at which I met the former Taoiseach, Garret Fitzgerald, and we discussed the Irish wealth tax. He told me the tax was abandoned because its yield was small, the administrative costs were almost as high and, although it affected only a tiny proportion of the population, it was politically very unpopular because even people with little wealth feared they would be affected.

While I cannot claim that my spell as Treasury minister changed the world, it was a valuable experience and an education in government. Moreover my reputation must have been fairly good since, after I left the Treasury, the founders of the Institute for Fiscal Studies approached me to launch the institute and become its first director. One reason why I accepted was the clear need for an independent outside body to match the Inland Revenue's expertise (see Chapter 7).

I found the Treasury civil servants a most able and agreeable lot. Roy recorded that on his arrival they seemed exhausted and demoralised by the long struggle against devaluation and were not good at suggesting constructive action.[‡] But subsequently the strong support he received from his department was invaluable. When Labour finally returned to office in 1997, nothing in my

---

[†]   Anthony, Lord Lester, has had as much influence as anyone else in the Lords in preventing bad laws and generally promoting civil rights.

[‡]   Jenkins, R., *A Life at the Centre* (London: Macmillan, 1991), p. 220.

view could have been more unwise than Gordon Brown's reliance on his own clique of special advisers (now known as SPADS) led by Ed Balls, while he ignored the advice of the Treasury on many of his most important decisions.

However, Roy Jenkins too had his special advisers, at a time when SPADS were virtually unheard of: David Dowler and John Harris. David Dowler was a civil servant, but a most unusual one. Originally, he had been Roy's Private Secretary in the Department of Civil Aviation, Roy's first ministerial post in 1964 that he had held briefly until the end of 1965 when he became Home Secretary. Roy was so impressed with him that he asked him to become his Private Secretary at the Home Office, and then at the Treasury when he became Chancellor. Naturally both departments greeted Dowler's arrival with moderate enthusiasm; he was a very political civil servant with a personal commitment to one particular minister that transcended any departmental loyalty. But they came to respect his obvious ability and wit. John Harris had been the Labour Party's head of publicity and campaign director in 1964, and was first brought into the Home Office as Roy's adviser and then he also transferred with him to the Treasury. John's political instincts and judgement were as good as anyone's I have known. His ability was later rewarded in 1974 in Wilson's second administration by his surprise appointment as Minister of State in the Home Office, when he became Lord Harris of Greenwich. After Labour's defeat in 1979 he joined the SDP and eventually became Chief Whip for the Liberal Democrats in the House of Lords until he died in 2001. He and David were generally known as 'the Treasury Twins' and were always at Roy's side. Roy rightly relied more on them for discussing the political and publicity problems he faced than on any other individuals. But however wise their counsel in general, they could be *plus royaliste que le Roy* in a way that was sometimes counterproductive. To them you were either Roy's supporter or an enemy.

For example, during negotiations about solving the problem of the sterling balances, one of the main obstacles to agreement was a young brigadier who had been appointed Ghana's finance minister.[†] I discovered that the Ghanaian minister had great admiration for Callaghan after Callaghan's skilful chairmanship of a Commonwealth Finance Ministers' Conference. I had been on reasonable terms with Jim during the few months when he had succeeded Roy as Home Secretary before I transferred to the Treasury, so I suggested I should seek Jim's help. David and John were appalled. 'You must on no account talk to Jim. He is a bad man. He is trying to screw us. Anyway he won't understand and will cock it all up.' I think they were wrong. He would have understood and would have helped.

Despite Roy Jenkins's dominance in the Cabinet, success in maintaining support for his austere policies was not a foregone conclusion. He told me there were only three Cabinet members whose support he could rely on consistently: Wilson, though he would seldom lead and left all the difficult arguments to Roy; Healey (except on one crucial issue); and, surprisingly, Barbara Castle, who in government proved a first-class minister. In the occasional dealings I had with her in her successive departments,

---

[†]   These were debts to Commonwealth countries incurred during the war. If
       the balances were withdrawn, the threat to sterling would have been greatly
       exacerbated. The problem was solved by guaranteeing their value in dollars
       while continuing to pay them the higher interest due on sterling.

Transport and then Employment, I was most impressed by her realism, skill and drive.

Roy's one clash with Denis Healey illustrated an important difference in their political skills. One of the major cuts proposed by Roy in his expenditure review when he became Chancellor was the purchase of a number of US-built FIII aircraft regarded by the Ministry of Defence and the Foreign Office as essential to our continued military presence East of Suez. Roy was against our role East of Suez; Healey strongly in favour, as he showed when in 1963 I had told him that in my view our role in Aden might not be sustainable. Roy's proposal for cancellation won the vote in Cabinet by eleven to ten. Healey not unreasonably asked for time for reflection. He had identified a weak link in the votes for Roy, namely Lord Longford, and arranged for an air marshal to meet him, who convinced Longford that the plane should be ordered. Healey was confident of winning the rerun. In turn, Roy, aware of Lord Longford's weak support, successfully canvassed two of the less committed votes against him, Patrick Gordon Walker and Cledwyn Hughes. The rerun came out twelve to nine for cancellation. Afterwards, Roy told me, Healey generously confessed, 'You are a better politician than me.'

Barbara Castle not only staunchly supported Roy's austerity measures but herself produced a proposal to reform Trade Union law that was a brave attempt at tackling one of the most serious problems of British industry at the time – the growing and increasingly irresponsible use of power by the unions and a rash of unofficial strikes that were causing increasing damage to industry. She dared to tread where Mrs Thatcher later succeeded. Her proposals, set out in a White Paper called *In Place of Strife*, included plans to force the unions to call a ballot before a strike was held and the establishment of an Industrial Board to enforce settlements in industrial disputes. Unfortunately the plans miscarried and resulted in an embarrassing defeat of the government by its opponents within the party and the unions. It was opposed by an unusual powerful alliance between the left wing of the party and right-wing trade unionists who strongly felt that industrial relations should be a matter for the unions and employers, and they should not be regulated by the courts. Wilson strongly backed Barbara. Roy also supported the reform but urged that it should be carried through rapidly, in a short Bill, before opposition in the unions and the party had time to build up. Harold and Barbara instead began a leisurely programme of elaborate negotiations with the unions.

As the debate in the party grew more strident, it became clear that Wilson and Castle were losing the battle. Callaghan led the revolt. Ignoring Cabinet decisions, he moved and carried a critical resolution in the National Executive Committee of the Labour Party and Wilson did not feel he was in a strong enough position to sack him. Anti-Wilson feeling in the parliamentary party over the Castle Bill was stronger than it had ever been on any previous occasion, and many of Roy's followers urged him to abandon support for the reform and challenge Harold for the leadership. They, and many others on the right of the party, were more anti-Wilson than they were pro-Castle Bill. Roy declined. To me it seemed that in any case the obvious leader of any challenge should be Callaghan, as the leader of the opposition to the Bill. However, after a Cabinet meeting that showed overwhelming opposition, Roy told Barbara he could no longer support her, because delay had meant that there was now no chance that the Bill would be passed and there was a danger that the government would break up. 'She accepted the news like St Sebastian receiving another arrow.'[†] Although his judgement of the mistaken tactics and the hopelessness of pressing on were justified – Harold and Barbara seemed ready to emulate Davy Crockett at the Alamo – Roy nevertheless wrote that 'they emerged from the affair with more credit than the rest of us'.

The event raises the question: could Roy Jenkins have become Prime Minister if he had used his dominance in the Cabinet and his strong support in the party to lead a coup against Wilson, as many of his devoted followers urged? I was one of Roy's strongest supporters but sceptical of the prospects of success of any coup. Roy's supporters were always much more eager to launch a revolt than he was. As he wrote, 'There was a dedicated group of commandos, waiting as it were with their faces blackened to launch a Dieppe raid against the forces of opportunism.' In fact the Dieppe analogy was wrong: many of them were dying to launch a full-scale invasion.

It is worth recording why Roy Jenkins had so many friends and why many of them were so devoted. When I first met him properly (at the meeting of The Group) I admired his ability and judgement, but thought he was rather a cold fish. Then, after I was elected to Parliament, he invited Janice and me home and we suddenly found that he and his wife Jennifer had admitted us into a circle of warm friends not usually found in politics. Jennifer was an integral part of that group and, as he acknowledged, 'was fully engaged in all the major decisions and enterprises of my life'. Roy was amusing and stimulating company, but what

---

† Jenkins, *A Life at the Centre*, p. 290.

appealed most was the same kind of integrity that attracted so many to Hugh Gaitskell. He wrote at the end of his autobiography, in assessing whether he might have reached the top of the slippery pole, 'I may have avoided doing too much stooping, but I also missed conquering.' It could also be said of him – as of very few leading politicians – that he never let down any of his friends.

This unwillingness to stoop was illustrated soon after my arrival at the Treasury. An influential press tycoon, Cecil King, the chairman of the *Daily Mirror* and nephew of Lord Northcliffe, an even greater press tycoon, wrote a signed article in the paper, then a very popular but highly responsible newspaper and probably the most influential paper among Labour voters, calling for an immediate change of Prime Minister. The strong implication was that his successor must be Roy. Frantic messages came from No. 10 that Roy must disown King and declare total loyalty. There was an emergency meeting in Roy's office with David Dowler, John Harris and me. The 'Treasury twins' were in no doubt: Roy should declare his loyalty to Wilson and confidence in his leadership, just as Churchill declared his confidence in Chamberlain in May 1940.

Roy thought for a while and then said, with rather bad temper, a reaction he sometimes showed when turning a proposal down, 'No, I won't. There has been too much double talk. I don't have confidence in Harold's leadership and I'm not going to say that I have.' In the event, no one commented that Roy had not issued a statement. The turmoil and Harold's anxieties subsided. As far as I remember, as a very new member of the Treasury team, I gave no advice but my admiration for Roy's integrity and judgement was enhanced.

Throughout most of his time in the Cabinet, Jenkins felt that
Wilson was a bad Prime Minister, whose opportunism, lack of
strategy and poor management had landed us in the economic
crisis and, like all his friends and many others in the parliamentary party, he obviously also felt that he could do much better.
But while he did not actively restrain his troops, he did not
encourage them either, because in his view there were always
good reasons against revolt. Wilson and his kitchen Cabinets
were paranoid about plots, including plots by the Campaign for
Democratic Socialism after it had long ceased to exist or by other
imagined conspirators. But there were three occasions when
Wilson's fears were justified. The first was in 1966 when Wilson
was in Moscow. Callaghan, then still Chancellor, took soundings
to see if a move against Wilson could succeed. Roy took no part,
although Wilson suspected that he did. The second occasion was
the time of the Cecil King letter, when Roy was encouraged to
challenge Harold. Jennifer once told me that Roy did not act
for two main reasons: it would be disloyal because Harold had
recently appointed him and, more importantly, a fight inside the
party and government at that time of crisis would probably have
shaken sterling, made the crisis worse and would have imper-
illed not only the future of the government but the prosperity of
the country.

Wilson's most vulnerable moment was during the battle for
trade union reform. On this occasion Roy's view was clear, that
to use the party's strong hostility towards Barbara's proposals, which Wilson enthusiastically supported, as the basis for
challenging Wilson would have been wholly opportunistic
and discreditable, since he had supported the reform himself.
Opportunism had been one of his principal charges against

Wilson. Moreover, by now he felt a certain loyalty to Wilson, who had given him constant, if sometimes lukewarm, support for all his many difficult decisions at the Treasury.

Did Jenkins miss his chance of becoming Prime Minister when he was Chancellor? Labour is not good at ditching its leader (as confirmed in its failure to get rid of Gordon Brown many years later). Roy's best chance would have come if Labour had won the 1970 election. He told me that Wilson had indicated to him before that election that if Labour won, he would take Britain into the European Community and then retire as a Prime Minister who had won three elections and made a decisive contribution to history. He would want Roy to succeed him. However, he added a proviso: he would not retire if Callaghan was likely to succeed – as he well might. In the event, Labour lost the 1970 election.

After that defeat the Labour Party changed and in its new mood Roy's prospects of ever being acceptable to Labour as leader were, in my view, unrealistic. When he stood for election on Wilson's retirement he came third. He then had two more chances of becoming Prime Minister: at the time of my by-election in 1973, and when the SDP was formed and the SDP/Liberal alliance looked momentarily as if it might break the mould of British politics.

Looking back on the first Wilson administration from 1964 to 1970, it is astonishing that a government of so many talents had such a disappointing record. No government since has been such an intellectual powerhouse. George Brown could be brilliant. I once went to a dinner at the Dutch embassy where the eminent Dutch Foreign Minister Josef Luns described Brown, before he arrived, as the best Foreign Minister he had ever come across, praising his insight and persuasiveness. Unfortunately, when

George turned up he was drunk, behaved most embarrassingly
and lost his reputation with the Dutch overnight. Denis Healey
was an outstandingly successful Secretary of State for Defence.
Barbara Castle, as already mentioned, was an excellent Minister
of Transport and later of Employment. Dick Crossman, too,
was a man of high intelligence, though he had two weaknesses
– he seemed more interested in the process of argument than its
conclusion and was completely unpredictable, constantly weav-
ing from left to right and back again. Tony Benn's exceptional
gifts (and shortcomings) I have already referred to. Although
he played a major part in the late 1970s and 1980s in making
Labour unelectable, he became a national treasure when he
finally retired from Parliament in 2001 'to devote more time to
politics', attracting large audiences of all political persuasions
to talks at which he charmed them with his reminiscences and
unorthodox comments. No one I knew could present misleading
arguments with greater eloquence.

Callaghan was a major force in the Cabinet, despite his failure
as Chancellor. He eventually succeeded Wilson as Prime Minister
in 1976 when Wilson retired. He was a most impressive personality, a formidable political operator and a good man to have on
your side. My own personal experience of James Callaghan was
only my brief experience of his early days at the Home Office,
when he became Home Secretary and his morale was bruised
and his reputation damaged. But he quickly recovered. I had
an interesting lunch with him shortly after he arrived and soon
realised that he had not given up his ambition to be PM despite
his recent setbacks.

He asked me about my view of the tasks ahead. I said there
were two areas where he could remedy a gap in Roy's reforms,

one of which was prison reform. The main recommendations of a commission, headed by Lord Mountbatten and appointed after the spy Blake had escaped from prison, had naturally concentrated on greater security. It was not calculated to enhance a programme of more effective rehabilitation. Apart from the abolition of flogging, prison reform had been largely neglected. The second gap was in the need for the introduction of an independent element into the investigation of complaints against the police. I argued that whereas the police opposed it, they could be won over because a more independent commission would not only increase public confidence but would be much better placed to dismiss worthless complaints at an early stage and save a huge amount of police time and costs. I was in charge of the police service and was appalled at how many trivial complaints without foundation were still investigated in great detail. Jim seemed to like both suggestions and said he was much encouraged by our lunch.

However, what surprised me was that during this lunch, which was in the Commons dining room, he constantly interrupted our conversation to exchange a word with nearly every Labour MP who passed our table, as if he was a candidate canvassing constituents. He had clearly not given up his ambition to be party leader.

This seemed to explain some erratic decisions in his early days as Home Secretary. One was the veto of a police merger. Roy Jenkins, strongly supported by the Police Federation as well as by the police establishment, had greatly reduced the unwieldy number of police forces and a merger of several forces in the north-east had been approved by the Chief Inspector of Constabulary. It hadn't yet been implemented when Roy left and local councillors on a police committee, which would disappear under the merger, persuaded their MPs to oppose it. There was no significant public opposition, but the councillors were well known to their MPs. In this case, a group of Humberside MPs asked Jim to intervene. To my astonishment, and to the dismay of the Home Office and my contacts in the police, Jim stopped the merger. Very apologetically he said to me, 'I know the case for merger is strong, but sometimes we should help our friends.'

Worse was a strange decision about gaming. I had just convinced the Home Office to recast the original draft of the Gaming Bill when Jim suddenly announced that we should drop the Bill and return to the recommendations of the Royal Commission. He personally had strong moral objections to gambling. And why offend the churches? I invited the Chief Constables from the major cities affected to an urgent conference in the Home Office. Unanimously they told Jim that should the Bill be dropped, the consequences would be disastrous. They gave him chapter and verse on the spread of illegal gaming under criminal control in their own areas. Jim gave way and the Bill went ahead.

Despite this shaky start, he redeemed his general reputation in time. The former Permanent Secretary at the Home Office, Lord Allen of Abbeydale, told me he proved a good Home Secretary. His standing in the party was such that he was elected as Prime Minister by the parliamentary party as Wilson's successor. Jim was easy to work with, exuded an aura of authority and was good with people. He was extremely active in Cabinet on issues other than home affairs. He led the opposition to the sale of arms to South Africa (in which I thought he was right). Later, quite irresponsibly, he also led the successful revolt against Barbara Castle's brave attempt to curb union power with her proposal *In Place of Strife*, and showed he had no qualms about blatantly flouting Cabinet decisions. Yet he could also rise above petty party interests. As Prime Minister he once vetoed a proposed personal attack on Mrs Thatcher during the 1979 election because, he said, she might become Prime Minister and no action should be taken to damage her standing.

My great disappointment was Tony Crosland. When I became an MP in 1962, I expected Crosland to be the leader of the social democrats in the party. He had been our intellectual inspiration and played a leading role in CDS. In 1959 he had been to Parliament as MP for Grimsby and when Labour formed the government I thought he would be an outstanding minister. To the dismay of his admirers, he proved neither a leader nor a good minister. In government he was indecisive, uncharacteristically cautious and ready to compromise on controversial issues, in contrast to his previous cavalier approach. One explanation was that his second wife, the journalist Susan Barnes, told him that he had a real chance of becoming leader of the party after all, which made him much more reluctant to offend different sections of the party. When Callaghan eventually succeeded Wilson in 1976, Tony became Foreign Secretary and perhaps he might have retrieved his reputation, but he died from a stroke soon afterwards. Former admirers were left with a sense of regret at what might have been.

In 1972, my clash with the Lincoln Labour Party was a very public affair. I had already decided to resign and fight a by-election but had not yet announced my decision. When I happened to meet Tony one day, he enquired, with a wry smile, how things were. 'What would you do?' I asked. He said it was impossible to advise me. One must act according to character.

I thought that very sensible advice. But my last encounter with him was no reconciliation.

In the Lincoln by-election some months later, which was regarded by the Labour party as an opportunity to punish a very public defector, numerous Labour MPs came to Lincoln to canvass against me, but not my friends and former Gaitskellites. None spoke against me – except Crosland. In the BBC special programme on the night of the by-election, Tony Crosland represented Labour. I had won handsomely and there were ugly scenes as my opponents yelled abuse, assaulted some of my supporters and pulled my female supporters' hair. Robin Day, who chaired the programme, asked me what I thought of Crosland supporting the very left-wing Labour candidate. I said that he must have felt embarrassed by what he had just seen and for supporting the kind of left-wing thugs he and I fought against in the past. Crosland was asked to comment. He replied, with great discomfort, I was told (I was not in the studio), 'I am a member of the shadow Cabinet, and so I supported the official Labour candidate.' Robin asked me to comment. 'Well,' I said, 'I suppose everyone must act according to character.'

Finally, there was of course Harold Wilson himself. He too was a man of outstanding intellectual ability, yet as Prime Minister he must bear the main responsibility for the inadequacies of his government. I held him in very low regard at the time because of his opportunism, his short term-ism – 'a week is a long time in politics' could be his epitaph – and his deviousness and apparent lack of principle. Fundamentally he did not belong to the right or left wing of the party, but to the management consultancy wing, and his main principle was: 'Keep the show on the road, as long as I'm in charge.' I once described him, in a phrase borrowed from that brilliant phrasemaker Ed Pearce, as 'a master of the pre-emptive cringe'.

In retrospect I think my judgement then was too harsh. Many other Prime Ministers have also regarded keeping their party together as one of their top priorities. 'Party first' is, after all, the first rule at Westminster. Wilson did have principles, for instance he had a passionate hatred of racial prejudice, and he showed great courage, even foolhardiness, in the battle for Barbara Castle's reform of the unions. Furthermore he should be given full credit for keeping Britain out of the Vietnam War without upsetting Anglo-American relations, despite strong pressure from President Johnson. Finally, in spite of his weakness and constant change of tack during the post-1970 debate on the European Union, in the end he did very skilfully succeed in keeping Britain in Europe in 1975 in the face of strong opposition from most Labour MPs. These were not inconsiderable achievements. He was also in his personal dealings a decent and considerate man.

If the Lincoln by-election of 1973 was the most exhilarating experience of my parliamentary career, my time in government was easily the most satisfying. Some particular personal experiences during my time in office were especially memorable.

In 1966, soon after my appointment to the Home Office, the Foreign Office asked me to host a lunch to entertain Polykarpos Georkajis, Interior Minister of Cyprus. He had been invited to Britain to study our police. It would not be a pleasant lunch, they warned me. He was a terrible man, a ruthless terrorist and killer, top of the wanted list when EOKA was fighting for union between Cyprus and Greece.† However the government

---

† EOKA stood for (translated to English) the National Organisation of Cypriot Struggle. It was regarded as a terrorist organisation.

was eager to be on good terms with him because, as a strong anti-Communist, he was considered a useful counter-weight in the Cypriot government to Archbishop Makarios, who had disturbing Communist connections. We met briefly to arrange our lunch and the Foreign Office assessment seemed justified, as he was unfriendly and thoroughly uncommunicative. I dreaded the lunch.

To my surprise it was a great success. He apologised for his rudeness at our earlier meeting – he had suffered from a hangover after a tour of London nightclubs. He was utterly charming, the soul of conviviality, fascinating in his accounts of his efforts to evade the police in his EOKA days. In fact, when he was being hunted by them, he conceived a great admiration for the British police, which was why he had come to Britain to study them. He planned to mould the Cypriot force on the British model.

A few years after our lunch, in 1970, he was assassinated, found murdered in his car.

Another memorable encounter was with Olof Palme, later Swedish Prime Minister. I had met him briefly at one of the Bilderberg Conferences when he was the Swedish Education Minister and considered a rising star. I met him in 1969 when I was Financial Secretary and he was then Prime Minister. I was asked to represent the government at a conference in Sweden about the future of the European Community. At the time, Harold Wilson had persuaded the Cabinet to reapply for British membership in one of his phases of pro-European enthusiasm. The other speakers at the conference were the eminent American economist, Kenneth Galbraith, and Olof Palme. My speech seemed to be a success, partly perhaps because Galbraith, while he wrote like an angel, spoke like Poor Poll. After the conference

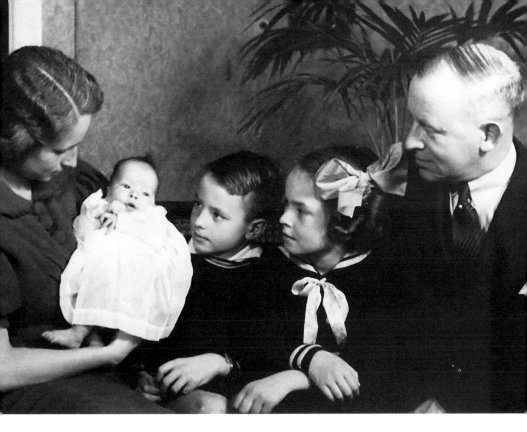

My parents with me and my sister Yvonne and our new baby sister Joke.

My mother, Louise Victorine Taverne (née Koch).

Wearing the shirt of HVV, Haagse Voetbal Vereniging, an amateur football club in The Hague, 1936.

My older sister Yvonne, 1951.

Oxford student, 1951.

Janice, another Oxford student, 1952.

Oxford Union, 1950. Front row: far left Peter Emery; centre, Robin Day, President; Professor C. E. M. Joad on his right and Randolph Churchill on his left. Back row: second from left Keith Kyle; then William Rees-Mogg; I am fifth from left; and second from far right, Jeremy Thorpe. The motion was 'that Columbus went too far'. Randolph Churchill launched a violent attack on Joad for having once supported the famous motion 'that this House would not fight for King and country'.

BBC *Bookstand* team, 1961. I'm seated in the middle with Dennis Potter standing on my right and Stephen Hearst standing on my left.

HELP YOUR

LABOUR CANDIDATE

Dick Taverne

CENTRAL COMMITTEE ROOM :

168 UPPER RICHMOND ROAD
PUTNEY, S.W.15

DICK TAVERNE at home with his wife Janice. They were married in 1955 and are expecting their first child early next year.

Dick Taverne is 30 years old and a barrister. He was educated at Charterhouse School, where he was head boy, and at Balliol College, Oxford. He gained First Class Honours at Oxford, was Chairman of the University Labour Club and an officer of the Oxford Union. In 1951 he was one of two representatives chosen by the Oxford Union for a debating tour of the U.S.A.

Before he was called to the Bar, he had experience of a wide variety of jobs : he was a building labourer, agricultural labourer, teacher, and a night security guard. He is also a part-time lecturer in Current Affairs for the Workers Educational Association. He has been a member of the Labour Party since he was 18.

IMPORTANT !

You will have received or will be receiving an official card from the Returning Officer giving your Polling Number and your Polling Station. This card should be carefully kept and taken to the Polling Station on Polling Day. Should you lose your official card *you can still vote.* Give your name and address to the Clerk in the Polling Station.

Remember your number and give it to the Number Taker outside the Polling Station. This will save you being called on.

Published by Frank Nodes, 168 Upper Richmond Road, S.W.15.
Printed by Rowling & Sons Ltd. (T.U.), 36 York Rd., S.W.11.

DICK TAVERNE
YOUR
LABOUR CANDIDATE

Polling Day :
THURSDAY, 8th OCTOBER
7 a.m. — 9 p.m.

A general election 1959 leaflet of the Labour candidate in Putney.

Janice in her lab coat at the London School of Hygiene & Tropical Medicine.

Lincoln by-election, 1962. The 'Daughters of the Revolution' canvassing in the snow: (from left) Susan Walston, me, Margaret Callaghan (later Baroness Jay) and Julia Gaitskell.

John Cronin MP,
Dingle Foot QC MP,
Janice and me, 1963.

With Roy Jenkins at the
Home Office, 1966.

Talking to Olof Palme,
the Swedish Prime
Minister, 1969.

ABOVE 'Lincolnshire Poacher.' This *Observer* cartoon, of me carrying the swag away from a furious Harold Wilson, featured the Sunday after my 1973 by-election victory.

LEFT On Steep Hill, Lincoln, the morning after the by-election, with my daughters: Caroline to my right, Suzanna on my left.

BELOW Welcomed into Parliament by my supporters.

Roy Jenkins, the President of the EU Commission, receiving the report of 'Les Petits Sages' from Ambassador Dirk Spierenburg (second right). The author is on the far left.

Visiting a branch of BOC, 1979.

At the finish line of my first London Marathon, 1982.

ABOVE Elevated to the House of Lords, 1996, sponsored by Lord Rodgers of Quarrybank and Lord Jenkins of Hillhead.

MIDDLE 'Parliamentary Science Communicator of the Year', awarded by the Association of British Science Writers and presented by Evan Harris MP, 2006.

BELOW The most beautiful of all our boats, *Ariadne*, a Najad 441.

I sat next to Palme and, throughout a long, very alcoholic dinner during which we both remained completely sober, he told me about the problems of his government, his hopes and fears and how he might achieve and avoid them. Had we had the chance to meet again socially, I felt we would have become close friends.

Soon afterwards, Palme paid a visit to Britain and at a formal dinner at the Swedish Embassy he invited me to the top table, way above my ministerial rank. Inexcusably, Ted Heath, then Leader of the Opposition, had been relegated to the ranks of lesser dignitaries. Janice was horrified to find she was due to sit next to Heath at the bottom of the last table. I admired Heath. He was a man of vision and principle. For example, after he became Prime Minister in 1970, defying public opinion, he treated Ugandan Asians who had been expelled by Idi Amin much better than Callaghan as Home Secretary had treated Asians driven from Kenya in 1968, when he deprived them of their rights as British passport holders. But Heath had few social graces and was reputed to be particularly uncommunicative to women he did not know. On this occasion he was likely to be in special ill humour because of the placement.

As my wife and I are both keen sailors, I suggested she should ask him how he had won the Sydney Hobart yacht race, Australia's premier yacht race, a few weeks previously. Heath, who had only done some dinghy racing before, had entered his boat and shipped it out to Australia. His 35ft boat was the first of several racing yachts he owned all called *Morning Cloud* and it was one of the smallest boats in the race. The winning boat has its time adjusted for its length, but his victory was still an astonishing achievement.

During dinner he told Janice in great detail how he had done it.

He had recruited a special crew, which he was able to do because of his position as leader of the Conservative Party, including the best helmsman, the best navigator (in the days before GPS), the best meteorologist, the best sail-maker and the strongest winch-grinder. He had personally learned everything to be learned about local currents and weather patterns and studied all local charts, old as well as new, and with all the relevant information at his fingertips presided over his team as over a Cabinet meeting. In the light of the forecast of wind and sea and currents, they decided to take a chance on the course to steer and with the expert helmsman steering, the sail-maker choosing and managing the sails and the other experts doing their special thing, they won. Janice came to the conclusion that he was not influenced by what makes most sailors like sailing: the sound of the wind in the rigging or of waves lapping against the hull. All he cared about was winning and he did.

My most bizarre experience as Financial Secretary involved John Stonehouse MP, who went swimming from a beach in 1974 and was presumed to have drowned since he did not return. He was eventually discovered living with his mistress in Australia. On extradition to Britain he was convicted of insurance fraud for taking out a large policy on his life before going for his Florida swim. It was also found that a fund he had set up to help Bangladeshi victims of a hurricane was missing £600,000 from its accounts. After his conviction it was discovered that he had been employed as a spy by the Communist government of Czechoslovakia.

In 1969 he was Minister of Posts and Communications, with responsibility for the oversight of independent television. At the time, what is now ITV consisted of a collection of separate regionally based companies. At first these were so profitable that it was said their licence to broadcast was a licence to print their own money and the government duly imposed a levy on their revenues. But in early 1970 the industry suffered from a recession and some of the companies ran into difficulties. There was pressure on the government to reduce the levy. I had talks with the chairman of one of them and asked Treasury officials to investigate. We concluded that to prevent the collapse of several of the companies and to stop them having to come back for more money, they needed a reduction in the levy by a total sum of between £6 million and £8 million a year. That sum now seems trivial; even though the pound was then worth more than fourteen times what it is today.

I invited John Stonehouse to a meeting at the Treasury and told him I had looked into the issue and accepted that the companies needed help. What was the minimum he judged sufficient to make sure they could survive? I believe his reply was '£3 million'. I was astonished. 'Are you sure that will be enough?' 'Well,' he said 'to be safe, £4 million.' We then had a tough bargaining session and eventually settled for £6 million. (Nobody complained it was insufficient.) It must have been the craziest negotiation in history between a spending department and the Treasury. In the press the next day I read how Stonehouse, after a very tough negotiation, had succeeded in squeezing the money out of a miserly Treasury. When I told Jack Diamond about Stonehouse's extraordinary conduct, Jack said Stonehouse was mad. He was a pathological liar. Many people lied for gain, or to avoid scandal, but he lied on principle.

The last unusual episode during my time as minister was my involvement in a prolonged controversy about a notorious murder case, the so-called A6 murder. In 1961, Michael Gregsten and a young woman called Valerie Storie were sitting in a car in a cornfield off the A6 highway, when they were disturbed by a man who held them up at gunpoint. He made them drive around, through St Albans, then turn back to a lay-by off the A6 at Deadman's Hill, where he shot and killed Gregsten and raped and then shot Storie several times. She was left paralysed for life. James Hanratty was accused of the murder. At his trial he changed his story at the last moment, claiming that he was in Rhyl in Wales at the time of the murder. This alibi became the main pillar of his defence. It was rejected by the jury, he was convicted of murder and was one of the last people in Britain to be hanged before the abolition of capital punishment.

Originally, a man called Peter Alphon was suspected of committing the murder. He had even been put in an identity parade but Valerie Storie identified someone else. Then a strange character called Jean Justice befriended Peter Alphon and claimed Alphon had confessed to him that it was he, Alphon, who had committed the murder. When this confession became publicly known, a Commons motion was put down, which I signed (before I was a Home Office minister), calling for a posthumous pardon for Hanratty. The government rejected the motion.

In 1966, after I arrived at the Home Office, the BBC ran a programme that claimed that Hanratty's alibi had been confirmed by a number of new witnesses and that he was innocent. Roy Jenkins appointed Detective Superintendent Nimmo to investigate. I asked if I too could look at the Home Office papers because I had signed the motion and hoped that exoneration of Hanratty would strengthen the case against capital punishment, which was still a highly controversial issue. After a conviction for murder, the Home Office used to retain every relevant document, because the death penalty was only implemented in a very small number of cases in which there appeared to be no scintilla of doubt about the guilt of the accused. Much to my dismay, after study of the documents I concluded that the evidence that Hanratty was guilty was overwhelming. Nimmo's report in March 1967 also dismissed the claims made by the BBC.

Then in 1971, Paul Foot, an investigative journalist of repute and a stalwart campaigner against injustice, published a book *Who Killed Hanratty?*, which claimed that new evidence confirmed Hanratty's innocence. The *Sunday Times* took up the case and the editor, Harold Evans, after consulting Roy Jenkins, asked me to review Foot's book, promising me the paper's two centre pages for my comments. I accepted and looked again at the Home Office documents (which ex-ministers can do) to see if Foot might be right after all. My conclusion was the same as before and in the review I submitted titled 'Did Hanratty kill?' I argued that the answer was yes. That was not the answer Evans wanted and at first he refused to print my review. When I protested to Roy he spoke to Evans, and while the two centre pages featured an article arguing that Hanratty was innocent, my review did appear, though in a shortened version in the book section. Afterwards I took part in several radio debates about the case.

That was not the end of the story. At the by-election in Lincoln in 1973, one of the candidates was Jean Justice, who stood against me as the 'A6 Murder candidate', to protest at my alleged role in blocking a pardon for Hanratty. The Hanratty family was persuaded to come to Lincoln to support him and, to my embarrassment, Jean Justice insisted on introducing me to James Hanratty's father. At the trial, Valerie Storie's evidence

had included a remark that what had struck her in the brief
glimpse she had of the killer were his staring blue eyes. I had not
based my conclusion of guilt on identification but what was most
striking about Hanratty's father were his staring blue eyes!

In 1975 there was a further investigation of the case, this time
by a prominent left-wing and anti-establishment lawyer, Lewis
Hawser QC. He reached the same conclusion as I did and on the
same grounds. His report was lost without trace in the continuing debate. A further book was published about Hanratty's
innocence.[†] I gave my views in an article in the *Daily Mail* and
was described in the press as the only man left in Britain who
still thought Hanratty guilty. Finally the argument was settled
once and for all in 2001, when Hanratty's body was exhumed
to obtain a sample of DNA. This was compared with that in
mucus preserved in the handkerchief within which the murder
weapon had been found wrapped. It was also compared with
that in semen preserved in the underwear worn by Valerie Storie
when she was raped. No scientific evidence from the crime had
previously been linked to Hanratty: the DNA from both gun and
underwear matched his DNA.

I had also come across a fascinating piece of hearsay evidence.
A witness in one of the BBC Radio 4 *You the Jury* programmes
I chaired was John McVicar, once described as Public Enemy
No. 1, who was one of the few prisoners who made good use of
their time in jail by getting a first-class degree in sociology from
the Open University. After the programme we got talking about
cases in which I had doubts about the conviction. (Our conversation took place before the establishment of the Criminal Cases

---

[†]   Woffinden, B., *Hanratty: The Final Verdict* (London: Macmillan, 1997).

Review Commission charged with examining dodgy convictions.) McVicar's own verdicts, mainly based on prison gossip, were always clear. For example, I mentioned my doubts about the guilt of a man called Curbishley convicted of armed robbery.

'You're quite right. Not guilty.'

'How do you know?'

'Because I know the bloke who did it.'

Then I asked him about Hanratty (this was many years before the DNA evidence).

'Guilty as hell.'

'How do you know?'

'Because in prison he used to boast about how he raped the girl and how it still gave him a hard-on.'

The moral of the Hanratty story is that public concern supported by strong media campaigns is no substitute for solid evidence. When people are convinced of the rightness of their cause there is a tendency to ignore inconvenient evidence, often with unfortunate consequences. One of many examples, in a very different context years later, was the widespread campaign against the MMR vaccine by sections of the media that should have known better. This led to a decline in vaccination against mumps and measles, and renewed outbreaks of measles – infections which the MMR vaccine had virtually extinguished – and a number of avoidable deaths.

CHAPTER 7

BREAKING THE MOULD

While I was enjoying my time in office, revolt was simmering in my home patch. The slightly fragile sense of political unity that followed the 1962 by-election and Labour's narrow victory at the polls in 1964 did not survive the more decisive win in 1966. The Left had seized firm control of the management committee of my local Labour Party, even before I had become an MP, and after 1966 they soon showed that they couldn't be moderate, realistic or tolerant.

I do not argue that all the causes championed by the Left during Wilson's first administration were without merit. CND had a serious case. I argued at the time that the route to the avoidance of nuclear war and the alternative of Soviet domination was through multilateral disarmament, and this was eventually achieved by patient negotiation. But the world did come close to a nuclear holocaust during the Cuban missile crisis in 1962. The Left were right to oppose the Vietnam War. During the 1960s and 1970s both Labour and Conservative governments argued (as I did) that the only alternative to inflation, deflation and massive unemployment was a wage freeze followed by statutory incomes policies. These propositions were opposed both by the Labour Left and the Conservative Right. They were right and we were wrong. Incomes policies in their various forms all failed. Mrs Thatcher's reforms of the unions that created a more flexible labour market were not only economically more successful but reduced the number of strikes, so that Britain was no longer regarded as the sick man of Europe. It was an essential element in the success of Tony Blair's government in its early days that he did not reverse these reforms.

However the Lincoln Left did not reject incomes policies because they believed that freeing the labour market was a better solution, but because any curb on union demands was an attack on the working class. Strikes were a call to the barricades in the class war and any criticism of the unions was a betrayal of socialism. They represented the Militant tendency, the jihadists of the Labour movement, whose influence was growing inside the Labour Party. Just as jihadists regard any criticism of the Prophet Mohammed or the Koran as an attack on Islam itself, the left wing in the Lincoln Labour Party regarded any doubts expressed about the fundamental socialist creed or the class basis of socialism as blasphemy. Most bitterly resented of all the government's actions was Barbara Castle's unsuccessful attempt to take the first tentative step towards union reform in 1969 with her proposals *In Place of Strife*.

Throughout my time in Lincoln, Leo Beckett was the effective leader of the local party, even before he became chairman in 1972. He worked in the research department of one of Lincoln's engineering firms and was a member of the Amalgamated Union of Engineering Workers (AUEW). Later he was divorced by his wife and married Margaret Jackson, who succeeded me as MP for Lincoln. She started on the far Left but later, like many early left-wingers, was transformed after 1997 into a loyal Blairite and a model of Labour orthodoxy in the Blair Cabinet. Leo gave up his job in Lincoln to be her full-time assistant and he too became, I was told, a sensible, moderate supporter of the official party line. But in my time he was a wholly, passionately devoted fundamentalist socialist who walked, talked, and breathed politics twenty-four hours a day. He firmly believed that if only the party was led by proper socialists, a militant working class would vote to a man for a programme of massive nationalisation and the overthrow of capitalism.

Leo's socialist religion would override reason. In the autumn of 1968, the very time when we in the Treasury feared Armageddon had come, the AUEW, then controlled by leaders like Hugh Scanlon with views not dissimilar to Leo's, called a national strike that would have caused an appalling economic crisis. At the Labour Party's annual conference in Brighton that year I discussed the threatened strike with Leo. Did he agree that the strike would have the most serious consequences for British industry? Yes, he did. Did he also agree that this would be likely to wreck the Labour government and bring the Conservatives to power? Yes, he conceded that it might. And was not a Conservative government the worst outcome he could imagine? Yes, it was. But he still supported the strike? Yes, he did. Incidentally the national strike was averted by one of my Lincoln supporters, Roy Lilley, a District Secretary of the union and an unsung hero of the time, who stopped the strike by an action for an injunction on the grounds that the decision to strike had been taken in contravention of proper procedure.

I should add that Leo was intelligent, charming and cheerful, and had a warm personality; I got on well with him, as did Janice, until the final break. At a 1970 party conference, when

he had complained about Wilson's double talk, he told me that
the reason they liked me in Lincoln, despite our differences, was
because they knew where I stood.

Soon after the 1966 election, as the incomes policy became
more restrictive, local disaffection with the Labour government came out into the open at meetings of the management
committee. In the summer of 1966, there was outrage when
Wilson denounced a seamen's strike which threatened to disrupt
Britain's trade as inspired by 'a tightly knit group of politically
motivated men', with the implication that Communists were
responsible (for which the evidence was admittedly thin). But
the real explosion came after the 1968 Budget, which imposed
cuts and tax rises that included the reimposition of prescrip-
tion charges. To Leo Beckett and his friends that was an act
of sacrilege. He bitterly attacked me for failing to resign from
Wilson's government, as no self-respecting socialist could remain
a member. They did not want 'a cabbage' as their MP. Labour's
regional organiser for the East Midlands, Jim Cattermole, later
told me that when he visited Lincoln in April 1968 Leo Beckett
asked how they could get rid of their Member of Parliament,
since no one who supported the Wilson government was acceptable to the Lincoln Party.

What made things much worse was that in 1968 I became
a minister in the Treasury, the department primarily responsible for the government's 'anti-socialist' policies. In fact, being a
minister at all was a black mark. Some constituents like to think
their MP is someone of distinction and I have often heard the
view when visiting other constituencies that their particular MP
ought to be in the Cabinet. But history suggests that, at a time
of government unpopularity, ministers suffer especially badly

in elections. They cannot ask parliamentary questions, only answer them. They cannot take up local grievances that involve criticism of government policies. When a local factory closed and I met the chairman with a deputation of employees, he pointed out that he was only doing what the government and Treasury recommended firms to do: rationalising and making the company more competitive. When local unions organised a march in Lincoln to protest against government and Treasury policy on mergers and closures, I could not take part. There were even complaints that I had not been elected to be a minister but to represent my constituents.

In fact, trade union reform was the subject of my first violent conflict with the leadership of my local party after the 1970 election, when our differences came to a head. In 1971 Heath introduced a Bill not a million miles different from Barbara Castle's failed attempt. A motion was passed at the party management committee that there should be a strike in Lincoln in protest. I argued that this would be quite unconstitutional, because the proposed Bill had been part of the manifesto of the elected government. When they ignored my objections, I said that if they proceeded with the strike I would oppose it publicly. They abandoned their plans for a strike but Leo Beckett and his colleagues furiously denounced my 'middle-class' concern with constitutional proprieties.

My final break with the local Labour Party came over Europe. While Labour was the government, relations with Europe were not a major issue. In 1967 Wilson announced that, despite Labour's earlier opposition, the government would seek to reapply for membership of the European Community, and in early 1968 he and George Brown, then Foreign Secretary, went

on a tour of European capitals to sound out opinion. Reports
from our embassies indicated that there were few signs de Gaulle
had withdrawn his veto, but Wilson stated that he 'would not
take no for an answer'. In the event, when de Gaulle again
said 'non', there was little Wilson could do about it. As Hugo
Young recorded in *This Blessed Plot*,[†] his history of our relations
with the Community, the tour was not a great success. George
Brown sometimes proved an embarrassing ambassador. Apart
from occasionally getting drunk, 'he was given to a buccaneering
familiarity with people whom, as a sound European, he always
thought he could deal with'. 'This little Brown,' de Gaulle alleg-
edly once said, 'I rather like him – despite the fact that he calls
me Charlie.'[‡] That would not go down well with that august
figure, about whom it was rumoured that if someone said to him
'Fine day, M. le President', he would reply, 'Thank you.'

There was no major parliamentary or party opposition to
Wilson's new application to join the European Community. It
was approved in the Commons by a majority of 488 to 62. Even
in Lincoln there was no hint that opposition to the EEC would
become a test of one's socialist credentials. The real battle started
after Labour's defeat in 1970, when de Gaulle was no longer on
the scene and Pompidou, the new French President, lifted the
French veto. Prospects for a successful application had already
looked much more favourable while Labour was still in government. As Financial Secretary, I played some part in preparing
a white paper on the pros and cons of entry, which on balance
came out pro. Indeed, in private conversation with Roy Jenkins

---

†   Young, H., *This Blessed Plot* (London: Macmillan, 1998), pp. 192–4.
‡   Young, *This Blessed Plot*, p. 192.

before the 1970 election, Wilson made it clear that he planned to take Britain into the European Community if we won.

All that changed when Labour lost in 1970 and the Conservative government led by Ted Heath made a renewed and successful application to join. It is not, of course, unknown for parties to oppose in opposition what they advocated in government. The majority of Labour MPs decided they did not like Europe after all, especially since a group of Conservative MPs had declared their undying opposition to joining, so the vote on entry offered a chance to defeat Heath's government. The Left now passionately denounced the Community as a capitalist rich man's club, membership of which would rule out socialism in Britain forever. A bitter debate took place within the party, during which Wilson displayed his worst qualities. There is little doubt that privately he still favoured British entry but publicly he swayed from one side to the other until finally, in the face of strong opposition from the Left, he came down firmly against. During this period he was truly 'master of the pre-emptive cringe'. I always expected this result and foresaw that it would lead to a fundamental change in the nature of the Labour Party. The influence of the social democrats or, as many of them still styled themselves, Gaitskellites, which had by and large prevailed until then, depended to a large extent on their broad identification with official policy. The Left generally had more support among the activists, but they were the dissidents and could therefore be accused of disloyalty. Loyalty was the supreme virtue in the eyes of the ordinary party member. But once it was official party policy to reject entry into the European Community, the pro-Europeans, i.e. the social democrats, became the dissidents. The Left promptly forgot its own history of dissent and now vociferously proclaimed the duty of every MP to toe the party line. It had already captured control of the two biggest unions, the TGWU and AUEW. Gradually, with Tony Benn as its leading voice in the shadow Cabinet, the Left extended its control of the party as a whole and its influence affected domestic as well as foreign policy. Labour became committed to a full-blooded socialist manifesto that called for the nationalisation of the top twenty-five companies in Britain. It was the start of infection by the Bennite and Militant virus, which was temporarily dormant after Labour's unexpected victory in 1974 but then later on so weakened the party that after defeat in 1979 it was out of power for eighteen years.

When a vote on entry into the Community was imminent, Wilson announced that Labour would vote against and imposed a three-line whip. In Lincoln in 1971 I made it clear that I would resist the party's whip and would vote for entry in support of the Conservative government. They made it clear that if I did, they would deselect me. Well, I did and they did. By then I had decided that our differences were irreconcilable, that the only course for me was to leave a party which was committed to policies that I certainly could not support and that I would resign and stand as an independent in a by-election. My views were not shared by my pro-European colleagues in Parliament. Although sixty-eight of them, led by Roy Jenkins, also voted for entry, which ensured a handsome majority of 112 in the House of Commons, they argued that the party would never split and urged me to compromise. My friend Bob Maclennan (now a colleague and general soulmate among Lib Dem peers) was a particularly strong, and almost persuasive, advocate of the view that I should accept my fate, keep my head down and one day, when the party returned to its senses, I could make a comeback. When I refused to compromise and later confirmed that I would fight a by-election, my colleagues strongly disapproved and told me in effect that if I swam against the tide I would drown. Instead I should wait till eventually the tide turned.

Apart from the reasons they gave, I could understand the reluctance of my fellow social democrats even to consider leaving a party for which they had worked all their political lives. None of their local parties forced them to choose between abandoning their support for joining Europe and deselection. I realised that facing what would be a bitter fight on my own, with the prospect of being regarded as a traitor by loyal party members, would be stressful and unpleasant and also that my actions would be some embarrassment to my friends. But it also felt wonderful to be free of having to defend the indefensible, free to say publicly exactly what I believed and free from the constraints imposed by tribal loyalties, which constantly urged one to compromise in order to avoid party splits that would damage the party's electoral prospects.

Two events, both engineered by my opponents, greatly helped my eventual by-election campaign. The first was a Granada *World in Action* TV programme about my constituency wars, produced by John Birt (who later became the BBC Director General and now Lord Birt), that was broadcast on the eve of the parliamentary vote on entry in October 1971. He approached Leo Beckett and his friends to see if they agreed to take part in the programme. They were enthusiastic at a chance to show up my treachery. My consent was also needed and when I too agreed, Leo apparently said he could not believe his luck. I agreed because I felt that if at some stage I was to fight as an independent, I would benefit from airing the issues before the largest possible audience. The core of the programme was a direct confrontation between Leo and me. I confirmed that I was going to vote for entry against the three-line whip and the views of the management committee. He accused me of intolerable arrogance in daring to ignore the wishes of my party, locally and nationally. How could I defy the wishes of those who had helped to get me elected? He repeated again and again, 'I was on the doorstep with you.' My position was uncomfortable because I was taken aback by the bitterness of his attack but I argued the case as propounded by that great political thinker Edmund Burke: however much I respected the views of those who worked for the party, I was not a puppet who voted as instructed by puppeteers. At the time, I felt I had not put my case aggressively enough but in the event moderation probably helped.

The TV programme had an astonishing impact. The *New Statesman* described it as 'politics in the raw' and it certainly made for unusually dramatic political television. Most of Lincoln seemed to have watched it and reaction was overwhelmingly in my favour and deeply hostile towards Leo. I was told that for a while he was even reluctant to show his face in public. At the eventual by-election over a year later, canvassers reported that the Granada programme was referred to by constituents time after time. It certainly registered our conflict in the public arena, as I had hoped, and helped to attract outside help when the by-election eventually took place.

Opinion in Westminster was mixed. At the next party meeting, Wilson singled me out for censure for having so publicly exposed party divisions. Most of my friends in the Labour Party were sympathetic but embarrassed. My own supporters in Lincoln were revitalised and my opponents temporarily dejected, so that for a while it even seemed possible that plans for my deselection would be shelved.

My supporters, however, did not have the staying power to attend endless meetings until late hours and in due course the Left recovered its nerve. In June 1972 the management committee voted by seventy-five to fifty to deselect me.

In fact, the vote did not reflect general party opinion. Wards and union branches that were strongly in my favour had been prevented from holding meetings. In wards or union branches that instructed delegates to support me, the instructions were ignored on the grounds that delegates must be free to exercise their own judgement. For example, the largest branch of the largest union in Lincoln, the engineering union, at a very well-attended meeting (and the largest of all those held) voted two to one against a motion for my retirement and instructed its six delegates on the management committee to vote for me. Five, who were friends of Leo's, nevertheless voted against me. After the management committee vote, a special committee of inquiry was set up by the National Executive Committee of the Labour Party to review the decision. It found unanimously that my deselection should be declared void because it had not been democratically conducted. However, the left-wing majority on the full NEC overruled this finding, actually to my relief. I could not see how the management committee and I could ever live in peace and by now I was set on fighting a by-election.

The second event that greatly helped me was the intervention of Tony Benn. After the vote to deselect me, I told my supporters that I planned to announce my resignation as their Labour MP and fight as an independent Democratic Labour candidate. I chose that designation to get the maximum Labour support and because it emphasised the undemocratic behaviour of the local party. My preferred title of Social Democrat would have caused confusion. When I had tried it out on various Lincoln people, they had not been sure whether Social Democrats were what the Nazis were or whether they were some sort of Communists. As for the simple designation 'independent', in Lincoln that was normally regarded as the label for independent Conservatives. Anyway, my Lincoln friends were determined to support me and about a third of the Lincoln Labour Party joined the Lincoln Democratic Labour Association (LDLA). Considering the strength of party tribalism and the fact that many of them had spent their lives in the party – canvassing, attending meetings and lending their homes for committee rooms – and now faced expulsion from the party for supporting me (as I warned them), that was a very high proportion. Indeed, many Labour Party members in Parliament and the country regarded me as a traitor. But I had never considered party loyalty to be the most important principle in politics. How could I represent Labour and argue for its re-election as a government when I believed some of its basic policies on issues vital to Britain's future were profoundly mistaken and likely to be disastrous in their consequences?

In the autumn of 1972, towards the end of the Labour Party annual conference, which Tony Benn presided over as that year's chairman, I publicly announced my decision to resign, to apply for the Stewardship of the Manor of Northstead (the Chiltern

Hundreds were already occupied by another retiring MP)† and to fight a by-election in Lincoln as a Democratic Labour candidate. Benn made the news of my announcement the centrepiece of his winding-up speech. He claimed I was neither democratic nor Labour. I was a candidate of the media, and the Labour movement would take on and defeat this new threat to democracy in the same way as they had defeated kings and landowners in the past. The printers should see to it that the truth was published about Labour and even the liftmen in Thomson House (then the headquarters of *The Times* and *Sunday Times*) should play their part (in a manner left unspecified). This extraordinary outburst was shown on television time after time and earned headlines in much of the next day's press. It made my resignation a national event.

In fact, the media, whose candidate Benn claimed I was, like my friends in Parliament, were almost unanimous in predicting my defeat. The *Sunday Times* described my action as 'suicidal'. Yet a poll in Lincoln, taken for London Weekend Television the next day, showed that some 49 per cent would vote for me, 16 per cent for the Conservatives and only 14 per cent for Labour. I thought this too good to be true. Labour's reaction was to postpone the date of the election as long as they could so that the emotions

---

†   These were two traditional 'Offices of Profit under the Crown' (actually unpaid and involving no duties) which, many years ago, were deemed incompatible with membership of Parliament. They are one of a number of historical anachronisms that riddle our constitution. An MP's resignation becomes effective when application for either post is accepted, which is always a formality, and the office becomes vacant again when an MP ceases to be an MP. I enquired whether there actually still was a stewardship but the manor had been engulfed by a lake in Yorkshire. When some Labour MPs heard about this they suggested that I should take up personal residence.

aroused by my dramatic announcement would die down, as I expected they would.

Shortly afterwards I held a town hall meeting to explain my decision. It was, I believe, the largest public meeting ever held in Lincoln, with 450 people in the hall and some 250 listening to loudspeakers outside, and was the best start to my campaign I could have hoped for. I was supported by Bernard Levin, a brilliant columnist for *The Times* and TV performer, who said that Lincoln had a choice between Dick Taverne and a Dictaphone. The other speaker was a surprise – Mervyn Stockwood, the Bishop of Southwark. I did not know him. He was a staunch champion of CND and other left-wing causes that I opposed and he seemed the last person likely to come out in my support. He made an inspiring, visionary speech about Europe.

In 1973, after my victory, I took him out to lunch to thank him. He started to ask me what the difference was between the Council and the Commission in Europe, whether the Community had a Parliament and other questions that showed he knew nothing at all about the European Community. 'You may be surprised,' he said, 'that I made such a good speech about Europe when I know nothing about it. Every word was written by my old friend Oswald Mosley.[†] When he heard about your troubles in Lincoln, he told me that you needed help but thought that if he supported you, it might not do you much good. So he said I should go and he would write my speech.'

I asked him what Mosley, now in his eighties, was like. 'He is excellent company. But occasionally his eyes will glaze over and he will say, "the Queen will still send for me, you know, to

[†] The leader of the British Union of Fascists interned during the war.

save the country". He is somewhat mad.' Mervyn Stockwood's speech was not Mosley's only connection with that by-election. Jonathan Guinness, chairman of the right-wing Monday Club, who was adopted by the Conservatives in Lincoln as their candidate, was Mosley's stepson.

When the by-election date was finally fixed, for 1 March 1973, the campaign proved an exhilarating experience. Individual donations from all over the country enabled me to employ an agent, Tony Elkington, a young member of the Lincoln Junior Chamber of Commerce, who showed great flair and imagination. He found a disused billiard hall near the centre of Lincoln which he transformed into workable headquarters and prominently displayed the name on it that I found rather embarrassing: Taverne House. He organised a campaign that was far more effective than that of the other two parties, who had to rely mainly on helpers from outside Lincoln. Labour MPs came pouring into the city to canvass for the Labour candidate, John Dilks. I was told over a hundred came, more than in any other by-election, certainly in that Parliament. I kept meeting them all over the constituency, which mostly led to an exchange of friendly banter.

We had enthusiastic help not only from numerous Lincolnians but also from a flood of outsiders – much the same sort of people who later rallied to the banner of the SDP when it was launched in 1981 as a breakaway group led by the Gang of Four. My supporters were young and old, though mainly young, of all parties and none. *The Economist* remarked on the way Conservative matrons worked side by side with shop stewards, whom they would have regarded as dangerous subversives only a few months before. Student members of university Labour clubs came to Lincoln to support me – and some of them were expelled from their Labour clubs for doing so.

Bill Rodgers and former colleagues who might have helped me were unable to come, because it would have led to their expulsion from the party, but they resisted strong pressure to canvass against me. Bill's wife, Silvia, canvassed for me instead. The most valuable supporter of all was John Harris, Roy's former aide, who was not only my principal campaign adviser but, being the effervescent character he was, greatly added to the gaiety of life at Taverne House. On election day itself I met old school friends and some from Oxford days, a few former colleagues at the Bar, and at least one Conservative MP, Sir Patrick Mayhew, later a Conservative Attorney-General. The wife of the former secretary of the Police Federation came all the way from Kent and gave strong support. Liberals were especially prominent, as their then leader Jeremy Thorpe favoured the idea of a Jenkinsite/Liberal alliance. By and large, the press must also have confirmed Tony Benn in his obsession with the role played by the media, because they gave me an easy ride, mainly, I believe, because an individual cocking a snook at the two major parties adds a bit of spice to conventional politics. I had particularly strong support from *The Times*, edited by my old colleague from Charterhouse and Balliol, William Rees-Mogg, who was then both pro-Europe and in favour of a new radical centre party. Later his views moved back again to the right.

John Dilks, Labour's candidate, was not helped by the unpopularity of the local party because of its left-wing views and autocratic behaviour. At a joint debate in a church hall that was traditional in Lincoln elections, which on this occasion was televised, he was asked what he would do if he disagreed with his party. 'If I disagreed with my local party,' he replied slowly and deliberately, and paused for effect. Someone yelled, 'You'd be out!' Loud and prolonged laughter.

The Tory candidate, Jonathan Guinness, was rather unfairly treated by the press. He was apparently a witty performer at his daily press conferences but was vulnerable because of his right-wing views, less fashionable in the Conservative Party led by Heath than they are today. On one occasion he said he would restore the death penalty. Someone challenged him about the elaborate precautions taken to prevent a prisoner sentenced to death from committing suicide. He said they were ridiculous. When challenged whether this meant he would not remove a convicted murderer's razor blades, he said he would not. Someone then dubbed him 'Razor Blades Guinness' and on election day he was sent a telegram: 'Best wishes – Gillette.'

I won the election handsomely, with 21,967 votes. There were 8,776 for Dilks, 6,616 for Guinness and eighty-one for Jean Justice, the A6 Murder candidate. I received about 60 per cent of both former Labour and Conservative votes. The result was much better than I expected. I was a little surprised that Labour achieved second place and this was almost certainly due to the enormous effort they put into the campaign, far more than the Conservatives had done.

All of my supporters who took part in the election seemed to feel they had taken part in a historic event. Indeed, I sent them a Christmas card afterwards quoting, perhaps pompously, Henry V's Agincourt speech about St Crispin's day:

From this day to the ending of the world,
But we in it shall be remember'd...
[Who] fought with us upon Saint Crispin's day.

It was remembered by many of them. In March 2013, two of my

strongest local supporters, who have remained friends ever since, Pat Coates and Frank Goulding, organised a reunion in Lincoln on the fortieth anniversary of the by-election, which was attended by some fifty surviving campaigners who came from all over the UK, from as far as Dundee, Sussex and Cumbria. Their enthusiasm was such they seemed ready to fight the by-election all over again. Several said it had changed their lives and inspired them ever since to become active local campaigners for a variety of public causes.

What were the reasons for my victory and what were the lessons, if any, to be learned from it?

Before the actual campaign, the Labour Party had tried to make Europe the main issue. It organised a poll in Lincoln's High Street and triumphantly announced that the result showed a two to one majority against Britain joining the Common Market. That may well have been an accurate reflection of popular opinion but, like Labour's commitment in the 1983 election to pull Britain out of the community and William Hague's attempt to make 'Save the Pound' the hoped for vote-winning slogan of the 2001 election, people did not care. Europe is rather like capital punishment: whatever the polls may say about strong feelings to restore the death penalty, at election time other issues matter much more. The European Union has consistently ranked low on the list of issues that determine how people vote. In fact, far from being condemned for going against the current of popular opinion and party policy, I gained support for sticking to my principles. Roy Jenkins found the same at the height of his opposition to the Labour line on Europe. He told me that taxi drivers would wind down their windows to say to him: 'Stick to your guns, mate.'

To adapt *The Sun* newspaper's famous verdict on the 1992

election, it was Edmund Burke 'wot won it'.[†] My main theme was that it is the duty of an MP to act as a representative, not a delegate. It was dramatised and somewhat simplified in a final leaflet we put through doors on election eve: 'Who do you want as your MP, a man or a mouse?'

The issue is indeed a fundamental one in British politics, especially relevant today when there is a widespread belief that a referendum is the ultimate expression of democracy. Burke's classic 'Speech to the Electors of Bristol' in 1774 famously refutes the proposition that a Member of Parliament ought to vote in accordance with the instructions of his constituents, and I have added some comments about its relevance to the new fashion for referendums.[‡]

My other main theme in the by-election, which seemed to evoke an increasingly positive response as the campaign developed, was linked to disillusionment with the two main parties. There were stirrings of a yearning for something new. I wrote a book about the by-election immediately after my victory called *The Future of the Left: Lincoln and After*, which ended with a few paragraphs about what would happen if the Labour Party split. Eight years before the launch of the SDP and fourteen years before the Liberal Democrat party was formed, I speculated, somewhat prophetically, about the prospects for a Social Democratic/Liberal party.

In my book I wrote:

Suppose that the majority, or even at first a minority, of the social democratic group in Parliament grow weary of the long struggle

---

[†] After Major's somewhat unexpected victory and *The Sun*'s final headline 'If Labour wins, will the last person to leave Britain please turn out the lights', it crowed, 'It was *The Sun* wot won it.'

[‡] See Appendix 1.

to make a coalition of incompatibles work. Suppose that they recognise that they have no chance in the party of playing a role more effective than that of a fig leaf of respectability, and that they pack up their bags and go. Politics in Britain would be transformed overnight. What might start as a Lib–Lab alliance would soon emerge as a radical or Social Democratic party.

Such a party would have great electoral appeal. According to a poll commissioned by *The Times* in September 1972, such an alignment would be supported by a larger proportion of people than would vote either Tory or Labour. There would be 'twelve million Jenkinsites'. A new party of this kind would be internationalist in its approach to Europe and the Third World, radical in its pursuit of social justice at home. It would promote industrial democracy and partnership in industry, redistribution of wealth – especially a redistribution of wealth which is accrued through the accident of birth – and a redistribution of power away from the centre to Cardiff and Edinburgh, Exeter or Leeds. Finally, as such a party would not consist of a coalition of people with a conflicting philosophy, it could discard the strict party discipline that stifles independent thought and action in the two main parties today. It could give Parliament a new lease of life.

No one can forecast with confidence that the Labour Party will split and it is extremely unlikely to happen just before a general election. A political divorce at any time can be as emotionally upsetting as a matrimonial one ... Those who leave the Labour Party will be called traitors. But there is no treason to parties. The only betrayal is of ideals and there is no worse betrayal in politics.[†]

---

†   Taverne, D., *The Future of the Left: Lincoln and After* (London: Cape, 1974), p. 159.

In retrospect I am rather proud of what I wrote. Public reaction to my own by-election victory, in the form of 2,000 letters of congratulation and support (and a dozen of condemnation and disgust), strengthened the view – which I first formed early in 1972 – that a social democratic party was not only desirable but feasible. In 1973 it seemed likely that divisions in the Labour Party would lead to a new Conservative government and I believed that there was a good chance that defeat would be followed by a split and the emergence of what later became the SDP. But in the first 1974 election, in the chaos of a miners' strike and a three-day working week imposed by a shortage of power, Heath unexpectedly lost. (Wilson himself had expected Labour to lose.) After a second general election in 1974, Labour won a small majority and Wilson's second administration carried on, somewhat stutteringly, until 1979, when Mrs Thatcher won. It was never likely that Labour would split while in power.

The split did happen in 1981, eight years later than I predicted. As in Lincoln in 1973, public enthusiasm for the Gang of Four's new party was electric and it soared in the polls. Then, in my view, the SDP made a fatal mistake. All the MPs who joined the SDP should have resigned together when the SDP was on a high after its launch. I held my seat in the first general election of 1974 (and if I had not made some serious tactical mistakes, I believe I could have won in the second as well) because I had fought a by-election and established a firm base. If all the SDP MPs had resigned en bloc in 1981 there would in effect have been a mini general election in which they would almost certainly have won easily, as I did in Lincoln. They would then have been in a much stronger position at the next general election in 1983, when most of them lost their seats.

I have mentioned two occasions after 1970 when there was a chance that Roy Jenkins might have become Prime Minister: one was after the launch of the SDP. For one day during the 1983 election the SDP/Liberal Alliance edged ahead of Labour in the polls, and if it had consolidated that position it might have replaced Labour as the alternative to the Conservatives, with a reasonable chance of later gaining power. Jenkins, as leader of the Alliance, could well have become Prime Minister then. But the Alliance fell back to third place in the polls and, under the bias of our electoral system, the third party scored well in votes but poorly in winning seats. Only a handful of ex-Labour SDP MPs survived.

The other time was in 1973. Just before the Lincoln by-election, Janice and I met the Jenkinses, for the first time since I defected, at a party given by one of the more elderly Labour MPs in the social democratic camp. At Roy's suggestion, we had dinner afterwards in an Italian restaurant in Notting Hill. I told Roy that I was pretty sure I would win but did not know by how much. If he joined me, I would win overwhelmingly and the victory would be his as much as mine. He would, of course, be expelled from the party but I assumed he would bring several Labour MPs with him. Given the disillusionment with the major parties – and I referred to the *Times* poll about twelve million Jenkinsites – we could start something really big and he could be Prime Minister in the next election, which I assumed would still be some two years away, or in the election after that.

Roy said he had seriously considered my scenario and found it attractive. He thought he might bring a dozen Labour MPs with him and he was often told by outsiders that he would become Prime Minister if he broke with Labour. (Typically, he added that this was advice frequently given to him during train journeys – and he always travelled first class.) However, there was a major obstacle. A new breakaway party would need the Labour moderates to come over in large numbers, of whom councillors would be an essential part. But as a result of recent local government reforms, in the local government elections the following May all council seats were up for election. Councillors needed a strong organisation to back them, which a new party would not be able to provide. The time was not ripe. I said I could see the strength of his argument. On the other hand, my by-election presented a unique opportunity for a break and such a good opportunity might not come again. He replied that the Labour Party in its current state would provide many other opportunities. Roy's wife Jennifer told me privately that one thing also holding Roy back was that he was not sure he wanted to face the personal bitterness and abuse, and no doubt this would have been much worse in his case than mine.

Was he right or did he miss his best chance? I think on balance he was probably right. I thought at the time that his estimate of the initial defection of a dozen MPs was an overestimate, though if we had won even more decisively than I did on my own, as we would have done, the huge national impact might well have persuaded more MPs to follow. They would probably not have included, however, the other three members of the Gang of Four. Bill Rodgers certainly told me he would not have joined us then. Breaking with the party to which they had belonged and for which they had worked all their political life would be a deep emotional wrench for them, much more so than for me or, I believe, than for Roy. Only months before he left the party I heard David Owen on the BBC *Any Questions* radio programme echo Gaitskell's words, that he would fight to save 'the party that

I love'. Without the 'Gang of Three' a new party in 1973 might
have had limited appeal to Labour voters.

I did not prize party loyalty as highly as they did. I was keen
on the prospect of an alliance and indeed ultimate merger with
the Liberals. Roy, too, would have had no objection to one. But
after 1981, in the early days of the SDP, I was one of very few
arguing that there was no room in British politics for two centrist
parties and that a merger, as opposed to a mere alliance with the
Liberals, was not only desirable because of common historical
roots but inevitable. But the tide had not yet turned in favour
of a Lib–Lab party. Instead, the Gang of Three envisaged
a new kind of Labour Party. David Owen positively disliked
Liberals and passionately opposed the eventual merger until
the end, persisting with a continuing SDP until it disappeared
after coming sixth in a by-election with even fewer votes than a
Monster Raving Looney candidate.

Another reason, I believe, that motivated Roy to avoid a break
with Labour in 1973 was the expected defeat of Labour in the next
election, as a result of its drift to the left. Conditions would then
be more favourable for a larger breakout by the social democrats.
On the other hand, there was one very powerful reason why Roy
might have missed his best opportunity. In the early 1970s he was
still at the height of his public standing. He still commanded the
House of Commons. He had been the outstanding success in an
unsuccessful government. If anything, his reputation with the
public had been enhanced by his dramatic refusal to compromise
his principles over Europe, despite lack of public enthusiasm for
the cause itself. (Burke ruled again.) Gradually memories of his
past achievements were bound to fade – and did.

In 1974, Labour did not lose the election but became the

government, with Harold Wilson as Prime Minister once again. For quite a while Roy was depressed and demoralised, as he had privately hoped Labour would lose and thought it did not deserve to win. The most he was offered was to be Home Secretary for a second time, which he accepted, possibly because of low morale. It was a humiliating demotion from his former position as Chancellor. Furthermore, when Labour finally lost the election in 1979 and the Gang of Four founded the SDP in 1981, he was, as I expected, no longer the dominating figure he had been in the 1960s and early 1970s. In 1976, on Wilson's resignation, he had come third in the contest for the Labour leadership, behind Michael Foot and Jim Callaghan. He then became President of the European Commission for four years, which, however important, was not an office that in Britain commanded the respect it deserved, even among some of those who knew what it was. Instead, on his return to British politics, it made him vulnerable to caricature as 'the fat cat from Brussels'. Lastly, while he proved a surprisingly effective campaigner in two by-elections in which he stood as a candidate for the SDP – the first in Warrington in 1981 when he lost, but gloriously, and the second in Glasgow Hillhead in1982, when he won triumphantly against expectations – he was no longer the orator he had been. In Parliament he was relatively ineffective. The House of Commons had changed, was much rowdier and his performances were less assured.

The aftermath of the Lincoln by-election led me to make two serious mistakes. For a while our momentum was maintained. At the council elections in June 1973, Lincoln Democratic Labour candidates won several seats and then took control of the council in April 1974. This success, the scale of my victory and the public enthusiasm, not only during the campaign but also immediately after the result, raised excessive hopes and expectations. We were slightly drunk with success. The first mistake we made was to set up a small organisation, which we called the Campaign for Social Democracy (CSD) – to revive memories of CDS – in the hope that we could act as a catalyst for breaking the mould of British party politics. Our intention was to stimulate the formation of CSD branches in other constituencies where there was promise of support. There were some green shoots in Newcastle and Norwich, where we held meetings that drew modest attendances, and in the Yorkshire constituency of Brighouse and Spenborough, where we had a crowd of 250 people. But in February 1974, before we could gain wider support and much earlier than we (or others) expected, Heath called an election. A miners' strike had led to such a serious disruption of power supplies that he had been forced to impose a three-day week. He thought he would win the election on the issue of 'who governs Britain'. In the event, other more usual bread-and-butter issues gradually dominated and Heath lost, although Wilson did not gain an absolute majority until a second general election in October 1974.

Our second mistake was that foolishly, urged on by enthusiastic supporters (and against the wise counsel of Bernard Levin), we decided in the first 1974 general election to contest four constituencies where we thought we had found suitable candidates to challenge strongly left-wing Labour MPs: Bristol, challenging Tony Benn, Penistone, Keighley and Tottenham. We did not expect to win but hoped to make a reasonable showing that would encourage others to consider a break. Our intervention attracted almost no notice and all three candidates easily lost their deposits. I still regret the sense of humiliation it brought on our unsuccessful candidates. Even our campaign in Lincoln, as we should have anticipated, was no longer a national event. I was briefly interviewed on one television programme and in the press only *The Times* (in Bernard Levin's column) and a piece in *The Economist* mentioned Lincoln and the fact that we were fighting four other seats as social democrats. CSD diverted a lot of our efforts, time and resources, which would have been much more profitably deployed in Lincoln itself.

Indeed, in retrospect CSD was a disaster. I should have realised that after our moment of glory in the limelight, party political life would return to normal. But our strategy was not entirely irrational. It was based on two premises: the first was that Labour would lose the next election, as was generally expected, and that this would be followed by a Labour split. Then our small organisation would have been of some relevance. The second premise was that we would have difficulty in maintaining the Lincoln Democratic Labour Association if it was a purely local group, not backed by a national organisation. Purely local support, I feared, would gradually erode and in the absence of allegiance to an outside body, personal differences would become more important (which in the event they did).

Independent MPs are not only rare but never survive for long. I knew that in a general election my majority in Lincoln would be reduced but in the event it almost collapsed, from over 13,000 to 1,300. One of the reasons was a quite widespread local feeling that I should have concentrated on Lincoln itself instead of haring off to other pastures.

There was an alternative strategy, namely to use our by-election victory to create a political island, a social democratic

republic of Lincoln, with a different style of politics, and to use
my position as an independent MP to promote ideas that were
not part of the political mainstream.

The local activities would have featured regular town meetings, not unlike the successful town meetings held in American
small towns, which have always struck me as a vital manifestation
of local democracy that we lack. Indeed I have always admired,
as de Tocqueville did in his famous reflections on democracy
in America, the strength of its local civic society. The historian
Lord Kenneth Morgan once wrote, 'The British don't do citizenship.' We could have tried to create a style of local Lincoln
citizenship different from politics in the rest of England, based
on the American model, which might have sought to realise in
concrete form the rather vague but attractive concept David
Cameron has since sought to promote as 'the Big Society' (for
which the word Big is singularly inappropriate). In fact, the
LDLA-controlled council did for a while succeed in establishing a special relationship with its public. After gaining control in
1974, it ran the council so skilfully that it reduced council taxes
while improving services and swept the board in the local elections of 1976. However, after that, gradually, as I had feared,
partly through personal clashes and partly because it lacked a
national base, its support eroded as the traditional parties took
over again and eventually the LDLA ceased to exist. But if I had
built up a strong local base instead of hawking the CSD round
the country, I would probably have retained a substantial majority in the first 1974 election and would probably have survived
the second, which I lost by 900 votes.

At the same time I could have used my position as an
independent in Parliament to propagate the case for a Social

Democratic Party. After the by-election I was approached by a number of impressive people to discuss ideas they felt had been neglected or ignored by the conventional parties. They included John Hoskyns, who later veered to the right and became head of Mrs Thatcher's policy unit in No. 10, and a young economist called Mervyn King, later Governor of the Bank of England. However, before the group became effective, general elections intervened and nothing ever came of it. I could also have sought to champion a programme for tax reform based on the work of the Institute for Fiscal Studies, which I had launched in 1971 and which was beginning to establish itself in the mid-1970s. In 1979 the IFS produced the Meade report, the most thorough and fundamental review of the British system of direct taxation that it had ever undergone (see Chapter 8).

Do I regret the mistakes and the loss of my seat? If politics were my whole life, the answer would be yes. As things turned out, I am glad I lost. Realistically, the chances of exercising influence as a lone independent would have been remote. The House of Commons is not like the House of Lords, where independents – that is the crossbenchers – number about a quarter of the active membership and are a significant force. They are not whipped but they are consulted in arrangements for debates and kept informed of planned future business as a group. In terms of votes, they actually hold the balance of power. In the House of Commons any independents, if they exist at all, are complete outsiders. All arrangements are designed to suit the political parties.

If Labour had been defeated in 1974 and the split in the Labour Party I anticipated had happened then it would have been a different story. A political life is not a comfortable one but to play a significant part in bringing about changes one longs to see is not an opportunity to be spurned. But with the Labour Party back in power, I would have faced five politically lonely, frustrating years, waiting to see if the mould of party politics would eventually be broken.

I had plenty of other things to do. If I had won in October 1974, I would probably have been less successful in nursing the Institute for Fiscal Studies beyond the stage of its infancy. I would have missed my enjoyable and valuable experience as a non-executive board member of two major companies and I would probably never have founded the charity Sense About Science, which has given me as much satisfaction as anything else I have done in public life. What is more, I would not have been able to enjoy family life to the same extent. It suffered while I was a Member of Parliament.

Did the Lincoln by-election have any lasting effect on British politics? One meeting I addressed in the early days of the SDP was reported in the local press with the headline: 'Prophet Speaks'. I was occasionally referred to as a John the Baptist – not an auspicious augury for a peaceful life. I suppose we did demonstrate that there was electoral life outside the conventional parties but I cannot claim that there is any evidence that Lincoln influenced the birth of the SDP. In fact, because its founders (with the exception of Roy Jenkins) originally envisaged the SDP as a new kind of Labour Party, they seemed to feel that too close an association with me might prejudice their support from loyal party members, many of whom in 1981 still saw me as a renegade. Memories fade fast in politics. I still meet people, including some who were still at school at the time, who recognise my name and mention the excitement created by that by-election, even if they do not remember where it was: 'East Anglia?' But by 1981, when the SDP was launched, most of the public had forgotten Lincoln. For those who do remember, I believe we left one very important message: never underestimate the popular appeal of Edmund Burke.

CHAPTER 8

THE INSTITUTE FOR
FISCAL STUDIES

The loss of my Lincoln seat in October 1974 was the end of my active role in party politics for the next twenty-two years. I stood twice as a candidate for the SDP/Liberal Alliance, at a by-election in Peckham in 1982 and in Dulwich in the 1983 general election, not because I was desperate to return to the House of Commons but because I felt I should do what I could to promote the Alliance when it became a reality, since I had argued the need for a new Liberal/Social Democratic party since 1973. It was never likely that I would win either seat and I was not upset to fail.

Even before the spectacular events in Lincoln, while I was still a Labour MP I had already become involved in a new career, launching the Institute for Fiscal Studies. At first, after I had left the Treasury because of Labour's defeat in 1970, I spent several months in rather aimless contemplation about what to do next. I was warned I would suffer withdrawal symptoms on leaving ministerial office and the loss of office was indeed a blow, because life in the Treasury with Roy Jenkins and my colleagues had been deeply satisfying, often exciting and fun, while the prospect of returning to life as a backbencher with all its frustrations was a bit like exchanging a role on the West End stage for a walk-on part in provincial rep.

My former chambers approached me to return to the Bar. (Many ex-ministers who were former barristers often did return in those days.) I rejected the idea for several reasons. The law had changed substantially since I left it and I had not only forgotten what law I knew, but would have to learn a lot of new law. Secondly, Privy Council work had shrunk. Partly as a result of a number of cases (like the plot against Mrs Bandaranaike) in which we had won victories against Commonwealth governments, countries like Sri Lanka and Nigeria had abolished the jurisdiction of the Privy Council over their courts. Thirdly, I did not want to repeat the strenuous life of combining Parliament and the law. Finally, I doubted whether, after the excitement of being a minister, I would find legal practice sufficiently satisfying. But what should I do instead?

Janice complained that while she went out to her wholly absorbing work in scientific research, my first two weeks before the new Parliament reassembled were spent lying on the sofa watching Wimbledon all day. I toyed with the idea of buying a boat in the Mediterranean to charter out as a business proposition. Sailing was my favourite relaxation, though not always relaxing in a gale, but the plan was of course a pipedream. Running a private charter boat is a precarious business at the best of times and a hopeless venture for an MP, especially one with constituency problems.

My next thought was to write a biography, an occupation that has kept several MPs harmlessly occupied and has even enhanced some reputations. I thought Sir Stafford Cripps might be one possible subject, as he had always fascinated me. He had been a passionate and incorruptible leading figure in the Labour Party in the 1940s and, from 1947 to 1949, a successful Chancellor of the Exchequer at a time of economic crisis, who had lacked an authoritative chronicler. Roy Jenkins rather encouraged me, though he warned me that Cripps's widow had all his papers and would not easily part with them. Then I reflected that the central driving force in Cripps's life had been his Christian faith (Churchill once said of him, 'there, but for the grace of God, goes God') and that probably disqualified me, a non-believer, as a sympathetic biographer.

Another idea I flirted with was a critical study of Eisenhower in Europe, where he had a high but, I thought, undeserved reputation that needed to be reassessed. From a rather superficial impression of his career, I believed that, although there was no doubt about his charisma, his victory in Europe had been largely due to his generals, while his lack of political nous and experience had led him to trust the good faith of the Russians and stop the allied advance to Berlin at the Elbe. If he, not the Russians had captured Berlin, as he could have done, the map between democratic West and Communist East Europe would have been drawn much further east. My view of him was also influenced by Robin Day's account of meeting him when Robin was on a debating tour of the US and Eisenhower was President of Columbia University. In a private conversation Eisenhower declared that he planned to get the best brains in America to draw a definitive line to mark clearly where capitalism ended and socialism began! It was also reported, I suspect maliciously and wrongly, that he had been horrified to learn that half the American population was of below-average intelligence.

Very soon after I started research, however, I found that

Eisenhower's contribution to Allied victory had been central
to success. He was a profound student of military history and
concluded that the greatest weakness of military operations by
Allied armies was always the link between them. In an opera-
tion as complex and hazardous as the invasion of the Continent,
with commanders as egocentric as Montgomery and Patton,
and with the risk of destructive rivalries between the British and
Americans, an integrated Allied command was vital to avoid
mutual mistrust and muddle. No one else could have achieved
this as successfully as Ike did, using his extraordinary personal
charm. As for halting at the Elbe, that was not a military but
political decision agreed with Stalin by Roosevelt and Churchill
at Yalta in February 1945.

The more I learned about Ike, the more I admired him. But I
decided there was no point in another book singing Eisenhower's
praises. In recent years there has been a general reappraisal of
Eisenhower's presidency, giving him high marks for common
sense, judgement, moderation and for his consensual approach.
Joseph Nye, in his comparison of the record of different Presidents
in foreign affairs, rates Eisenhower as one of the best, not only
as more effective than most of his peers in extending US power
but also more ethical in how he went about it. [†] Unlike most
Presidents, who are unstinting in their praise for the military,
he warned about the dangers of the military-industrial complex
and told military advisers who advocated use of the atom bomb
during the crises in Korea, over Dien Bien Phu in Vietnam and
when conflict blew up in the Taiwan straits, 'You boys must be

---

[†]   Nye, J. S., *Presidential Leadership and the Creation of the American Era* (Princeton:
Princeton University Press, 2013).

crazy.' In any case, my local difficulties in Lincoln would have left me no time to do the necessary research for a biography.

I received two offers for jobs, as already mentioned, that were superficially attractive. The first was to become special adviser to the Police Federation, a post held by Jim Callaghan until 1964, when Labour became the government, and then by Eldon Griffiths until 1970,when he was appointed a junior minister in Heath's government. The second was to be a non-executive director of the security firm Securicor, my former employer when I was a night-watchman. I rejected both, as they wanted me to be their parliamentary representative, which I believed would conflict with my duty as an MP.

Then, out of the blue, came an enquiry from a group of professional people: was I interested in launching a new institute? Merchant banker Will Hopper, investment trust manager Bob Buist, stockbroker Nils Taube and tax consultant John Chown had been appalled by the history of the Finance Act of 1965. Soon after the 1964 election, James Callaghan, the new Chancellor of the Exchequer, made a speech announcing his plan to make far-reaching changes in the tax system, including the introduction of a capital gains tax and a fundamental reform of corporation tax. They felt the proposals had been ill-thought out. Subsequently they were dismayed to find, in John Chown's words, 'the same half-baked proposals rehashed in the Budget speech, and the Finance Bill, when published, read as if the draftsman had simply been given the Callaghan speech and been told to turn it into legislation.'[†] The four met for a

---

† IFS Archives, *The First Five Years: IFS 30th Anniversary*, p. 4. The Finance Bill of 1965 was subject to a record number of amendments and its reform of corporation tax was not exactly a model of lucid legislation.

weekend and later wrote 'A Charter for the Taxpayer', to which
The Times devoted a whole page in April 1967. They added
solicitor Jeremy Skinner and accountant Halmer Hudson to
their group and subsequently established the Institute for Fiscal
Studies as a company limited by guarantee.

The declared aim of the institute was to change British fiscal
policy or, more specifically, 'to alter the climate of opinion
within which changes to the British tax system were considered;
to improve the procedures by which changes in the tax system
were effected; and to help create a more rational tax system.[†]
But how was this aim to be achieved? They had no money, no
patronage, no staff and no track record. There were obvious
problems in attracting high-quality staff without a track record
and no chance to establish a track record without high-quality
staff. Who would back the IFS without either? After the 1970
election, they decided that, as an ex-Financial Secretary, I was a
suitable person to approach to be its first director. They offered
me a modest salary from their own resources, guaranteed for a
year, and asked me to launch the new institute.

At first I was uncertain. Despite my Treasury experience, I was
not a tax expert or an economist and the task was completely
different from anything I had ever done before. I was also not sure
how interesting the job would be. Everyone is affected by tax but,
as *The Economist* once observed, few subjects match tax reform
for economic importance and utter lack of sex appeal. Or in the
words of David Lipsey: 'Detailed tax policy is a subject for nerds.'[‡]

I decided to accept the challenge. There was, in my view,
an urgent need for a centre of independent expertise in tax

---

†   Ibid., p. 5.
‡   Op. cit.

administration as well as in tax law and also in the interaction between tax and public spending. Much as I admired the dedication and intelligence of the top civil servants at the Inland Revenue, if they disliked a proposed reform – and they often did – they could prove conclusively that the administrative difficulties were insuperable, and unfortunately their objections were often justified. My suggestion that we should look at the merits of a wealth tax was a good example. Few proposals for tax reform properly considered the practical problems. There was a yawning gap between the knowledge of administrative and practical detail possessed by the legal and accountancy professions, and the expertise of academics interested in economic effects, who often had little time for, or interest in, the finer problems of administration.

Furthermore there was something radically wrong with the way proposed tax reforms were transformed into law. Many details of fiscal legislation were in my day debated in the middle of the night when MPs and ministers were exhausted; few MPs understood its complexities. The more that opposition spokesmen were baffled by a minister's explanation of some intricate clause in a Finance Bill, the more effusively they would congratulate him (seldom a her in my day) on the lucidity of his exposition. In 1998, in a debate in the Lords about improving our tax laws, a former Conservative Treasury minister recalled one occasion when he was congratulated by his opponent on the clarity of his exposition, only to receive a note from his civil servants: 'Minister, your explanation was of the wrong clause.' No one noticed.

Much tax legislation used to be contained in schedules to bills. During discussion of one proposed Finance Bill when I was in the Treasury, Roy Jenkins said he wanted a short Bill and was disturbed to find that some particular technical tax changes were long and complicated. 'Well,' he was advised, 'you can always put them in a schedule.' So we did. A schedule is hardly ever properly discussed in detail. In fact, there is an apocryphal story that when the unhappily married town clerk of Birmingham was responsible for drafting a long Bill on water management at the end of the nineteenth century – a time when divorce was rare and very expensive – no one noticed that a minor paragraph of a long schedule contained the words: 'And the marriage of the town clerk of Birmingham is hereby dissolved.'

Lack of transparency was another major weakness. Before the IFS was established, the contents of the Budget were a closely guarded secret until their dramatic revelation in the annual ritual of the Budget Speech. There was little prior consultation or public discussion, no IFS Green Budget. Tax policy was also kept separate from decisions about expenditure. Consequently the whole system of tax and spending was in an appalling mess. Some social and economic objectives were pursued through grants and subsidies; others by tax allowances. The result was one full of contradictions and inconsistencies because each provision was proposed and debated with little if any regard for its effect on the system as a whole.

For example, after a popular campaign championed by MPs, a special tax allowance was introduced for the blind. Everybody cheered. But what about the deaf? Were they less deserving? If an allowance for the deaf, what about the lame, or other categories of the disabled? Moreover tax allowances benefit high-taxpayers most and non-taxpayers not at all. A tax allowance that reduces taxable income by £1,000 benefits someone liable to a marginal rate of 45 per cent by £450, someone with a marginal rate of 20 per cent by £200 and provides no benefit at all to someone who pays no tax. Grants which are tax-free benefit every beneficiary equally; grants which are taxable give most help to those least well-off. Thus grants or benefit payments are a much better way of helping people you want to help.

A plethora of allowances and exemptions also complicate the system, creating massive opportunities for tax avoidance. In the 1970s this was especially true of savings. The yield on savings for basic rate taxpayers varied enormously, depending on the kind of savings they chose or were advised to choose. In some cases they would receive two-fifths of the real yield on the underlying investment; in other cases four times that yield. If the saver was able to invest through a tax-free pension fund, the range of return was even greater, up to six times the basic yield. These anomalies were only understood by masters of the Eleusinian mysteries that enveloped the taxation of savings.

Furthermore the greater the complexities of our system, the larger and more lucrative the tax avoidance industry becomes. Each year, two vast armies, staffed by officers of great talent and infinite ingenuity, clash in a battle of wits over the Finance Bill. Before the Budget, the staff officers of the Inland Revenue seek to shore up their defences wherever their opponents have discovered particularly significant loopholes in the previous year. After publication of the Bill, accountants, solicitors and barristers probe the new defences and nearly always discover new weak spots. The whole exercise is almost as unproductive a use of top-class brains as the City's efforts to invent ever more sophisticated financial instruments to make ever higher profits with little apparent public benefit – indeed often with disastrous consequences for everybody.

For all these reasons, I was convinced of the need for a new institute, but what were the prospects of financing it? I asked advice from some senior civil servants and a few industrialists I knew and they were mostly discouraging. However, after much thought, I was confident that we could persuade some potential backers. Supplied by my new friends in the tax world with a wealth of persuasive arguments, I found I was able to convince a number of captains of industry that it was worth providing the starting capital for our new institute, with its aim to promote a more rational tax system. A wholly rational tax system is, of course, an impossible dream because in the real world political pressures will always distort the best-laid schemes of the wisest counsellors. Just as the greatest happiness of the greatest number will always prove a mirage while the least misery of the smallest number is a more realistic target, the most we can hope for is to mitigate as many of the inefficiencies and harmful effects of the tax system as possible. That does not mean that the less we tax, the better, but that we should tax in a way that is as effective as we can make it to achieve our social and economic aims.

In retrospect, I believe I made three important contributions to the success of IFS: by successfully promoting the launch, by setting up the Meade Committee and by persuading John Kay to be its first professional director.

The launch, in 1971, and its follow-up went well. At that stage we were in no position to obtain funding from grant-making foundations, so funding from industry was the only hope. Marks and Spencer was the first major company to prime our pump. They not only gave us £2,000 (worth nearly £30,000 today) but encouraged other companies to follow suit, though mostly for smaller sums. I vividly remember a gathering of major suppliers to M&S, invited by that great and good man Sir Marcus Sieff who was then its head, to hear me make my pitch. I am not sure the attendance was entirely voluntary. At any rate, after I finished Marcus announced that we were a good cause, M&S was supporting us and he hoped others would follow suit, and then glared at the audience of his suppliers, not without a hint of menace. Sheepishly, rather nervously, they glanced at each other and, one after another, hands slowly went up. The subsequent actual offers of support were modest – a few hundred pounds each at the most – but still a handsome haul for a penniless institute. Other major companies also made substantial contributions.

There was a slight hiccup at the start. In 1970–71 the BBC ran a series of television trials of current affairs issues. It was in many ways the forerunner of the Radio 4 programme *You the Jury*. In the TV trial, each side called four witnesses instead of two and the jury itself was not the audience but was composed of thirty law-students. Neither advocate knew in advance whom the other side would call as witnesses. I was asked to suggest an economic subject and to be one of the advocates. To their surprise, I said I would like to oppose the motion 'that direct taxation should be reduced'. Was I a masochist? Surely no motion could be more popular? I persisted, perhaps partly to show that the nascent IFS, at that stage entirely dependent on business support, had a director who would not be a lobbyist for minimal taxation or the special interests of business.

The debate went surprisingly well. I argued that while direct taxation should be reformed, because I did not defend the current, absurd, top marginal rate of 83 per cent, a high standard of public services was essential to a more civilised and equal society, that this implied a substantial level of taxation and that direct taxation was the fairest form of tax.

It was the former chairman of the Conservative Party, Sir Edward du Cann MP, who had proposed the motion. Two of his four witnesses whose evidence I remember were Sir Paul Chambers, the chairman of ICI (Imperial Chemical Industry), then one of Britain's most successful companies, and Ludwig Erhard, the Finance Minister and later Chancellor of West Germany, who had been the architect of the post-war German economic miracle. I managed to get Sir Paul to agree that he loved his job, that he was successful at it and that he could not work or try any harder than he was doing now. So would he be more devoted or more successful if he paid less tax? He had to agree he would not. But was he suggesting that this was only true of someone as dedicated and public spirited as himself, while other managers in industry were more selfish and greedy and would only do their job properly if they paid less tax? He seemed to have some difficulties with the answer. As for Ludwig Erhard, fortunately his evidence (given by radio interview in the days before international interviews by television) was something of a farce. His English was poor. He admitted that Germany's position was quite different, because they had had the huge advantage of little or no military expenditure, and that he knew little of the special problems of economic management in Britain.

My witnesses were Des Wilson, Director of Shelter, and a great social campaigner of the day; Kenneth Mellanby, an eminent ecologist; Gunnar Myrdal, the famous Swedish economist; and a dour, little-known Scottish economist, Chuck Brown, who turned out to be my star witness. He had made a thorough study of incentives and found, as most academics know, that taxation has two opposite effects on effort: some, do less work, if they can afford to do so, because they value leisure more. Others work harder because they need the extra money. Most people seem to be unaware how tax incentives work. One example was that of the lawyer who complained bitterly about the disincentive effect of high taxation. To enable him to achieve a decent standard of living, high taxes forced him to work eighty hours a week! The man I hoped to be my most impressive witness, Gunnar Myrdal, was not much more effective than Ludwig Erhard, because evidence down an audio line has less impact than evidence in person.

I lost by fifteen votes to fourteen, which I regarded as a victory. We met the jurors for drinks afterwards and one of the jurors told me he did not press his voting button strongly enough, which would have made it fifteen all. However, some IFS supporters greeted my performance with well-concealed enthusiasm. It certainly shook some of the IFS founders, who wondered if by mistake they had recruited a fanatical egalitarian, bent on turning Britain into a Scandinavian social democratic paradise. I should add that I do accept that very high tax rates have harmful effects – they lead to tax avoidance and evasion and distort behaviour in all sorts of undesirable ways. But I also believe that the harmful effects of high taxes are overstated – high tax Nordic countries such as Denmark and Sweden are among the most contented, civilised and prosperous countries in the world. Moreover, the argument I used against Sir Paul applies strongly to the current popularity of bonus payments, for good performance as well as bad.

The debate was soon forgotten and it did not prevent IFS making steady, if slow and unspectacular, headway. We recruited a secretary and a research director, Thelma Liesner, a Cambridge economist who supplied the economic expertise I did not have and who deserved most of the credit for our progress in the first few years. We published a number of papers on a variety of subjects such as corporation tax,[†] the taxation of wealth and inheritance, and the black economy. They were commissioned from outside experts, because a new institute did not have the reputation to attract first-class academic staff. If I had been less distracted by events in Lincoln, progress would no doubt have been faster.

In 1974 I reached the conclusion that to make a significant impact we had to be more ambitious. We needed a big idea. Since the fundamental weakness of our tax system was the failure of reformers to look at the system as a whole, I decided we needed to set up a high-powered authoritative commission to examine what a good system would look like if we started from first principles, with a blank sheet. There was a precedent. In Canada, Kenneth Carter had been appointed in 1962 to do precisely that and his commission's report, published in 1966, seemed to have made a big impact.

The reaction of the IFS executive committee was enthusiastic. My first task was to find the right chairman and, fortunately, I managed to persuade Professor James Meade to accept. He had just completed a major project and was wondering what to do next. James was a wonderful man. In an obituary he was described 'as one of the greatest economists of his generation, [who], more than anyone since John Maynard Keynes, influenced the way

---

† John Chown's *The Reform of Corporation Tax* was our first publication and was written before the launch of the IFS.

in which economic policy is now discussed in Britain.'[†] James wrote with a beautiful simplicity, which could disguise the depth, and sometimes the complexity, of his ideas. He was profoundly modest and even diffident. When his ideas were challenged at a public meeting, he would often confess that he might be wrong. This would obscure the tenacity and determination with which he pursued them, often dismissing all criticism.

He was also a man of infinite patience. He once told me that since he and his equally wonderful wife Margaret liked to read books together, he would read them aloud. I asked whether this might sometimes be tiring. He confessed that during a reading of David Marquand's majestic life of Ramsay Macdonald, which he had just completed, when a passage started with the words, 'This incident needs consideration in greater detail', his enthusiasm would sometimes flag (though at some 800 pages, the book is not in fact unconscionably long for a biography). I first met James at a conference about a year earlier and, to my great delight, he told me that he had strongly supported my stand as an independent in the Lincoln by-election.

The idea of the IFS project appealed to him and he started work on it at once, even before the members of the committee had been recruited. A few months afterwards he confessed to me that on reflection he felt appalled by the enormity of the task I had asked him to undertake, especially as he had recently been seriously ill and was now seventy years old. Nevertheless, he persisted and his role was basic to the committee's success. He wrote most of the report himself but he was supported by an exceptionally talented group of colleagues whom I persuaded

---

† Layard, R. and Weale, M., 'Obituary: Professor James Meade', *The Independent*, 29 December 1995.

to join the committee. Several had already taken part in earlier activities of the IFS. A vital role was played by the deputy chairman, Donald Ironside, who organised the work and acted as chairman during the discussions so that James Meade could concentrate on arguing for his ideas. Ironside was later voted 'Accountant of the Year', an annual award given by a special committee of the Chartered Institute of Accountants, for his special contribution to the Meade Committee in translating the language of accountants and tax lawyers into language intelligible to economists, and vice versa.

I was also fortunate in my choice of young economists. John Flemming, the best-known, was appointed chief economist at the Bank of England soon after the committee reported. The next in seniority was a young economist in his mid-twenties whom I had got to know after the Lincoln by-election because he was interested in promoting new approaches to economic policy and thought I might be a useful spokesman. I thought he would be an asset to the committee – he was Mervyn King, later Governor of the Bank of England. He in turn recommended an even younger Oxford economist, John Kay.

John Kay proved the most influential member of the committee after James Meade. When we held a series of well-attended seminars after the report's publication, James would deal with the more difficult questions by saying: 'I think John Kay should answer this question.' John and Mervyn King would later write their own version of the Meade report: *The British Tax System*, which is a surprisingly readable book on tax.

The committee reported in January 1978, little more than two years after its establishment. I had originally asked them to report within twelve months because I envisaged a report on general principles, fearing that a detailed examination of tax reform would take many years. A Royal Commission on the Taxation of Income and Profits had reported in 1955 after many years' labour. To limit the scope of their studies, the committee decided to look at direct taxation only, as it felt that general recommendations about the system would be of limited value, or would carry little conviction, without an examination of the administrative problems that its recommendations might raise or solve. To take only two years was therefore a triumph. We prepared the launch of the report meticulously with elaborate private briefings of editors and specialist commentators, and as a result its publication received more publicity than most Royal Commission reports. The *Financial Times* devoted five pages to it, including one full-page summary of its findings and an editorial that described it 'as a radical analysis of the British system which has long been needed'. James Meade had also just been awarded the Nobel Prize and he received a special telegram from President Carter congratulating him on his well-deserved reward for his work on tax. The prize was for his work on international trade many years earlier, but at least it showed that the fame of the Meade Committee had spread abroad.

The report proposed to replace income tax, with its complex different exemptions for savings, by a much simpler expenditure tax, not to be confused with VAT. A person's annual income would still be the basis for tax liability, but all forms of savings and investment would be deductible, while all forms of dissaving, such as sales of property or shares or realisation of life insurance, would be taxable as part of income (less, of course, any amount reinvested). Result: you would be taxed on what you spent. Corporate taxation would be based on cash flow rather than profits. The committee argued that the system would result in a drastic simplification, sweeping away the need for a capital gains tax and special rules for close companies, trusts and various savings institutions, which were a bane in the life of those affected at the time. The committee also proposed a radical reform of social security, to abolish the 'poverty trap' and cut the high marginal rates paid by those on benefits as their income rises. (These reforms were perhaps a more carefully thought-out version of the changes in the welfare system proposed by the coalition government of 2010.)

The committee's central proposal for an expenditure tax has never been implemented, though some of its particular proposals have been. For example, some of the worst anomalies of the taxation of savings have gone. The nearest the expenditure tax ever came to realisation was when I persuaded the SDP National Conference in 1984 to adopt it, but it never made the Alliance manifesto of 1987, and in any case the Alliance came nowhere near forming a government. Thirty years after the publication of the Meade report the IFS felt another look at what would make a good tax system for the twenty-first century was needed. Alas, the Mirrlees Review found the system was still the product of often incoherent changes rather than strategic design. So it goes, and given the intensely political nature of tax issues, no doubt it always will. However, the Meade report has proved, as I said in the report's preface I hoped it would do, 'a rich quarry for tax reformers and a valuable reference point for students of taxation for decades to come'. It also firmly established the reputation of the Institute for Fiscal Studies.

The progress that followed was due to my third major contribution: to persuade John Kay to become its director, while

I became chairman. I was told he was already in the running for a prestigious university chair but I argued IFS would be a much more exciting choice. We were beginning to raise serious money. The Meade Committee had been financed by major grant-making trusts and foundations, such as the Gatsby Trust and the Esmée Fairbairn Foundation who were impressed by the result and were now ready to fund other projects. Finance from companies was boosted by a meeting of top chairmen and chief executives, sponsored by the Governor of the Bank of England, Gordon Richardson (later Lord Richardson of Duntisbourne), who strongly supported my appeal for funds. I could therefore offer John the promise of being able to recruit high-quality staff of his own choice and plan his own programme of research. He would be able to develop closer contacts with industry, government, the press and the world outside in general than as professor in any university. IFS would also guarantee, indeed would require, complete independence. Fortunately, and I believe wisely, John accepted and was the first of a series of very able directors, noted for their success in the media as well in academe, who have made IFS what it is today. In due course he was succeeded by Bill Robinson, Andrew Dilnot, Robert Chote and now Paul Johnson.

John Kay recruited a group of top university talents, most of them very young. One of them started work for IFS during the vacations when he was still an undergraduate. He looked about fifteen years old. He was Andrew Dilnot, who proved, when he later became director, no less eloquent on television in explaining the intricacies of tax than John himself. John managed his young staff well because they admired his academic ability, the scope of the research programme and his exceptional eloquence and wit, in speech and on paper. He is one of the cleverest people I know and what I admire most is his immunity to conventional ways of thinking about almost any topic. Not that he is without weaknesses. No one could describe him as one of nature's diplomats. One of my last services to IFS was to act as peacemaker between him and the Director of the Economic and Social Research Council, Sir Ian Byatt. The ESRC are key funders of economic research through the specially nominated ESRC research centres. IFS had been overlooked, despite its high reputation, apparently on the curious grounds that we were good at raising our own money, so we did not need their support. John was furious and said he would resign. I persuaded Ian Byatt that he really meant it, that this would be a tragedy and a scandal, and that it was quite ridiculous for the ESRC not to give its prestigious support to IFS – just because we had been good at raising funds from other sources. IFS has been one of the ESRC's specially nominated research centres ever since.

Ten years after I had launched IFS I resigned, as by then I had become a rather passive chairman and was making no significant contribution. IFS itself was clearly flourishing. Now it seems to be regarded as the ultimate source of fiscal wisdom, with everyone vying for its endorsement of their claims. I have watched its transformation from the infant I once nourished with a degree of pride and satisfaction. But I believe those who start an enterprise should not hang around too long, and by then my mind was on other things.

CHAPTER 9

A BEGINNER IN THE
BOARDROOM

In 1972 another unexpected invitation came my way. I was asked to become a non-executive director of Equity and Law, an old-established life assurance company founded in 1844. Then in 1975 I was asked to join the board of BOC, an industrial gases company, on the recommendation of one of Equity and Law's directors who was also on the BOC board.[†]

Why did I join these boards? I had no commercial experience. To become a director of two major companies was certainly a milestone on the long journey from my early days in the Labour Party, when I even had doubts about the morality of owning shares. But I thought it would be a chance to learn about an entirely new world and find out how decisions were taken in important parts of industry and what role was played by non-executive directors.

Many years ago, I heard Bob Boothby, the colourful maverick Conservative MP, describe being a non-executive director as the nearest thing to a permanent hot bath. Once every few months, he said, you are collected by a company car, have an extremely

---

† Its official title at the time was BOC International, later changed to the BOC Group, but referred to here as BOC.

good lunch after which the executives give an account of their activities and future plans. The chairman, who is probably a friend – normally the reason you are on the board – may occasionally ask your views. You nod sagely in agreement or raise an eyebrow and question if the matter might not deserve further consideration. Then you are driven back to your home (or club). For this exhausting contribution to the success of British industry, you are paid a modest but not insignificant fee.

But how did boards actually operate and what did corporate governance contribute to the record of British industry, which was hardly one of unqualified success? I certainly had time to find out. The general view in the City and industry is that non-executive directors should serve no more than six years. I rather exceeded this limit, ending my connection with Equity and Law, and the successor companies into which it was merged, in 2011 after thirty-nine years. I was a board member of BOC for a mere twenty years, from 1975 to 1995.

In fact non-executive directors perform a number of important roles. As independent outsiders they can add an extra perspective to discussions of strategy. On behalf of the different stakeholders, principally shareholders, they act as a check on management, whose personal ambitions may sometimes conflict with a company's interests. For instance, a programme of acquisitions may benefit management by expanding the empire which they control, but may not improve, and may even harm, the company's efficiency or profitability. Furthermore, non-executive directors, through board remuneration committees, fix top executives's pay – a task they have singularly failed to carry out to most people's satisfaction.

As I had hoped, my time on these boards proved a valuable

and interesting experience. But what use was I to them? I was
very much an outsider, a stranger to the culture of industry, my
background limited to public affairs and the law. However, this
did, I believe, prove useful in raising and asking searching questions. I am often amazed how few people ask questions and do
not seem to be naturally inquisitive, when learning something
new is one of the most exciting experiences in life. Curiosity
is one of the great virtues, next to enthusiasm. It has been the
inspiration behind many of the achievements of science. Also, as
Artemis Cooper wrote in a biography of Paddy Leigh Fermor,
'the greatest blessing a guest can bring to his host is the right kind
of curiosity. And it bubbled out of Paddy like a natural spring.'
At dinner parties even the apparently most boring neighbours
can be interesting if you probe them about their work and their
likes and dislikes. Janice is very good at this, but she is seldom
asked about her own job and interests. When asked, the reply
'scientist', or more specifically microbiologist, parasitologist or
immunologist, is usually a conversation-stopper.

My colleagues on the BOC board were good at cross-
questioning management about anything to do with its operations. But when we were visiting one of our subsidiaries in Brazil
in 1979 and were lucky enough to have meetings with several
members of the government, they asked very few questions and
became somewhat restless when I quizzed ministers in some
detail about their policies towards the environment, regional
and social inequalities, and the Brazilian economy. For me it was
a unique opportunity to learn more about an important country I had never visited. But the only board comment about our
ministerial meetings was from a South African colleague, who
said, 'these meetings have really cheered me up. I have found

a government that cares even less than ours about its poorest citizens and a country where inequalities are even greater.' (This was in pre-Lula days.)

Despite my long service at Equity and Law, my contribution there was limited. Indeed my first impression was that I had been invited by mistake. One of the leading tax experts at the Bar had just retired from the board and whoever recommended me must have thought that a silk and politician, who was a former Financial Secretary and who had recently launched the Institute for Fiscal Studies, would know about tax and law and would therefore be a suitable replacement. I explained that I knew nothing about insurance or insurance law, was not actually an expert in tax, had left the Bar six years ago and had no experience of corporate life of any kind. As for any supposed political influence, I told them I was about to resign my seat and fight a by-election as an independent, with every prospect of an early end to my parliamentary career. Despite these confessions they pressed the invitation. I also noted that just about all board members had a title, so I thought perhaps another reason for inviting me was that a proletarian on the board, and a Labour, or rather ex-Labour MP at that, would give the board a more democratic flavour.

Life assurance, I found, was a business in which, as a lay board member, I did not really have the qualifications to make a major contribution. The products, various life assurance and pension policies, are designed by actuaries and almost all the senior executives were actuaries. The board might question the mix of products and their suitability for the market at which they were aimed, but mostly these were highly technical issues that non-actuaries were not well qualified to judge. One of the important decisions for the board of a public company is normally the payment of the dividend. In proprietary (non-mutual) life companies it is enshrined in the company's articles that the dividend must be a fixed proportion of the annual bonus paid to policy holders and judgement of what bonuses can be afforded is primarily based on mathematical calculations made by actuaries. Only a brave, possibly reckless, layman rejects actuarial advice. Investment policy is also crucial to a life company's success, but while the bankers on the board could offer useful advice, I could not.

Despite the high quality of my fellow board members, who were eminent, highly intelligent, charming, cultured and open-minded, the board was not, in my view, an effective one. In fact, in my first few years on the Equity and Law board, meetings were not altogether different from Boothby's description, except that I arrived on my bicycle not in a company car. Meetings were preceded by a first-class lunch prepared by a chef who was also, I was told, the chef at Buckingham Palace. The wines were exquisite. After lunch the board was generally in an affable mood and not necessarily over-critical in its examination of the executives' reports. Some cynical executives even hinted in private that these arrangements were not altogether accidental. Later on, under a new regime, board meetings were held before, not after, lunch. That seemed to me a very sensible arrangement, which allowed me to enjoy lunch and its wines without inhibition. Once a year, in the summer, there was a most agreeable dinner with senior executives to which wives were also invited. (There were no women on the board.) It was held in some style in the boardroom at the top of Equity and Law's premises in central London, dinner jackets naturally de rigeur. Previous general managers looked down on us benevolently from their portraits on the walls; outside were the green and pleasant fields of Lincoln's Inn.

I believe the board would have functioned more effectively if it had not been so large. There were over a dozen non-executive directors. The sense of personal involvement and responsibility is much stronger when there are fewer (as there were at BOC) and consequently the talents of the board were not fully exploited. Indeed the amount of time we were expected to give to our duties was undemanding. We met every three months and there were no special meetings to discuss strategy, which probably explains the biggest and most costly mistake Equity and Law made.

In the early 1970s, just before I joined the board, Equity and Law had decided to set up a branch in Germany. It had already established a successful subsidiary in the Netherlands with a new approach in a sleepy Dutch market and it believed it could repeat that success in Germany. However the German market proved to be very different, much more closely regulated and much less open to innovative newcomers. A minority of board members had opposed the venture and, when it nevertheless proceeded and ran into difficulties, urged us not to throw good money after bad. But the majority backed the general manager and the local executives in Germany, who kept predicting an early turn around and future success. I regret to say I backed the majority. If I had been more experienced, I would have looked at optimistic forecasts more critically. If there had been special board strategy meetings to review the risks and benefits of our German venture in depth, we should have realised how serious the difficulties were and how the risks greatly exceeded likely benefits. The company would have saved many millions and an enormous investment of management time. By the time we became part of the French insurer AXA (soon to become the second largest insurance company in the world), the German branch had made no money in sixteen years and had failed to establish a significant market presence.

One of the duties I enjoyed most was visiting local branches. In the course of my long association with the company, I got to know its senior executives and many of its local managers and staff, and found a corporate culture very different from my early prejudices about the way the profit motive worked. Profits did not come before service. The board was told that our mission was to maximise shareholder value, but in the field shareholder value meant little or nothing. The interests of policy holders came first and no risks were taken that might prejudice the security of their investments.

Staff throughout the company believed they made the world a better place by helping people to save for a comfortable retirement. They were honest and dedicated and on the whole happy in their work. They often told me they did not want to work for any other company, because Equity and Law was like a family. The place did not buzz with entrepreneurial excitement and the more ambitious employees were somewhat restive. When in 1988 AXA eventually became the owners of the company, some of the Young Turks were excited by the sense of energy and drive that the top French management brought with them.

One useful part I did play was in initiating a change of chairman when Equity and Law first became involved in a takeover in 1987, an episode not without its comic aspects. For some obscure reason (I had not been one of those consulted) Sir John Witt had been succeeded as chairman by a very congenial but rather colourless member of the board, whose main qualification, it seemed to me, was that he was another solicitor and Equity and Law, as its name indicated, originally provided life insurance for members of the legal profession. I thought that he was not the man for difficult takeover negotiations. Several of my colleagues agreed and I canvassed the opinion of the rest. There was a general view that we should ask him to step down. But who was to approach him? It was decided that the most senior industrialist on the board, Lord Cave, was the right man. But to spare his feelings, he asked the chairman to resign in such a tactful way that he did not realise he was being sacked. In desperation Lord Cave then suggested that the chairman should talk to me, since I had initiated the rebellion, although Cave did not say so. At the end of the next board meeting, he hailed me cheerfully: 'Dick, I gather you want to talk to me. Why don't we have lunch?' I murmured that I was not free, but would come to see him in his office. Again he greeted me as his long-lost friend and I had to explain, somewhat bluntly, that while he had done a great job so far, we now faced a very difficult new challenge and the view of the board was that we needed a new chairman with different skills and experience. He received the news as cheerfully as Caesar received his meeting in the senate by Brutus and his co-conspirators.

What followed was exactly what one of my colleagues predicted. Who was to succeed? Lord Cave had ruled himself out because of other commitments. He was therefore asked to sound out other directors. One obvious candidate was Sir Douglas Wass, a recent board arrival who had been a fairly junior civil servant at the Treasury when I was a minister and who later became its head. He would normally have been appointed to the House of

Lords when he retired from the Treasury, but he had disagreed strongly with some of Mrs Thatcher's policies and was therefore condemned to being a mere knight. But he was then head of a consortium bidding to build a cross-channel bridge and felt he would not have the time.

Lord Cave reported that unfortunately there was no consensus about the succession. However several members had asked whether he himself might not be available after all. As rapporteur he did not of course feel able to put himself forward, but his own circumstances had now changed and he could make himself available if board members so desired. The result: we unanimously appointed Lord Cave. He would no doubt have been a good chairman, but unfortunately he died of cancer some months later. By then a channel tunnel had been chosen instead of a bridge, Douglas Wass was free and duly became an excellent chairman.

Why did I stay on so long? There was no time limit on board membership then and it seemed we would all have happily grown old, or even older, together, when in 1987 Equity and Law was taken over by Compagnie du Midi, which in turn became part of AXA. AXA decided to replace the whole board, except for Douglas Wass and me. It was thought I would be useful for keeping the French in touch with government and the political background generally.

Later, in 2000, AXA bought Sun Life and merged it with Equity and Law to become AXA Sun Life. To reconcile the interests of AXA shareholders with those of former Equity and Law policy holders involved difficult negotiations with the Financial Services Authority of a highly technical kind. It all ended with a complex court settlement that set up a special board sub-committee to protect Equity and Law policy holders from unfair discrimination in favour of AXA shareholders. I was asked to chair this committee, which I did for nearly ten years. It had a curious role. We met three times a year to check, as we did most conscientiously, whether policy holders' interests were being properly looked after. No policy holders ever enquired about our work or showed any sign that they were even aware of the existence of these guardian angels protecting their savings.

While I enjoyed my association with Equity and Law, I would not have missed my experience as a director of BOC for the world. It brought me into contact with some of the prominent people in apartheid South Africa and taught me a lot about corporate governance.

When I joined the board in 1975, the BOC chairman was Sir Leslie Smith, a man of vision whose views on the role of non-executive directors were refreshingly unconventional. He championed the idea that some of them should spend at least one day a week on their duties, to acquire a thorough knowledge of the company's operations and the quality of its management. No permanent hot baths for Sir Leslie's directors. In fact, he envisaged the evolution of a new breed of professional, career non-executives, whose ambition was not to be chief executive officers or chairmen of companies, but who would divide their time between a limited number of companies, spending a day or so a week on each. Although I was not likely to become one of this new breed, of professional non-executives, I did have some spare time (I had recently lost my seat in Lincoln and IFS was not a full-time occupation) and was approached because he was looking for someone with political, preferably governmental, experience. He also approached Michael Shanks to be another guinea pig. Michael was one of my Balliol contemporaries, a distinguished economist who had recently retired as Director General of the Social Department of the European Commission. Alas he died in 1986.

BOC was a company with subsidiaries all over the world, mainly in the business of industrial gases, a business then dominated by eight major international companies. One of three American ones was Airco, in which BOC had recently acquired a controlling share, thus reducing the eight to seven. However the American Federal Trade Commission (FTC) had ruled that this acquisition was anti-competitive and, unless the decision was overturned, BOC would have to dispose of its shares. BOC appealed against the decision. Sir Leslie thought I might be helpful in preparing the appeal, as the FTC's reasons had political and international economic implications. I was given an office and the assistance of two old BOC hands to teach me about the gases business and to assist me in preparing the Airco appeal. I was to devote a day a week to my board duties.

In 1978 we won the Airco appeal. The details of the case were rather technical but memorable for its summary by Jay Topkiss, the American lawyer who represented BOC in the US Federal Court. In a nutshell, the FTC had ruled that to enter the American market BOC should have done so by establishing a new subsidiary company in the US or by acquiring a number of minor existing American companies, routes that would have increased competition. Instead, by acquiring a major company, as Airco was, competition had been reduced. BOC had argued that, on the contrary, acquiring Airco was the only realistic way of entering the market and that by strengthening the challenge from Airco, competition in the US would be increased. Topkiss

admitted that BOC wanted to establish a strong presence in the
US, but the issue, he argued, was not the desire to enter the
market but how to achieve it. Could it have done so by the route
the FTC required? This had not been proved; indeed BOC had
argued that this approach faced almost insuperable obstacles. As
Topkiss put it, he personally had long nurtured a strong desire
to be closely associated with a lady called Sophia Loren, the
beautiful Italian actress of the time, but desire was not enough.
The question was how to achieve it: how, where and, perhaps he
added ungallantly, how much?

My own contribution to the success of the appeal was to
persuade the British government that what was at stake was
important to future British investment in the US and to make that
view clear to the court. After some research I had found that other
major British companies had either tried or considered entering
the American market by what was called 'greenfield entry' or by
acquiring small American companies as a base, as advocated
by the FTC, but had found it was not feasible. This meant that
the FTC ruling would be a major obstacle to British investment
in the US and, as a foreign investment generally promotes competition, placing obstacles in its way would have an anti-competitive
effect. I also discovered that some continental companies had had
the same frustrating experience. In the event, with help from the
British Embassy in Washington and from my former colleague
in government, Edmund Dell, who was by then President of the
Board of Trade, the British government agreed to take part in
the appeal as *Amicus curiae* (friend of the court) and put in its
own brief on BOC's behalf. With the help of David Hannay
(now Lord Hannay), who was then head of the cabinet of the
European Trade Commissioner Christopher Soames, I also

persuaded the European Commission to support the British case
and send a telegram to Henry Kissinger, the American Secretary
of State, asking him to stress to the court the importance of their
decision to international investment. The court was thus left in
no doubt about the international significance of its ruling.

At first, Michael Shanks and I were the only BOC non-
executives with a major commitment of our time. In due
course our commitment somewhat decreased while that of our
colleagues on the board increased, and we were soon no longer
a separate part of the non-executive board. Indeed, Sir Leslie
was a pioneer who contributed to a general change of attitude
towards corporate governance. Indeed nowadays non-executives
are expected to give a serious commitment of time to their duties.
Personally I found that the chance of learning in detail how the
company operated and mixing quite a lot of my time with
the senior managers made my role infinitely more interesting.
The board paid regular visits to overseas subsidiaries, principally
in the USA, our biggest market, but also to Australia and South
Africa, in each of which BOC had a dominant market share.
We also visited Japan, Hong Kong, Singapore, Malaysia and
Brazil. I paid personal visits to Nigeria and Indonesia. In the
latter case a government minister who attended a meeting of
the Indonesian company was most intrigued to learn that this
was my first return to the land of my birth.

Politically, my visits to South Africa were a unique experience.
I went there four times, the last time in 1989, shortly before the
end of apartheid. What most struck me on my first visit in 1976
was the extent of the contacts between prominent people in the
white and black communities, including prominent members
of the ANC who had survived the ban on the party and were

not in prison. White universities were officially allowed to take black students only if there was no equivalent course in a black university. But the University of the Witwatersrand ignored the restriction and admitted a substantial number of black students.

I met the chairman of a major food company who suggested I should meet his (black) head of industrial relations. The latter had been detained in solitary confinement under the 90-day detention law for his political activities, but was known to the chairman, who had contacted him and asked if there was anything he could do. 'Yes,' was the answer, 'give me a job when I get out.' In due course he became a senior executive. I took him out to dinner – and was ticked off by the restaurant proprietor for doing so in a white restaurant but, perhaps surprisingly, we were allowed to stay as I was not a South African and did not know the rules. My guest turned out to be no moderate. He told me that in discussion with liberal whites he and his friends talked of the day when they would be 'sharing power' but that when the day came, they would 'grab it'.

During a later visit I met Dr Nthato Motlana, the head of the Committee of Twelve of Soweto, who were the de facto unbanned leading representatives of the outlawed ANC. He described his own time in solitary confinement and delivered a tirade against Chief Buthelezi, the Zulu chief, then regarded by many in the liberal community as the great hope of an eventual reconciliation between black and white. Buthelezi, he argued, had no credibility with the black population outside Kwazulu, his tribal homeland, because he was unwilling to face jail. His opposition to the regime would always stop short of action that might endanger his freedom. Further, he claimed, Buthelezi was too attached to the official trappings of a homeland leader, including a police escort wherever he went, though Motlana acknowledged that Buthelezi had resisted the carrot of so-called independence for Kwazulu.

He gave a graphic account of their personal feud. Motlana's ally, Bishop Tutu, and Buthelezi's sidekick, Bishop Zulu, had tried to bring the two together, but they had ended a meeting of supposed reconciliation by abusing each other in a way no white man would ever abuse a black man or vice versa.

BOC chartered a private plane to fly me to Ulundi, the capital of Kwazulu, where I met Buthelezi and the Council of Inkatha (the leadership of the Zulus) in full session. Three things impressed me particularly. Most of the council, but not Bishop Zulu, were in military uniform, which suggested they might not play an entirely peaceful role after the end of apartheid. Secondly, I learned that Inkatha received substantial economic support from the German Social Democratic Party. I was received by the full council because they clearly had the wrong idea about my political importance, or of BOC's role in the order of things, because Buthelezi enquired whether I might be able to help them with financial support, from Britain or presumably from BOC. Thirdly, he confirmed his hostility to the ANC. He complained bitterly that foreign journalists and politicians visiting South Africa seemed obsessed with the Soweto Twelve and often ignored Inkatha. I found Buthelezi an impressive figure but, in the event, when apartheid ended, he did not cover himself with glory and Inkatha virtually disappeared as a force in national South African politics.

Some liberal German friends I had met many years earlier at one of the Königswinter conferences, who now worked in South Africa, introduced me to other eminent opponents of the regime, including the wonderful Bishop Tutu, with whom I had a memorable and entertaining dinner, and Helen Suzman, described by her biographer as 'the doughtiest of fighters for human rights anywhere in the world'.[†] They also organised an illegal evening in their house (all curtains drawn) with a prominent Dutch Reformed Church minister, the Reverend Beyers Naudé, who was subject to a restriction order forbidding him to meet more than one person at a time. On his behalf I smuggled a message hidden in a greetings card to an exiled anti-apartheid campaigner in London, the only act of smuggling I have ever engaged in. I never discovered what the message was.

My most interesting meeting, however, was with the Minister for Education, Gerrit Viljoen, a former head of the Broederbond, the inner sanctum of Afrikaner nationalism, and later chairman of the Constitutional Commission. It took place in 1989, not long before the release of Nelson Mandela.

There had recently been some relaxation of the oppressive apartheid laws, such as the repeal of the Immorality Act that made interracial sexual intercourse a crime. I asked him if he could foresee a time when they might repeal the Group Areas Act, which prohibited black Africans owning property in white areas. Of course, he said. That gobsmacked me. Could he foresee a time when there might be black members of Parliament? Certainly, that could happen very soon! If they were being so progressive, how could he justify the fact that black pupils had to pay for their school books while they were free for whites? He said of course it could not be justified but last year they had increased spending on black education by 28 per cent (or some

---

[†]   Renwick, R., *Helen Suzman: Bright Star in a Dark Chamber* (London: Biteback, 2014).

such figure) and it was a question of priorities. The former high priest of Afrikanerdom talked like a Western liberal!

In retrospect I believe that the peaceful change from apartheid to black majority rule – which presented a dramatic contrast to the horrors that followed independence for Algeria, as vividly described in Alastair Horne's great book *A Savage War of Peace* – was successful for three main reasons. First and foremost was the extraordinary statesmanship, humanity, heroic courage and integrity of the ANC leaders, not just Nelson Mandela. His co-defendants in the Rivonia trial, people like Walter Sisulu and the elder Mbeki, deserve enormous admiration.[†] They all decided to tell the truth throughout and admit charges of sabotage of which they were guilty, even though these potentially carried the death sentence. But they made it plain that they always took great pains to avoid endangering human life. As Mandela wrote in his foreword to Joel Joffe's book, 'We were determined to put apartheid in the dock, even if this were to put our own lives in jeopardy.' Ironically, another person who in the end played a vital part was the pro-apartheid, Afrikaner judge Quartus de Wet, who displayed implacable bias against the defendants throughout the trial. After the inevitable guilty verdict, he surprisingly used his discretion not to impose the death penalty but to sentence the accused to life imprisonment instead and thereby enabled Mandela to play his historic role. Led by their outstanding leaders and people like Archbishop Desmond Tutu, the ANC was not a race-based organisation and welcomed white members and reconciliation with their former oppressors.

[†] See Joffe, J., *The State vs. Nelson Mandela* (Oxford: One World, 2007).

Secondly, white nationalist leaders like Gerrit Viljoen, and
even dyed-in-the-wool supporters of apartheid like F. W. De
Klerk, in the end allowed realism to prevail over dogma. And
thirdly, a not unimportant part was played by members of the
white community, including some leading businessmen, who
maintained contact with the ANC.

A footnote about BOC in South Africa: at one board meeting when we had a report on industrial relations in our various
companies, it transpired that industrial democracy was most
advanced in our South African company – almost certainly to
avoid entrenching nationalist trade unions. The impression of
my visits was certainly one of good relations on the shop floor.

Generally I formed a favourable opinion of the quality of
BOC's managers. Their job satisfaction was high, not least
because most believed that their work benefited society (as did
those in Equity and Law). In fact I got the impression that they
probably found their work more satisfying than many backbench
MPs and were rather less concerned with money than several of
my former colleagues at the Bar who spent a great deal of their
time discussing the size of their fees on their latest briefs.

What use was I to the BOC board? I believe I played an important part in the special circumstances of BOC's acquisition of
Airco and I found my experience as an MP was good training
for getting the most out of visits to BOC branches and overseas
subsidiaries. Also, some of our board meetings were very like
meetings of government committees or even Cabinet meetings.

The board that Leslie Smith chaired functioned as a good
board should. Apart from reviewing business reports, we were
constantly encouraged to focus on strategic issues – new acquisitions or initiatives, the company's weaknesses and strengths, and

new threats or opportunities. Periodically the chairman would enquire if we were happy with the information before the board – no question of non-executives only learning what executives thought safe for them to know. A weekend strategy meeting was the highlight of the year. We were always asked what subjects we would like to discuss. One year, for example, we asked to review which countries or parts of the world were likely to see the biggest growth in their demand for industrial gases, in which were we strongest and weakest, and where did we face the greatest challenge from our major competitors. Although this was a time when China had not yet developed as a major economy, the analysis presented to the board clearly showed that China's market would grow faster than any other and that none of the major gases companies had a significant presence there. The meeting undoubtedly influenced the focus of the company's activities. Within a year BOC had a stronger presence in China than any of our rivals.

The board showed an admirably critical approach to management reports and to suggestions for new initiatives or acquisitions. Proposals for the latter mainly featured in BOC's second business, medical equipment connected with anaesthetics in hospitals, a business that was only moderately successful and eventually sold. On one occasion, a new American manager put the case for an acquisition and confessed afterwards that he felt his presentation had flopped. We told him he had been too keen to sell his proposal: of course he thought his proposition was a good idea, or he would not have put it forward. We wanted to know the risks and possible weaknesses, to which he had given less attention than to projected benefits.

Most company takeovers, particularly hostile ones, ultimately

disappoint, sometimes because of conflicting loyalties and rivalries between the staff of the acquirer and the acquired. After our
takeover of Airco (which was not contested), we reviewed a list
of international mergers that had failed. What measures could
we take to make ours a success? At considerable expense we
employed brand consultants, who advised that we needed a new
name to create new loyalties. In any case, BOC's official name
at the time was BOC International, stressing its international
character, as opposed to the former 'British Oxygen', which had
sounded rather territorially restricted. BOC International was
an altogether uninspiring name. After deep thought and widespread consultation, the consultants came up with their solution:
the 'Green Square Corporation'. Visually the logo would look
good on letterheads and on the side of the company's tank-
ers. Astonishingly they had not considered that the new name
suggested that the merged company was both inexperienced and
old-fashioned! Our head of PR, Nigel Rowe, proposed a simple
alternative: why not the 'BOC Group'? We agreed without further
debate and could have saved ourselves a lot of consultant fees!

In fact, the problem of potential rivalries had already been
solved. To the surprise and delight of Airco employees, we
made Airco's chief executive, Dick Giordano, the CEO of the
merged company. On the whole the British staff were satisfied
because BOC was a British company with a British chairman
and mainly British shareholders. The Americans were happy
because an American CEO was a guarantee that they would not
be discriminated against. One of BOC's strong points was that it
was nationality-blind. At different times we had a South African
as head of UK gases, a Briton in charge of Australia, an Iranian

in charge of the gases business in the US and a Hong Kong Chinese in overall charge of gases internationally.

Dick Giordano, who was the chief executive for most of my time on the BOC board, was a very able man of high intelligence and forceful personality. He and Leslie Smith formed a harmonious and effective team: Leslie in charge of the board, Dick of the management. Dick used his time well and was never flustered. His desk was always clear and he always had time to see you and discuss whatever issue you wanted to raise. When I first met him he was a progressive democrat who favoured a wealth tax. Gradually he went native, became part of the British business establishment and his outlook became more conservative. He even became hooked on deer stalking in Scotland. Unusually for an American, he was awarded a knighthood, though at first his nationality prevented him using the title. Later he became a British as well as American citizen, but long before he became officially British, when he talked about 'we', it was clear that he meant 'we British'. When he retired, after his successful spell at BOC followed by a period as CEO of British Gas, he returned to the USA and became a proper American again.

He had his weaknesses. In particular, he was never good at judging the British style, especially of people who did not project themselves as aggressively as Americans do, and he cared a lot about money. It was a term of his appointment that he should receive an American-scale salary and for a while he was always referred to in the press as 'Dick-Giordano-the-Highest-Paid-Executive-in-British-Industry'. (His pay at the time was only a fraction of that paid to CEOs of top British companies today.) He really did believe that it was the mission of boards to 'maximise shareholder value', a belief that in my view lies at the heart of the weaknesses of Anglo-Saxon, certainly British capitalism.

He introduced a system of bonuses for executives. I have never understood the justification for most bonuses, even when restricted to successful performance. Managers are paid a salary to do their best: why do they need another incentive to do what they are employed to do? The bonus system at BOC, however, seemed to work quite well as a management tool. Part of it was based on the performance of the company as a whole – in a bad year no bonuses were paid – part on the performance of the individual executive, judged by criteria agreed with his immediate superior. One senior executive told me he had been opposed to bonuses, but became converted to them in practice because it made senior managers discuss with junior managers what was expected of them and made the latter think more deeply about their performance. Compared with those currently paid to bankers, BOC bonuses were very modest.

I was impressed by the importance of honesty in the culture of BOC and found the same was true in Airco. There was never any attempt to hide what should not be hidden. The rare case of dishonest conduct was rigorously dealt with. Less impressive was concern with gender equality, especially in the Australian subsidiary. There were no women on the BOC board (nor in Equity and Law or most of British industry at the time) and little serious attempt to recruit them despite regular declarations of good intentions.

In the Australian company, the head of industrial relations was an attractive young woman, who had several degrees from different foreign universities. We met her in Sydney in 1978, during a visit when board members were accompanied by their wives.

She told Janice and me that whenever she wanted to raise an issue with her immediate superior (male, of course) they could only talk out-of-doors walking round the block, because private discussions in the office would be assumed to mean they were having an affair. She also found it tactful to hide her academic qualifications. In front of both of us at a dinner, she raised with the head of gases in Australia the need for more concern about injuries to employees shifting heavy gas cylinders. His reply: 'Please get off my back. Why don't you go home and breed?'

I believe BOC was one of a number of British world-class companies before it was taken over in 2002. It was efficiently run, a viable competitor in a very competitive industrial gases market dominated by seven international majors. It did not claim to be the best – each of the seven had its own strengths and weaknesses – and there were some aspects of the gases business and some countries in which we operated where we recognised we were not as good as our rivals. In fact, I believe a reasonable guide to British corporate performance is a company's claim to excellence. Those who boast how good they are tend to be second rate. Good companies acknowledge their weaknesses.

What did strike me as a major weakness of British industry in general was the orthodox view of corporate governance. There have been many improvements in the law and attitudes since my days in the boardroom, including the Higgs report, the Companies Act of 2006 and, more recently, the Kay report. But not all the myths that prevailed in the 1970s and 80s have been dispelled. The conventional wisdom, laid down in the Cadbury report, the corporate bible of the time, was that the interest of shareholders must reign supreme. The Cadbury report also declared that 'the basic system of corporate governance in Britain is sound'. It seemed a good illustration of our national vice, which is not that we always run ourselves down, but a tendency to smugness and complacency. If our system worked so well, why was our general industrial performance not better?

According to the Cadbury gospel, boards were accountable to shareholders 'who elect the board and can make their views known to the board ... by communicating them ... through attendance at general meetings'. BOC AGMs were purely ritual occasions. The election of directors was a formality as we were assured beforehand of massive support from institutional investors. Indeed at one AGM I received a record number of votes against my re-election, not, I was told, because many shareholders took a poor view of my performance as director, but because they objected to my political past. I was still re-elected by a majority of North Korean proportions.

We never faced serious criticism. In one year of relatively poor results that caused the chairman and CEO to prepare for the AGM somewhat apprehensively, the only questioner after the presentation of the annual report congratulated the company on the excellent way it managed its affairs. Most of those attending would be employees or ex-employees there to meet old friends or small shareholders there for free coffee and biscuits. The best attended company AGMs offered free alcoholic drinks. BOC AGMs never lasted long – unlike those at Rolls-Royce, which, according to Sir Ian Fraser, one of my fellow directors who was its chairman, went on for hours because shareholders knew exactly how a Rolls-Royce should be redesigned.

Whatever the merits of the reforms since my time, I fear one of

British industry's most fundamental weaknesses will persist while shareholders retain the unqualified right to sell a company to the highest bidder. When times are tough, German companies cut dividends and do all they can to maintain investment and retain staff; British companies do everything they can to maintain the dividend. Propping up the share price is the best hope of avoiding a takeover.

In 2006, BOC was taken over by a smaller German gases company, Linde, not because it suddenly became inefficient but because an earlier, unsuccessful, joint bid by two other gas majors, ruled out on competition grounds, had put the company 'into play'. When Linde subsequently put in a high bid for the company's shares, the board apparently felt bound to accept a bid which would give shareholders an immediate gain bigger than they could hope for if BOC remained independent. As many as two-thirds of all mergers and takeovers fail, in the sense that they do not achieve their promised benefits, except for the bidder's management who gain from controlling a bigger company.[†] One successful investor I know advises all his friends that in a hostile bid, you sell the bidder's shares and, if you can get in early, buy those of the company subject to the bid.

Hostile bids more often than not actually harm rather than promote the public interest. The victim's management, however efficient, is generally displaced; jobs are lost and in takeovers by foreign companies the research centre of a British company is likely to be moved abroad. There were industries and companies that were badly run and have benefited greatly from foreign

---

[†]   Clarke, P. J. and Mills, R. W., *Masterminding the Deal* (London: Kogan Page, 2013).

ownership, such as our motorcar manufacturers. Protectionism protects inefficiency. But I do not accept that it would be impossible to introduce some 'public interest' criterion that would not leave the decision solely to those who will benefit financially. Again it does not seem to me self-evident that in a takeover continental corporate models that give the workforce a say, or at the least that require them to be seriously consulted, make such companies less competitive and less successful. Some form of industrial democracy does not seem to harm companies in Germany, the Netherlands or Scandinavia.

I greatly regret that I was no longer on the board in 2006 when BOC was sold. BOC had not suddenly become less efficient. It seems the board was advised it was their legal duty to sell. I would argue that this view could have been challenged then, even before the 2006 Companies Act widened a board's accountability to include a duty to a company's members which must include the interest of its employees. In 1989, in the Paramount v. Time-Warner case, a Delaware Court (in the heartland of capitalism) ruled that a board was not legally obliged to regard the short-term benefit of shareholders as the only relevant consideration.

Sometime after the Linde takeover I visited Leslie Smith, by then long retired. We agreed the sale of BOC had been a tragedy. We also agreed that there should have been a campaign to fight the bid. In the early 1960s there had been a dramatic and successful challenge by a minority of directors of the textile company Courtaulds, when a board majority recommended acceptance of a bid for the company by ICI. The rebels somehow persuaded a majority of shareholders to take a long-term view rather than realise an immediate profit by selling their shares. Leslie felt that the BOC board of his day would have put up a doughty fight.

Perhaps we, like the Courtaulds rebels, could have won. Who knows? The issue was never tested. The doctrine of 'shareholder value' prevailed.

Hinc lacrimae rerum.[†]

---

† Virgil's *Aeneid*: 'This was the source of our sorrows.'

CHAPTER 10

SENSE ABOUT SCIENCE

The last stage in my intellectual odyssey took me unexpectedly into the realms of science. My journey had begun among the classics, philosophy and ancient history, had led me into the less academic surroundings of the Middle Temple, Westminster and Whitehall, then to the study of taxation and public spending and into the world of commerce, and then took me back again to Westminster, to the gilded chamber of the House of Lords.

In 1996 I returned to politics as a life peer (officially as a Liberal Democrat), a curious mule-like constitutional creature that boasts neither pride in ancestry nor hope of posterity. The coalition government in 2012 argued that a body involved in making laws should be elected, which seems at first sight a reasonable proposition. A Bill was introduced which aimed at making peers more accountable to the public but it purported to do so by proposing that 80 per cent of them should be elected for a fifteen-year non-renewable term. The other 20 per cent were to be appointed by an independent committee, as they are now. Not surprisingly the Bill was defeated. Why would election to a secure seat for fifteen years without any possibility of re-election make peers more democratically responsive?

So life peerages survived, since the kind of elected second

chamber proposed by the coalition government did not make sense, but a golden opportunity was missed to make the House a more effective upper chamber. The most urgent need today is to reduce the enormous number of peers and introduce a time limit for their service, not leaving them to judge themselves when they are past it. In the meantime life peers live in a politician's nirvana. We have a platform of sorts, lifelong security of tenure, no constituency obligations, no accountability to anyone, and we are free to say the most outrageous things without anyone being able to do anything about it. In practice, of course, noble Lords and Baronesses are rarely outrageous.

In the Lords, I began to focus on the public understanding of science. Previously, the only public pronouncement I had ever made about science was that casual comment on the day I first met Janice about zoology, a remark that had such happy consequences. She was always a persuasive advocate for science because she found her career in scientific research so absorbing and satisfying that she could not imagine anything more worthwhile. I came to realise that science is the intellectual discipline that more than any other is based on the combination of reason and evidence. I have always tried as far as possible to base my views on both. Of course, political views start with social values and one cannot always base policy purely on reason because what is achievable is limited by what is practicable. But Tony Crosland's appeal when I first took up politics seriously was his willingness to subordinate ideology to evidence. He showed that there was no evidence that nationalisation would lead to a workers' paradise, which persuaded me to support Hugh Gaitskell's attempt in 1959 to abolish Clause IV of Labour's Constitution. It made me a social democrat rather than a socialist.

When politicians disregard evidence it can have devastating consequences. For instance, Tony Blair's conviction that Saddam Hussein had weapons of mass destruction and had to be deposed became so strong that it was impervious to evidence. Blair ignored warnings from intelligence experts that the evidence of Saddam's possession of these weapons was 'thin', 'weak' and 'patchy' and that he was no more a danger in 2003 than he had been for a decade. 'Lack of evidence for what he believed troubled him [Blair] no more than the lack of evidence for the creation troubles a religious zealot.'[†] Hence the notorious 'dodgy dossier' that helped persuade doubters to vote for the decision to go to war, the greatest mistake Blair ever made that cost countless lives and severely damaged his reputation.

I first became interested in science politically through concern about the environment. I was an early convert to green causes, having fallen under the spell of Rachel Carson after reading her famous book *Silent Spring*, published in 1962. In the 1970s I joined Greenpeace and Friends of the Earth. I was impressed by the Club of Rome's dire warnings in *The Limits to Growth* (1972) that economic growth must come to a halt. In fact, I swallowed the whole green agenda hook, line and sinker.

I still support many green causes. One decision that Janice and I have never regretted, which we took in 1974 at the height of our green enthusiasm, was to give up owning a car – not a difficult decision if you live in central London. It improved our quality of life and made a small contribution to that of our fellow Londoners. However, one by one my new idols turned out to have feet of clay.

---

†   Marsh, K., *Stumbling Over Truth* (London: Biteback Publishing, 2012), p. 239.

My re-education started at the Cambridge Union sometime in the late 1970s or early 1980s (I do not remember the exact date). Kenneth Galbraith and I were invited as the principal speakers to oppose the motion that 'conservationists should not be allowed to stand in the way of economic growth'. It was proposed by John Maddox (later Sir John Maddox), the formidable editor of *Nature*, who made *Nature* one of the two top science magazines in the world (*Science* being the other), and the economist Wilfred Beckerman. Galbraith and I won the vote by a big majority. But on reflection the next day, I decided that we had lost the argument. Based on *The Limits of Growth* and the conventional wisdom of green lobby groups, my arguments had been shown to have serious flaws.

In due course I found that the forecasts in *The Limits of Growth* were factually discredited. Rachel Carson, whom many still regard as an ecological saint or a divinely inspired prophet, proved to be wrong in her predictions in *Silent Spring* about the effects of DDT. It does not cause cancer in people, as she claimed, and while she was right to oppose the indiscriminate spraying of DDT in agriculture, the worldwide ban on DDT, including its use to prevent malaria, which followed the publication of her book, resulted in many millions of deaths that could have been avoided. The World Health Organization described DDT as the agent that saved more lives than any other, estimating the death toll from malaria caused by its abandonment as hundreds of millions. As Professor Robert H. White-Stevens, an agriculturalist at Rutgers University, observed: 'If man were to follow the teachings of Miss Carson, we would return to the Dark Ages and the insects and diseases and vermin would once again inherit the earth.'

I found that Greenpeace and Friends of the Earth were so convinced of the rightness of their causes that they ignored any evidence that undermined them. Three particular events led me somewhat reluctantly to the conclusion that Greenpeace often does more harm than good. The first was a successful campaign launched in 1989, STINC – 'Stop Toxic Incineration in Cleveland'. A company called Ocean planned to build a new state-of-the-art incineration plant in Cleveland, north Lincolnshire, to burn toxic industrial waste instead of dumping it in landfill sites, one of the least environmentally friendly ways of waste disposal. Greenpeace claimed that since incineration would cause the emission of some dioxins – often described dramatically, but wrongly, as 'the most dangerous chemical known to man' – the plant would have a devastating effect on the health of the local population. Greenpeace had never heard of Paracelsus, who centuries ago taught the simple lesson 'it all depends on the dose'. Of course, a large amount of anything can poison you. As many scientists have pointed out, large doses of aspirin are lethal, while small doses are beneficial. In Cleveland, the amount of dioxin released by the proposed incinerator would have been small, no more than that naturally present in the atmosphere. Moreover, incineration plants of a similar design built elsewhere had caused no harm to health. This evidence was ignored: protest marches were organised and petitions were signed by thousands. Plans to build the incinerator had to be abandoned in the face of passionate public opposition – and toxic industrial waste continued to be dumped in landfill.

The second event that made me think again was another immensely successful campaign by Greenpeace in 1995 to stop Shell disposing of a huge disused oil rig called Brent Spar in the deep waters of the Atlantic. Greenpeace claimed such disposal would pollute the ocean, partly because the rig was full of poisonous residues, partly because the sunken rig would cause irreparable harm to marine life at the bottom of the sea. It organised a Europe-wide campaign to boycott Shell petrol stations and, as part of a brilliant publicity campaign, TV screens showed shots of brave Greenpeace warriors in their small inflatables harassing the huge tugs that were towing Brent Spar to its supposedly life-destroying destination. A powerful international corporation was finally forced into a humiliating climb-down and had to order its tugs to tow the rig back to a Norwegian fjord to be disposed of on land.

As Greenpeace later admitted in a grovelling apology, there were no poisonous residues in the rig. Furthermore, disposal on land was environmentally less friendly and much more costly than sinking it in the Atlantic, as was later confirmed by the Natural Environmental Research Council. Finally, Greenpeace never mentioned that when its own ship *Rainbow Warrior* was irreparably damaged by French saboteurs in New Zealand in 1986, it deliberately sank the ship off the coast because, it claimed, the wreck would form an artificial reef of great benefit to marine life.

The third event was the testimony given in 1999 by the director of Greenpeace, Lord Melchett, before a House of Lords Select Committee on GM crops.† Genetically modified (transgenic) crops are, in my view, a test case for the rational evidence-based approach to scientific issues. The possibility that some trans-genic crop might one day be found to harm human health or

---

† House of Lords, *EC Regulation of Genetic Modification in Agriculture 1999*, Evidence, p. 43, q. 107.

damage the environment cannot of course be ruled out. But so far, since their first introduction in the early 1990s, no harm has been found despite many false alarms. Every National Academy of Science in the world and every other impartial and expert body that has examined the issue has concluded that there is no evidence of harm to human health or to the environment. Hundreds of millions of Americans have eaten food with some GM content for well over a decade without ill effects and indeed without a single law case, which in the US speaks volumes. GM technology has reduced the need to spray pesticides. The potential development of GM drought-resistant crops able to grow in arid regions of the world is only one example of the invaluable contribution the technology can make to help feed the expanding world population.

What explains the persistence of such fanatical opposition to GM crops by Greenpeace and Friends of the Earth? Opposition has become an article of faith, as clearly demonstrated by Lord Melchett in his evidence before the House of Lords. He was asked whether his opposition to GM crops was absolute and definite, or could be influenced by further research or future evidence about safety. He replied, 'It is a permanent and definite and complete opposition.' It was essentially the same answer given by the Pope's representative asked by Galileo to look through his telescope at the newly discovered moons of Neptune, who replied that he refused to look at something which his religion told him could not exist.

The campaign against agricultural biotechnology, specifically against transgenic crops, has done much harm and continues to do so. In fact, in Asia and the Americas, the application of genetic engineering to agriculture has been highly successful and has spread rapidly. Millions of small-scale farmers who grow GM pest-resistant cotton, for example, have grown richer and found their health improve because they have had to buy less pesticide and spray their crops less often. Yet many potentially beneficial new developments have been held back by the bitter opposition of Greenpeace and Friends of the Earth. In Africa, progress in agriculture was frustrated, as chronicled in Robert Paarlberg's superb book *Starved for Science: How Biotechnology is Being Kept out of Africa*[†] because NGOs persuaded governments, who were dependent on them for their (praiseworthy) support in health and education, that they should stick to traditional African farming methods. Disastrously, the cultivation of GM golden rice that could remedy vitamin A deficiency, the cause of blindness in half a million children a year, has been delayed for over a decade by onerous regulatory hurdles urged on governments by NGOs.

I made speeches and asked questions in the House of Lords about biotechnology, the misleading claims made by the organic movement and other scientific subjects, and wrote a book, *The March of Unreason*.[‡] Looking back, the only modification I would now make to what I wrote then is that, having studied the various assessment reports of the International Committee on Climate Change, I now fully accept its conclusions that there is overwhelming evidence of an important manmade contribution to global warming and that this is moving towards dangerous levels. In the book, while I was never a climate-change denier,

---

[†]   Paarlberg, R. L., *Starved for Science: How Biotechnology is Being Kept out of Africa* (London: Harvard University Press, 2008).

[‡]   Taverne, D., *The March of Unreason: Science Democracy and the New Fundamentalism* (Oxford: Oxford University Press, 2005).

I had more reservations about the ICC's approach than I have now. Unlike the more gloomy doomsters, I believe the solutions to climate change lie through technology, not dramatic changes in our way of life. For example, I believe it is unlikely people will stop driving motorcars but we can develop motorcars that are affordable and efficient and do not use fossil fuels.

It was an article I wrote for the magazine *Prospect* in 1999 about the 'Dangers of Anti-Science', citing opposition to GM crops as the main example, which led to my new career. Several people asked me what I was going to do about the threat from the forces of unreason. Was there not a need for a new effective organisation to take them on? I therefore called a meeting of representatives of the Royal Society, the Medical Research Council, the Wellcome Trust and other institutions concerned with science and argued that there was a need for a new organisation to promote the evidence-based approach more proactively and aggressively. On the whole, despite a tendency to claim that they themselves were already successfully pursuing similar aims, those present gave my proposal a reasonably fair wind and several said that in principle they were willing to cooperate. Most importantly, two industrialists who also attended (not themselves connected with the biotechnology industry) announced that they were convinced by my arguments and that they would each give me £15,000 to get going. They were Lord Stevenson of Coddenham and Nick Butler, then policy adviser to Lord Browne of Madingly, chairman of BP. Dennis Stevenson was particularly supportive in getting Sense About Science (SAS), as I named our new organisation, off the ground. In its early days he gave us free use of part of his office. Amid the strong criticisms to which he was subjected for his later role as chairman of HBOS, no one mentioned that he was a wonderful and highly successful supporter of new ventures and innovation, for which he was deservedly awarded a peerage. Without him, for example, there would be no Tate Modern and there might have been no SAS.

My next task was to find a director, to do for SAS what John Kay had done for the Institute for Fiscal Studies, and I found the ideal person. She was a sociologist (recommended by another sociologist), a young woman called Tracey Brown, who had just finished working for a risk-assessment firm. The only apparent problem was that she was eight-and-a-half months pregnant with her third child. I rang her up and suggested I should come to see her at her home in Kent. She rejected this emphatically and insisted on coming to London. I asked: 'What happens if you have your baby on the train?' 'I'll cope' – which was undoubtedly true, but I did not know this at the time. I do not claim to be an especially good judge of character, especially at first sight, but on this occasion within minutes of meeting her I was confident she was the director I needed. Some years later, when SAS was well-established, an eminent member of the Royal Society confessed to me, 'When Tracey says "jump", we all jump.' She proved to have an excellent sense of strategy, a great flair for publicity and for raising money, and would nearly always offer an original slant on how to handle controversial issues. She recruited a talented and enthusiastic young staff (at first nearly all female, with only one male) and managed them with tact and understanding. Not unsurprisingly, she kept being offered jobs at a salary well above what we could afford, which she refused.

We soon came under intense fire from eco-fundamentalists,

those environmentalists who are more concerned with ideology than evidence and are particularly strongly represented in the anti-GM lobby. Tracey was attacked because as a student she had been a member of the Revolutionary Communist Party (of whom I had hardly heard and which was not exactly a major force in British politics). Judging people by their student politics would of course have disqualified most of the leading luminaries of New Labour. James Callaghan, after meeting a student at Dundee University called Alastair Darling, is reputed to have declared: 'If I have anything to do with it, I will see that that Trot gets nowhere in the Labour Party.' Today he is one of relatively few politicians who is almost universally trusted for his honesty, good sense and moderation. But this did not stop frequent reference to Tracey's old RCP connections. I was, of course, dismissed as an apologist for GM. Had they known about it, they would no doubt have drawn attention to a paper I wrote at school in praise of Marxism.

SAS itself was attacked as a pro-GM lobby, financed by the agricultural biotechnology industry. In fact we had scrupulously rejected all offers of support from companies connected with GM crops. Furthermore, to guarantee our independence and academic reputation, one of the first things Tracey and I did was to assemble a stellar board, which no one could accuse of allowing SAS to be a sectional interest group. I persuaded Dame Bridget Ogilvie FRS, former Director of the Wellcome Trust, to become my deputy chair. Other board members included the former editor of *Nature* Sir John Maddox; the philosopher Baroness Onora O'Neill; the eminent Oxford plant biologist Christopher Leaver FRS; the science journalist and author Dr Simon Singh; the broadcaster Nick Ross; Diana Garnham, Chief Executive of the Science Council; Professor Janet Bainbridge, former chair of the Advisory Committee on Novel Foods; a prominent GP and author Mike Fitzpatrick; and Paul Hardaker, a meteorologist and chief executive of the Institute of Physics, who became my successor as chair.

Within a few years we had several thousand scientists on our books willing, indeed eager, to argue in public the scientific case against popular misconceptions or unfounded scare stories. Most scientists had refused to take part in public debate because their work and views were often misrepresented by journalists who were not specialist science correspondents and had little idea of the nature of scientific evidence or the scientific method. In an argument about vaccines, for instance, scientists might be asked a question such as: 'Can you guarantee this vaccine is absolutely safe?' Of course, nobody can, as there are no absolute certainties in science. Resulting headline: 'Scientist says vaccines are not safe.'

As our reputation grew we began to attract substantial funding from grant-making trusts and foundations such as the Esmée Fairbairn Foundation and, most gratifyingly, from a host of voluntary personal contributions from scientists, which by the time I retired as chairman constituted over a quarter of our income. Many fledgling institutes have to depend at their early stages on corporate funding but then succeed in becoming rigorously independent. It was the story of IFS and was repeated with SAS.

SAS soon established good relations with the media, publishing papers in a 'Sense About...' series that dispelled myths about a wide range of subjects, from GM crops and claims for the supposed nutritional advantages of organic food to fear of phone masts and of mobile phones themselves ('Mobile phones fry your brains' screamed one newspaper headline).

We proved a relentlessly effective enemy of misinformation and attracted wide publicity by ridiculing celebrities' endorsement of quack products and television programmes. They would explain, for example, how to cleanse your body of all chemicals. Exposing bad science was one of our most effective activities, since every time bogus science is pulled apart it reveals how good science works. A major success was a leaflet titled 'I Don't Know What to Believe', which explained the importance of peer review of scientific papers. The leaflet was the subject of half a million downloads and had wide distribution in schools. Another popular success was a campaign called 'Ask for the Evidence', which spread like Japanese knotweed, with rather more beneficial effect.

We did not campaign alone. The Science Media Centre, set up about the same time, played a vital role in answering media inquiries and putting journalists in touch with expert advice. Professor Edzard Ernst deserves special praise for his exposure of false claims made for different forms of alternative medicine, particularly homeopathy. He had been appointed to a chair at Exeter University as Professor of Complementary and Alternative Medicine because at the time he was not unsympathetic to its practice, and his chair was established with the support of alternative medicine practitioners. However, when his research showed little or no evidence of its efficacy except as a placebo, as a good scientist he published his findings in a series of papers. Together with the science journalist Simon Singh, he also wrote a book titled *Trick or Treatment*, which, with its meticulous scientific analysis, should be compulsory reading for

anyone who genuinely wants to know whether alternative medicine works. Professor Ernst did not endear himself to those who
had sponsored his appointment. Indeed, there was an attempt
by the Prince of Wales's office to muzzle him, with allegations
of misconduct, which led to his suspension from his university
for some eighteen months. The allegations were shown to be
completely without substance.

Others who are high on any list of honour for debunking
scientific nonsense, to mention only a few, are Ben Goldacre for
his book on *Bad Medicine* and his column in *The Guardian*, Francis
Wheen for his book *How Mumbo Jumbo Conquered the World* and
Professor David Colquhoun of University College, London, who
runs a website called 'DC's Improbable Science' and who has
single-handedly forced a number of universities to stop award-
ing phony Bachelor of Science degrees for courses in subjects
such as reflexology, aromatherapy, naturopathy and other forms
of quack medicine. Reflexology, for example, holds that pressure
on certain areas of the foot can, through special pathways to
inner organs such as the kidney, repair troubled functions of that
organ and thus improve a patient's health. Another organisation
called HealthWatch also deserves mention for its promotion of
evidence-based medicine.

Gradually there has been a discernible change in media reporting of science in the UK. Professional science correspondents
have nearly always observed high standards of accuracy but when
there was a hot scare story they would often be brushed aside
to make room for spokesmen from Greenpeace, Friends of the
Earth and the Soil Association, the body which promotes and
regulates organic farming, all of whom used to be treated with
great deference as if they were the ultimate objective authority

on environmental matters. No longer. There is still a widely held popular belief, despite overwhelming evidence to the contrary, that organic food is more nutritious, tastes better and is more environmentally friendly than conventionally grown food, but its sales have begun to decline. Organic farming can claim some environmental merit for its concern in preserving the quality of the soil but this benefit is vastly outweighed by its inefficient use of land. Why does organic food cost more? Not because organic farmers seek to exploit the public but because organic crops have lower yields. A less efficient form of farming is the last thing needed when there is a desperate world shortage of good agricultural land and a need to feed ever more people. As the famous environmentalist James Lovelock observed, if the world relied on organic farming for its food it could feed only a third of its population.

When I started SAS, the gap between the two cultures described by C. P. Snow in his famous 1959 Rede Lecture appeared as wide as ever. But there has been noticeable progress in the media and even in government, which has appointed chief scientists to all its departments – although ministers often disregard their recommendations. British schools have been stopped from teaching creationism, special thanks to Richard Dawkins and others who expose the extraordinary ignorance and perversity of those who refuse to acknowledge the overwhelming evidence in favour of evolution, which should now be treated as a fact as much as the fact that the earth goes round the sun. Particularly important, since 84 per cent of the public gets its information about science from television, the BBC has appointed a science editor for BBC News and has issued new guidelines on giving 'due weight' in observing impartiality in its treatment of scientific issues. The views of cranks no longer have to be given equal time with the views of acknowledged experts. Sense no longer has to be balanced by nonsense, though not all producers have yet discovered the difference.

I found the cause of promoting the public understanding of science one of the most satisfying chapters of my public life and wondered why I had not taken it up before. Science is not just about promoting health and wealth. As a politician, what particularly concerned me was that it has seldom been acknowledged or realised that since the Enlightenment science has played an essential part in the history of democracy and civilisation. Because science rejects claims to truth based on authority and depends on the criticism of established ideas, it is the enemy of autocracy. Because scientific knowledge is tentative and provisional, it is the enemy of dogma and makes us more tolerant and understanding of others. Because it is the most effective way of learning about the physical world, it erodes superstition, ignorance and prejudice, causes of the denial of human rights throughout history. It is the enemy of narrow nationalism and is one of the activities in this world, like the arts, which is not motivated by greed.

What can compare, for example, with the recent achievement of the Large Hadron Collider, a venture of international collaboration by 10,000 scientists and engineers from 113 countries, free from bureaucratic and political interference, who put aside all national, political, religious and cultural differences for the one purpose of exploring and understanding the natural world?[†]

[†]   The Hadron Collider has already brought practical benefits in the invention of the World Wide Web and many of the technologies used in medical imaging, and has contributed to the emerging field of proton beam cancer therapy. The excitement that the Hadron Collider Project has generated was described in a stirring article by Brian Cox in the *New Statesman* of 21 December 2012.

One surprising event was that in 2006 the Association of British Science Writers voted me 'Parliamentary Science Communicator of the Year'. It was particularly gratifying because I had learned no science at school. The nearest I ever got to a scientific education was during a debating tour of America when, at an agricultural college in Des Moines, Iowa, I was asked what subject I had majored in. As I thought Greats or *Literae Humaniores* might not be very informative, I simply answered Classics. Perhaps because of my English accent, or the unfamiliarity of the subject, I was introduced as 'Dick Taverne, who majored in Plastics.' I still lack much understanding of basic science. Every word of my book *The March of Unreason* was checked by Chris Leaver FRS, a board member of SAS and, as mentioned, an eminent professor of plant science at Oxford.

The recognition of my contribution in Parliament was accompanied by a sum of £500 to give to an educational institution of my choice. I gave it to a young friend, Marcelo Staricoff, a former research scientist who had decided that teaching was his real vocation and who was then an exceptionally successful teacher in a primary school in a deprived area of Brighton.[†] He was delighted, but insisted that I should present the prize in person.

First I was shown his class. One wall was covered with questions the children had been encouraged to put up for discussion, such as 'where do babies come from?' and 'can you come back from the dead?' Then the bell rang for my talk to the whole school of about 150 children. As they passed us on the way to the assembly room, nearly every child touched or hugged him.

---

† He is now a headmaster of another primary school, singled out for high praise by OFSTED.

(Teachers are of course forbidden to touch children.) One ten year old gave him an especially warm hug. 'When he first came into my class he threw a chair at me,' Marcelo said. 'His mother is an alcoholic and his father is in jail. Today he is in charge of arranging the sound equipment for your talk.'

I had been apprehensive about giving a talk about science to 7–11 year olds, but they had clearly been stimulated by Marcelo to an interest in science. In fact, I was barely able to finish at all because of the stream of questions and interruptions. I started by saying that science had changed a lot of beliefs – for example, that the earth was flat. First interruption: 'That's what me dad says.' Loud laughter. I asked who watched David Attenborough's programmes about animals on the BBC. Most of them did. (Marcelo did not know that.) I asked how they thought an alba-tross, after a year away and flying thousands of miles, could find its way back to the same island, the same nest and the same part-ner. Several explanations were offered such as, 'He flies very high and knows his way by the islands,' until a girl popped up, 'Built-in memory, sir.' Had I known it at the time I could have told them some birds have magnets in their beaks and eyes and can navi-gate by the earth's magnetic fields. Why did Australians at the bottom of the world not fall off? Derisive laughter. 'Everybody knows that. Gravity, sir.' My meeting could have gone on long after the scheduled forty minutes. If all 7–11 year olds could get so enthusiastic about science, I wondered what we might achieve in secondary schools.

When I stepped down as chairman of SAS in April 2012, following my self-imposed rule that founders should not hang around for more than ten years, I made the contribution of science to civilisation the subject of my valedictory lecture, entitled 'What Has Science Ever Done For Us?' I argued that, apart from making us wealthier and healthier and live longer, there is a historic and logical link between the birth of modern science and the beginnings of liberal democracy, that science has made us more democratic and tolerant and that it has played an important part in the development of human rights.[†]

But how important is the role of reason and the evidence-based approach to democracy today? Historically there may have been a link between the birth of modern science and democracy. There are still obvious reasons why it is desirable that policy should be based on evidence and that we should support science for its contribution to our health and wealth. But it is now generally accepted in established democratic societies that freedom to criticise and tolerance of dissent are basic principles on which we cannot compromise. Are science and democracy still interdependent?

The basic rights on which democracy depends are not as secure as many assume. Freedom of speech and thought is constantly threatened or denied in many parts of the world, not only by political ideology and dogma in the autocracies that still remain, but by religious fundamentalism, particularly militant Islam. As a humanist and rationalist I do not subscribe to beliefs that contradict the laws of nature, such as belief in the power of prayer, the resurrection of Christ or the Virgin birth, let alone that truth is to be found in what was written in sacred texts of doubtful authority very many centuries ago. I object to faith schools in Britain, which treat children not as children of Catholic, Protestant, Jewish or Muslim parents, but as

---

[†]   See Appendix 2 for an edited version.

Catholic, Protestant, Jewish or Muslim children. We do not label children as Conservative, Labour or Liberal Democrat children. Moreover the experience of faith schools in Northern Ireland shows how divisive their influence can be.

Furthermore, I believe we should not underestimate the underlying dangers of irrationality. If people have never learned to exercise their critical faculties and are even encouraged to abandon them, for instance by being taught to believe in miracles, they are more likely to be susceptible to irrational fears unsupported by evidence, as well as to comforting myths. Such fears can easily be whipped up by demagogues or irresponsible newspapers. One example is the belief that immigrants come to Britain to sponge on our welfare state, a belief immune to contradiction by facts or rational argument.

However, most Christians do not take the Bible literally and do not blindly accept everything their church tells them. Most Catholics do not obey their church's teaching on birth control and are often models of tolerance and social responsibility. I also recognise that religion is an important part of many people's lives and inspires them to promote many good causes. Most Christians do not seek to thrust their own beliefs on others, except in some cases over abortion, gay rights and euthanasia. Most believe they can come to terms with science and, generally, except in the United States, accept the truth of evolution. The biggest threat from religion to freedom of speech and social tolerance today, in my view, comes from Islamic fundamentalism.

There are many Muslim countries in important parts of the Muslim world where Islamism is not in control and which are democratic, or have moved towards democracy. Indonesia, for instance, the largest Muslim state, has a secular, not a

theocratic, constitution and is steadily becoming more democratic. The same is true of Malaysia. There was substantial
progress, too, in Turkey, until the government began to imprison
journalists for reporting dissent or expressing views critical of
the government. It now seems determined to reverse the reforms
of President Kemel Ataturk and introduce elements of sharia
law. Many moderate Muslims, such as members of the Quilliam
Foundation, champion a tolerant and democratic society, as did
most young demonstrators who played a leading part in the
Arab Spring.

But Muslim moderates and democrats have not so far
been the beneficiaries of the revolutions in the Middle East.
Where Islamists are elected, hopes of a liberal democracy are
suppressed. In the world of militant Islam, dogma and autocracy prevail and the conflict between ideology and science is
once again demonstrated. Physics may be tolerated by Islamists
because it can serve the interests of the state. But evolution is
not taught in the madrassas, because the truth of the Koran
must not be questioned and doubt is not allowed. Human rights
that are seen as contradicting the Koran, especially women's
rights, are suppressed when militant Islam seizes control and the
rule of law as we know it gives way to sharia law.

Even in established Western democracies freedom of speech
and expression are affected. The fatwa against Salmon Rushdie
so restricted his freedom that he later confessed he would not
have written *The Satanic Verses* if he could have foreseen the
consequences. In Japan one of his publishers was shot. Many
in Britain, to their eternal shame, said the book should not have
been written and also argued that it was irresponsible to honour
Rushdie's literary achievements with a knighthood because of

the offence he caused. In the Netherlands, Theo Van Gogh was murdered for making an anti-Islamic film. Later, the riots and deaths, which followed when a Danish cartoonist ridiculed the prophet, proved to the world that mockery of Islam is dangerous. Yet it is an essential part of freedom not only to be free to criticise political views with which we disagree but to mock and criticise oppressive religious practices, even if it causes offence. As Lord Justice Sedley said in Redmond-Bate *v.* DPP (1999), 'Freedom only to speak inoffensively is not worth having.'[†]

To appease Islamists there was an attempt by the Blair government in 2006 to create a new offence, a law against incitement to religious hatred, which was fortunately (just) defeated. It would have been a denial of free speech. We should be allowed to express hostility to, even hatred of, religious beliefs that make people cut off the hands of petty thieves, stone women for adultery, mutilate girls' genitalia, oppose women's education, as well as the beliefs of religious fanatics who shoot people who work in abortion clinics, or who claim rights to Palestinian lands because of what was written in ancient texts of doubtful validity. Tolerance is a basic element of democracy and that includes tolerance of views which we may find abhorrent. We must be careful that opposition to Islamism does not lead to hostility towards Muslims in general. But in a democracy we must also be careful that, subject to the words of Lord Justice Sedley, we do not become tolerant of intolerance that inhibits free speech.

[†] In my term as a teacher at Mill Hill Junior School (see Chapter 3) young Stephen Sedley was my brightest pupil.

POSTSCRIPT

Throughout these memoirs, I have extolled the virtues of reason. I do not subscribe to David Hume's view that reason is the slave of the passions but it is not the leading star of life or politics. In Tom Stoppard's play *Jumpers*, when George Moore's wife calls the church 'a monument to irrationality,' he answers vehemently:

> The National Gallery is a monument to irrationality! Every concert hall is a monument to irrationality! … And so is a nicely kept garden, or a lover's favour, or a home for stray dogs. You stupid woman, if rationality was a criterion for things being allowed to exist, the world would be one gigantic field of soya beans!

Quite, though I fail to see the connection between reason and the massive cultivation of soya beans.

Reason and evidence have little to do with most of the pleasures and foibles of life or with one's successes and failures. A huge influence on my life was luck. It was sheer luck that I met and married Janice. I was launched on my political career in 1958 by a chance meeting in the street with Bill Rodgers. Sense

About Science prospered because someone casually mentioned Tracey Brown to me as a good director. Fate and life are not linked by reason.

One thing I look back on with a lot of satisfaction is running four London marathons, the first at the age of fifty-three and three more at three-yearly intervals. What can be a more irrational activity than running 26-and-a-half miles? It is not particularly good for your health. Training for a marathon takes many hours a week for several months and the last five miles put the great torturers of history to shame. But finishing it: 'I've done it!' Each time my finishing-line verdict was, 'Never again.' Then you think that if you train more conscientiously, next time it will be easier and faster.

It all began in my mid-forties. Janice suggested keeping fit, taking exercise beyond tennis or squash, perhaps a run round the block. I started running round Warwick Square Gardens (less than a quarter of a mile), close to our house in Pimlico. Then, spurred on by a friend, around Battersea Park – nearly four miles. On sailing holidays I enjoyed running over the hills in Brittany and, having got up to managing ten miles, I looked the marathon in the eye. I never quite made my target of breaking the three-and-a-half hour barrier but always stayed under three hours fifty minutes.

Sailing was – and is – a favourite pastime. As usual, Janice started it. She had sailed dinghies on Lake Victoria in Uganda (where she was born), taking care not to capsize because of crocodiles. Once, before we were married, she took me out in a dinghy on a Dutch lake – no crocodiles and much enjoyed! And, some years later, we spent an Easter sailing on the Norfolk Broads. Then, in 1964, jointly with a friend, we bought *Isle of*

Dreams, a 21ft, gaff-rigged, clinker-built wooden boat, which was resting in a mud berth in the Thames under Hungerford Bridge, for £600. Since then we have sailed different bigger and better boats (two of the early ones were catamarans) round England, in Scotland and Ireland, explored nearly every port in Brittany, sailed to Holland (and through Holland which is possible without lowering your mast), Denmark, Sweden and Norway, and finally swept three times through Biscay to the Mediterranean, enjoying Spain, Portugal and Italy on the way to exploring Greece and Turkey. We have kept boats in Greece for over twenty years. We have sailed into Venice (what could be more glorious?) and into Istanbul. We have chartered a boat in Maine and in the Seychelles. From time to time, I would be invited to August conferences in Aspen, Colorado, meetings on interesting subjects with various world experts which offered valuable political experience. All were declined because sailing, not reason, came first.

Sailing can become an obsession. I was told one story by someone who had watched a single-handed sailor skilfully moor his boat to a pontoon. They got chatting and he asked, 'Have you ever had problems sailing single-handed?' The reply: 'Yes. Once, when I was returning from a day's sail, I faced an unexpected gale on the nose. I had a hell of a struggle and took hours to bring down my working jib and stow it. I eventually managed to hoist a tiny storm jib. I made it back to harbour but only got home after midnight. There I found a note from my wife. "I'm fed up and have gone off with your best friend."' 'How awful, what did you do?' 'Well, I got myself a furling jib and have had no problem since.'

Looking back on my public life so far, what has given me most satisfaction or regret? My greatest sadness about politics is Britain's loss of standing in the world through its failure to play the role it could have played in Europe. As Dean Acheson famously observed, 'Britain has lost an empire, but has not found a role.' Economically and socially we have fallen between all the stools: we never adopted the social approach to capitalism, which has been tried one way or another in the Scandinavian countries, Germany and the Netherlands. Neither did we chase the highly competitive, free-market enterprise society of the United States. My choice, naturally, would be the former. The more egalitarian Scandinavian countries, like Denmark, come top on most of the criteria for a well-adjusted society, for example, low numbers of teenage pregnancies and abortions, generally high standards of education, low rates of homicide and depression and so on. In a scale of social dysfunctionality the most unequal developed countries come off worst.[†] But Labour governments have failed to make Britain a more social democratic country in the Scandinavian-style. Under both political parties, British industry has lost competitive edge. We have become a country with a grandiose financial hub and a patchy manufacturing sector, with a poor overall record of long-term investment.[‡] But we do inequality superbly.

At the heart of our decline, in my view, lie failures of policy

---

[†]   Wilkinson, R. and Pickett, K., *The Spirit Level: Why More Equal Societies Almost Always Do Better* (London: Allen Lane, 2009).

[‡]   The decline in size of our manufacturing sector, it should be said, has often been exaggerated. In an article in the *Telegraph* (18 April 2010), Roger Bootle pointed out that at 12 per cent of GDP it is much lower than Germany's (24 per cent), but about the same as that of France and higher than that of the USA. On the other hand, its record since the article was written has not been impressive. Its share of GDP started to decline even before the financial and economic crisis and since then its exports have performed poorly despite a very large devaluation of sterling.

towards Europe. I have been a lifelong enthusiast for Britain's active participation in a closely knit European Community and I joined the pro-Europe Strasbourg Club as an undergraduate. The founding of the Community was a contract between nations, some previously bitter enemies, to limit the influence of counterproductive nationalism and rivalry in favour of a degree of shared sovereignty for mutual benefit. What an inspiring concept. And it worked! The original idealism of the European Union has faded but the basic principles still survive and one of its many achievements is that it has proved a magnet of democracy for previous autocracies. The outstanding economic progress in its early years has stuttered, partly through the flaws in the design of the single currency for the eurozone. But the EU market has become the biggest economic market in the world and the establishment of the Single Market has produced, and continues to produce, large economic benefits for its members.

In 1957 the leadership of Europe was open. Russell Bretherton was our observer at the birth of the European Union, the Messina talks which led to the Rome Treaty. He was an Under-Secretary at the Board of Trade, Britain having declined to send a member of the Cabinet. It has been widely reported that Bretherton made the following farewell speech: 'Gentlemen, you are trying to negotiate something you will never be able to negotiate. But if negotiated, it will never be ratified. And if ratified, it will never work.' There is no documentary evidence that he actually made this statement, which reflected the very opposite of his own views. But it sure as hell spoke for the Conservative Cabinet at the time and enraged our friends.[†]

---

†   Young, H., *This Blessed Plot*, p. 93.

The Cabinet believed and hoped that the talks would fail, while Bretherton advised that as they would succeed we should participate. The other six nations desperately wanted Britain to join and Bretherton later said that, had we agreed to do so in principle, we could have had any kind of Common Market we wanted. In 1957, the French, for example, who under de Gaulle vetoed our application in 1962, saw British entry as a condition of their own entry and were prepared to pay a British price for that.

Five years later, because of the signal success of the European Community, the Macmillan government realised that our future lay in Europe. When after two rebuffs by de Gaulle we eventually joined the Community in 1972, several important features of its structure, such as the agricultural and fisheries policies, were fixed in a form that was against our national interests. We were also left paying too much into the EC's budget. But except in the formation of the Single Market and the Community's enlargement, admittedly two very important aspects of the EU, our participation has generally been half-hearted and has left the leadership to Germany and France. Most of our political command, except for Macmillan, Heath, Jenkins and an early, better Blair, missed the whole point – that an active EU membership would lift our influence in the world and raise our prospects of future prosperity. Meanwhile, to boast about our special relationship with the USA is one delusion, while claiming in Europe to safeguard our particular 'red lines' is another.

Despite the serious problems now faced by the European Union, which might well have been avoided or mitigated had we joined at the start and been more committed members, our growing isolationism simply orchestrates national decline. When

Margaret Thatcher died, many Conservatives praised her for 'making Britain Great again', when in fact her legacy to the Conservative Party was a deep distrust and hostility towards Europe that has reduced our international influence. Britain cut off from the EU is of use neither to the US nor to emerging powers such as China, India and Brazil. What is forgotten is that in one part of her famous 1988 Bruges speech, generally cited as a searing indictment of the European Community's shortcomings, Mrs Thatcher actually made some very sensible remarks about it that pro-Europeans could strongly endorse:

> On many great issues the countries of Europe should try to speak with a single voice. I want to see us work more closely on the things we can do better together than alone. Europe is stronger when we do so, whether it is in trade, in defence, or in our relations with the rest of the world.

The issue of Europe has been, and still is, one of the main issues in my political life, which has generally been satisfying, enjoyable and, I believe, productive. I had an unusually rewarding time as a minister, even though I was not in the Cabinet, because I was part of Roy Jenkins's very successful team both at the Home Office and the Treasury. I derived great satisfaction from starting things, such as the IFS and SAS. Even my attempt to start a new Social and Liberal Democratic Party, which was premature and unsuccessful at the time, showed that there is political life outside the conventional party tribes.

However, I was perhaps somewhat casual in my approach to Parliament (except when I was in office), not giving it the full attention it deserved. You don't go into politics for fame, and usually not for money (although recently some ex-Cabinet ministers have ended up as chairmen of privatised industries). It is to make things better. It is part of a serious approach to the job to mix with journalists, generally good company anyway, and with fellow MPs, of whom the same is often true. But with very few exceptions, the few journalists we had to dinner had been friends before I became an MP. Few fellow MPs became really close friends and I spent as little time as possible in the House of Commons tearooms and bars. I asked very few parliamentary questions (they cost a lot of public money and seldom achieve much, except publicity for the questioner). I was mainly concerned to keep my private life private and give family life as much time as possible.

Surprisingly, being a minister left much more time for family life than being a backbencher. It meant I had only one job and could even go to the cinema some evenings or the theatre or to concerts and generally enjoy the wonderful cultural opportunities London has to offer. One reason why I did not regret leaving the House of Commons after my defeat in the second general election of 1974 was that it gave me more time at home. Just before that election my younger daughter Caroline, then aged ten, overheard Janice and me discussing my prospects. She asked if I was going to lose. I said I probably would. 'Does that mean you will be at home at weekends?' 'Yes.' 'And in the evenings?' 'Yes.' 'Oh, I do hope you lose.'

Two wonderful Lincoln supporters of mine, the Richardson sisters, Linda and Biddy, kept an archive of my public progress and recently sent me an article from the *Sunday Times* magazine of 6 March 1967: 'Spot the Prime Minister – who will occupy 10 Downing Street twenty-five years from now?' It illustrates the absurdity of such prognostications. Favourite at odds of 5/1 was Richard Marsh, Minister of Power at the time, a member of Wilson's Cabinet at the age of thirty-eight. Dick was widely regarded as a future Labour leader. To me he had an attractive quality of nonchalance in his approach to politics, but it led to his sacking two years after the *Sunday Times* article for a series of private, cynical and disrespectful remarks about the Prime Minister. He then left politics and, as Lord Marsh, later became head of British Rail. Second favourites were Bill Rodgers and me, both at 10/1. Among a list of twenty names, most of them long forgotten, were people like Peter Emery (the 'immaculate conception' of my student days) at 100/1, Shirley Williams at 500/1 and a complete outsider, at odds of 1000/1, one Margaret Thatcher. So Bill and I were reckoned to have a hundred times better chance of being Prime Minister than Mrs Thatcher!

At the time of writing, I find myself enjoying a final fling in politics as a Peer. The influence of the House of Lords is limited, as it should be, since the House of Commons, the elected chamber, must have primacy. But the Lords fulfil an essential role as a revising chamber, a role which it performs well because of the expertise among its members in nearly every aspect of national life. For example, I am surrounded by formidable allies fighting against the tide of populist resentment of immigrants and of the EU, which threatens to sweep us into national isolation and also threatens Britain's generally deserved reputation for tolerance. A Bill introduced in 2014 to fix a date for an 'In or Out Referendum' on Europe in 2017, which passed through the House of Commons without detailed scrutiny, was torn apart in the Lords by diplomats and former civil servants with long experience in EU negotiations. They demonstrated unanswerably that a major renegotiation of our relations with the EU could not possibly be completed by 2017.

Debates in the Lords are very different from those in the Commons. They are short on drama but long on detailed argument. There is no jeering and cheering as at Prime Minister's Question Time. Courtesy prevails. Even the most boring speeches are treated with respect: 'I listened to the last speaker's carefully considered remarks with great interest.' After a rare intemperate outburst, the answer might come: 'That was a very spirited contribution from the noble Lord (or Baroness).' Most importantly, no party has a built-in majority. A quarter of the members of the Lords have been appointed as independent 'crossbenchers'. Even those peers who have been nominated by a party do not necessarily vote the party line. As a result, the outcome of many votes is unpredictable and depends on the merits of the arguments advanced in the debate – an unusual phenomenon in the House of Commons. The Lords have played an important part, largely unnoticed, in amending illiberal legislation and occasionally even preventing it from being passed.

Apart from the anachronistic absurdity of being called 'Lord' or 'Lady', membership of the Upper House is a satisfying, and I hope useful, way of enjoying the autumn of one's political career.

APPENDIX 1

Burke's Speech to the Electors of Bristol, 1774

Burke's doctrine that an MP should be a representative, not a delegate, played an important part in my 1973 by-election. I therefore reproduce his historic Speech to the Electors of Bristol, plus my reasons for questioning the contemporary fashion for regarding the referendum as the ultimate expression of democracy.

His constituents' wishes ought to have great weight with him [the MP]; their opinion, high respect; their business, unremitted attention. It is his duty to sacrifice his repose, his pleasures, his satisfactions, to theirs; and above all, ever, to prefer their interest to his own. But his unbiased opinion, his mature judgment, his enlightened conscience, he should not sacrifice to you, to any man or to any set of men living ... Your representative owes you, not his industry only, but his judgment; and he betrays, instead of serving you, if he sacrifices it to your opinion...

Government and legislation are matters of reason and judgment, and not of inclination; and what sort of reason is that, in which the determination precedes the discussion; in which one set of men deliberate, and another decide; and where those who

form the conclusion are perhaps three hundred miles distant
from those who hear the arguments...

Authoritative instructions; mandates issued, which the member
is bound blindly and implicitly to obey, to vote, and to argue for,
though contrary to the clearest conviction of his judgment and
conscience, these are things unknown to the laws of this land...

Parliament is not a congress of ambassadors from different and
hostile interests; which interests each must maintain as an agent
and advocate, against other agents and advocates; but Parliament
is a deliberative assembly of one nation, with one interest, that of
the whole; where not local purposes, not local prejudices, ought
to guide, but the general good ... You choose a member indeed;
but when you have chosen him, he is not member of Bristol, but
he is a member of Parliament.

Burke's arguments are as valid against the referendum as an
instrument of democracy as against treating MPs as delegates. Reluctantly I have to concede that the referendum is now
an accepted part of our political procedures for fundamental
constitutional changes. But in my view the belief that it promotes
trust in democracy is a fallacy. Of course, if you ask people, 'Do
you want a say?' they will answer, 'Yes.' But in a referendum
people often vote Yes or No for reasons little to do with the issue,
if they vote at all. In 2008 Ireland held a referendum on the
Lisbon Treaty and voters rejected it. One of the main debates
was about abortion, not mentioned in the treaty. The following
year they voted again and approved the treaty. In France, whatever the referendum question, the outcome generally depends
on the popularity or unpopularity of the government. In Britain,

Eurosceptics also campaigned for a referendum on the Lisbon Treaty. It would have been as meaningless as it was in Ireland. The treaty is a long and complicated one, which even many politicians never read. Europhiles might well have opposed some clauses; others might well have been acceptable to sceptics. But voters could not pick and choose.

If a referendum is regarded as the ultimate democratic criterion, the demand for its use will grow. Why not a referendum on MMR or GM crops or nuclear power, or lower taxes, as in California? Exeunt Locke and Burke; the champions of parliamentary government. Enter Rousseau, the champion of the doctrine that the will of the majority should always prevail, even over minority rights or the rule of law, Rousseau, the favourite of autocrats and dictators.

The electors of Bristol were well-advised.

APPENDIX 2

**Sense About Science Annual Lecture April 2012:
'What Has Science Ever Done For Us?'**

*In Chapter 10 I stress the important role science played at the time of the
Enlightenment in the birth of democracy and making us more civilised. This
theme was more fully developed in my farewell lecture on my retirement from
the chair of Sense About Science, which is reproduced here.*

I thought it would be a suitable beginning of a lecture to a
predominantly scientific audience to start with a slide in classical Greek.

Idiotes, the origin of the word idiot, in the ancient citizens's
democracy of Athens, meant someone who took no part in
public affairs.

One of the aims of Sense About Science when it was launched
ten years ago was to stop scientists being idiots, at least etymo-
logically. At the time, most scientists were reluctant to take part
in public discussion, let alone political debate. The meaning of
the word has, of course, changed. Otherwise politicians cannot
be idiots, which runs counter to experience. Sense About Science
has succeeded in substantially reducing the number of scientific

idiotai. We now have a list of over 5,000 scientists who are willing, often eager, to take part in public discussion and debate.

Pericles, the great Athenian statesman, said that Athens
differed from other states in regarding the man who holds aloof
from public life as useless. I would not go as far as that. But a
decline in civic participation, and indeed a decline in concern
about politics, is a slippery and dangerous slope that weakens
democracy. If we are in no way involved in the management
of our collective affairs, we should not be surprised if no one
is listening to us. So I do believe it is an important achievement
that there has been a significantly increased participation in
public discussion by scientists.

On the other side of the coin, I regret that the number of
my fellow politicians who know or really care about science has
not notably increased. There is just one graduate scientist in the
House of Commons (compared with some half a dozen Fellows
of the Royal Society in the Lords). There is not just a gap in
politicians' knowledge. There is a gaping black hole.

When politicians say 'I know nothing about science' it is often
a boast rather than an admission. They're all for science in
principle – because it helps economic growth and provides new
drugs to cure disease, because it helps to make us wealthier and
healthier. But generally they have little clue how science works
and aren't that interested in finding out.

The same is true of the public generally, and of much of the
civil service and the media. A poll taken a few years ago showed
that overwhelmingly people think science is a good thing. But the
same poll showed that an overwhelming majority also believe no
new product should be allowed to be marketed unless science has
first proved it absolutely safe. So much for an understanding of

scientific method. Again, the popularity of alternative medicine hardly demonstrates public dedication to the evidence-based approach. And as for understanding risk, just look at the success of the lottery.

Well, what has science ever done for us? OK it has made us healthier. But what has science done for us, apart from helping to feed the world, cutting infant mortality, exploring the universe, explaining the origin of the planet and our species, letting us fly, watch television, radically expanding our lifespan, inventing anaesthesia, making us wealthy beyond the dreams of any previous generation?

My theme today is that it has made us more democratic, more tolerant and more compassionate. When I started Sense About Science my aim was not only to expose bogus science but to increase public awareness of the role of science in making us more civilised.

The Enlightenment was in my view one of the most glorious events in the history of mankind. It saw the birth of modern science. I don't deny the contribution of medieval Islam, or the technological achievements of Chinese civilisation, or especially the astonishing insights of the ancient Greeks. In a fragment of one of the first books ever written, about nature, the Greek philosopher Xenophanes, who lived in the late sixth and early fifth century BC, even wrote about the impossibility of absolute certainty:

The gods did not reveal, from the beginning
All things to us, but in the course of time,
Through seeking we may learn, and know things better...
But as for certain truth, no man has known it...
For all is but a woven web of guesses.

That period saw not only the first stirrings of the search for scientific explanations of the world about us, but also of democracy. Even then the two were linked.

But consider what the Enlightenment in Europe achieved in the late seventeenth and eighteenth century. It challenged authority as the arbiter of truth; dethroned theocracy; overturned years of sterile metaphysics; challenged superstition; and put reason and science at the centre of the explanation of the world.

Consider what it achieved in Britain. The witchcraft statutes were repealed; smallpox vaccination was introduced; madness ceased to be regarded as a supernatural occurrence; the Royal Society was founded (1662); the Divine Right of Kings was abolished; and liberal democracy was born.

Not a bad record.

Voltaire, generally regarded as the chief patron of the Enlightenment, declared that the three key figures of the Enlightenment were Bacon, Newton and Locke. Bacon was the prophet of modern science, Newton revealed the laws of the universe and Locke demolished Descartes and rebuilt philosophy on the bedrock of experience. Thomas Jefferson said Bacon, Newton and Locke were the three greatest men that ever lived. They were certainly an extraordinary trio. But how were they responsible for linking modern science and liberal democracy?

First, and crucially, they challenged dogma. Bacon was the great empiricist. He championed reasoning by induction, proceeding from observation and experiment to ever-broader conclusions. I'm a Karl Popper fan and Popper pointed out, as did Medawar, that Bacon was wrong, because the first step, observation, does not involve looking at things in an open-minded but empty-headed sort of way. How do you know what you are looking for? What question do you have in mind? Instead you start with an idea, a possible explanation of the facts in which you are interested. Instead of observation leading to theory, theory comes first. Then, Popper argued, to support the hypothesis, the good scientist will look for facts that falsify it. If you claim that all swans are white, you don't keep looking for more white swans to confirm your claim, but see if you can find a black one. And if you look in St James's Park you may find one.

Whatever the flaws in Bacon's approach – and Popper himself understated the complexities of his falsification principle – Bacon's message was a practical one: to observe and study the real world and base conclusions on these observations and studies. That is how our knowledge of the world improves. Knowledge gives power over nature, and this leads to real benefits. But greater knowledge depends on constant criticism and constant criticism means rejection of dogma. It follows that science does not do certainty. Some new hypothesis may always provide a better explanation of the facts.

As for Newton, Popper said his *Principia* marked the greatest intellectual revolution in the history of mankind. I find its impact mind-boggling. It was written in Latin. It was crammed with mathematics, largely unintelligible to all but dedicated mathematicians – Newton was not exactly the Brian Cox of his day. As Tim Ferris summed it up in *The Science of Liberty*[†] it not only demonstrated that the solar system works according to mathematically precise rules, which apply on earth as in the heavens, but provided a handbook that could be used for calculating a million practical matters, such as the strength of bridge girders,

---

†   Ferris, T., *The Science of Liberty* (New York: HarperCollins: 2010), p. 55.

and even the amount of rocket fuel needed to dispatch astronauts to the moon. Newton, more than anyone else, showed that reason, not superstition, could explain the world.

Incidentally, it is extraordinary that many of the books which changed the world are indigestible. *Principia* is one. Another is Keynes's *General Theory of Employment, Interest and Money* – very hard going for non-economists, although generally Keynes wrote beautifully. Then there was *Das Kapital*, a deadly volume, but Marx like Keynes coined some memorable phrases. The Communist manifesto ended with a stirring battle cry: 'Workers of the world unite. You have nothing to lose but your chains.' Scientists have no similar battle cry, except maybe Adlai Stevenson's injunction, 'Eggheads of the world unite. You have nothing to lose but your yokes', or for scientists he might have said, 'You have nothing to lose but your brains.'

Of the glorious triumvirate, my favourite is John Locke, who based his political philosophy on Bacon's practical, empirical approach and his friend, Newton's reason.

'In an age,' he wrote, 'which produces such masters as the incomparable Mr Newton, it is ambition enough to be employed as an under-labourer in clearing the ground a little and removing some of the rubbish that lies in the way to knowledge.'

Inspired by science, his approach to public affairs was tentative, anti-dogmatic, and therefore anti-authoritarian, and profoundly tolerant of dissent. 'Where is the man,' he wrote, 'that has incontestable evidence of the truth of all that he holds, or of the falsehood of all he condemns, or can say that he has examined to the bottom all his own or other men's opinions?' Locke argued that sovereignty must reside in the people. From his rejection of dogma and certainties, it followed that respect for the wishes of the majority must be tempered by checks and balances, by respect for the rights of minorities, for the rule of law and for human rights, essential parts of parliamentary democracy.

It is clear that democracy, like science, depends on the right to criticise. However inefficient the political process may be, if you can't openly challenge what has gone wrong, the odds are against progress. But in politics today you must never say you have changed your mind or that you were wrong. TV interviewers spend much time trying to get politicians to admit they have changed their minds – which they in turn vigorously deny. Mrs Thatcher reacted to the suggestion she might have to do a U-turn with one of her most famous and admired remarks, 'You turn if you want to. The lady's not for turning.' But politicians should take pride in being prepared to change their minds. As Oscar Wilde said, 'Experience is the name everyone gives to their mistakes.' And the eminent physicist John Archibald Wheeler said, 'Our whole problem is to make the mistakes as fast as possible.' (It would not perhaps be the most appealing election slogan.)

Parliamentary democracies make progress, because in the end politicians have to abandon policies that don't work and must change their minds. Democracies are the best system for coping with mistakes and learning from them. In a way it proceeds by trial and error. And if you are not prepared to make mistakes you will not take risks. And if you are not prepared to take risks, you will have no innovation. That is why democracies have proved more prosperous than autocracies.

Incidentally, there was once a politician who had no qualms about changing his mind. He was that mercurial figure, George Brown, who was Foreign Secretary from 1966 to 1968 in the first

Wilson government – not to be confused with Gordon Brown. When he was challenged with having changed his position, his answer was simple: 'Yes, I have. I was wrong'. His challenger came back, 'How do we know you won't be wrong again?' George replied, 'I will be wrong again, but at least I'll admit it.'

Locke's antithesis at the time of the Enlightenment was Rousseau, the great romanticist. Rousseau actually wrote that science and technology were ignoble. He was the guru of anti-science. 'Let us begin,' he wrote, 'by laying facts aside.' He admitted that his noble savage might never have existed, but that did not stop him describing how this primitive saint lived his Arcadian existence in harmony with nature: 'I see him satisfying his hunger at the first oak, and slaking his thirst at the first brook; finding his bed at the foot of the tree which afforded him a meal and with that, all his wants are supplied.' Rousseau also preached that the will of the majority must always prevail and his influence on the French Revolution was profound. It started stirringly with the *Declaration of the Rights of Man* by Thomas Paine, so that Wordsworth could exclaim: 'Bliss was it that dawn to be alive, but to be young was very heaven.' But gradually it succumbed to mob rule, and Paine's *Rights of Man* was overwhelmed by Rousseau's will of the people. In the history of politics after the Enlightenment, there was a profound divide between followers of Rousseau, the champion of unreason and the will of the majority, and those of Locke, the champion of science and parliamentary government. One led to tyranny; the other promoted democracy.

When I argue that democracy and science are linked, I am sometimes asked: didn't Communism claim to be scientific and didn't the Nazis use technology effectively in the Second World War? And how about China today?

In fact Communism denied the basic principles of science. Though denouncing religion, it said, 'There is no God and Karl Marx is his prophet.' Soviet rulers claimed that Marxism applied the laws of nature to history and society, but there was no question of testing Marxist theory to see if it was contradicted by facts, as it was. Doubt was not allowed and dogma ruled. Any scientists who questioned Lysenko's doctrines of Lamarckism and 'vernalisation' disappeared into the gulags, or were shot or forced to recant – just like Galileo. Bourgeois class-ridden genetics was banished. A new 'creative' Darwinism had to be adopted, based on dialectical materialism. The only scientists allowed any freedom were those useful to the state, for example some distinguished physicists who worked on the atom bomb. When a meeting was called to denounce them for their bourgeois approach, Stalin cancelled it and said to Beria, 'Let them get on with their work. We can always shoot them afterwards.'

Even today, when autocracy is no longer absolute, as a recent comment in *Nature* pointed out, favouritism and corruption pervade science and a stifling bureaucracy and a perplexing jungle of regulations and restrictions are the despair of aspiring Russian scientists. Science did not flourish under Communism and Communism certainly did not lead to prosperity. As Khruschev once said, 'We have nothing to hide. We have nothing. And we hide it.'

By the way, the Russians did make good political jokes. My favourite was made by Gorbachev when he met Ronald Reagan. They got on very well, as Gorbachev did with all Western leaders, but at some point Reagan said to him, 'You know, there is one fundamental difference between America and the Soviet Union. Anyone can come into my office and say: "I don't like

the way Reagan is running the government of America."'
'Nonsense,' said Gorbachev, 'there is no such difference. Anyone
can come into my office in the Kremlin and say, "I don't like the
way Reagan is running the government of America."'

Let me briefly mention Nazi Germany, which appeared to
combine dictatorship with scientific success, particularly in
military technology. In fact the Nazis made little pretence to
be pro-science, most of which was dismissed as Jewish science.
Hitler declared the end of the Age of Reason. They championed alternative medicine, especially homeopathy, which was
invented by a German, Hahnemann, and they favoured organic
farming, which was founded by Nazi party members and fitted
neatly with the doctrine of Blood and Soil. In some ways, they
were pretty green. As for technology, except for rocketry, this
was a field in which Britain, I learned to my surprise, was generally superior.[†] The great strength of the Germans in the Second
World War was the quality of their army. It has taken German
science a long time to recover from the Nazis.

But what about China today? Will it disprove the thesis that
science is linked with democracy? It has given scientists a degree
of freedom that Soviet and Nazi scientists never had. Their best
students are encouraged to go to the top universities abroad and
their rulers don't seem to worry that they will be corrupted by
foreign democratic influences. China invests hugely in science.
Yet it is still an autocracy that puts dissidents in prison. In fact,
reports in *Nature* suggest that Chinese science has its weaknesses.
It is not strong in basic science, has produced little innovation
and good connections often trump academic expertise. It is also

[†]   Edgerton, D., *Britain's War Machine: Weapons, Resources and Experts in the Second
       World War* (London: Allen Lane, 2011).

clear that their political system is under stress. I believe it is too early to say whether science and autocracy will coexist in China.

What about claims that science has made society not only more democratic but more tolerant and more compassionate?

Throughout history, dogma, superstition, prejudice, and hysterical fears based on ignorance have been responsible for the denial of human rights and for any number of atrocities. Reason and civilisation go hand in hand. As Voltaire said: 'Those who can make you believe absurdities can make you commit atrocities.' Dogma, often based on passionately held ideology, has been responsible for many of the worst things that people have done to each other. Stephen Pinker in his book, *The Better Angels of our Nature*, lists as examples the Crusades, the European Wars of Religion, the French and Napoleonic Revolutionary Wars, the Russian and Chinese Revolutionary Wars, the Second World War, the Holocaust and the genocides of Stalin, Mao and Pol Pot and could have added many more.[†]

Pinker could also have added that millions of lives have been lost through bad science. One of my heroines was Rachel Carson after I read *Silent Spring*. Later, I learned that her unfounded claims that DDT caused cancer led to a ban on what had been one of the most successful agents there has ever been for saving lives, preventing some hundreds of millions of people dying from malaria. It can be argued that her untruths about the effect of DDT and pesticides were responsible for as many deaths as Hitler, Stalin and Mao combined. Again consider the deaths from the denial by the government of South Africa of a link between HIV and AIDS.

[†]   Pinker, S., *The Better Angels of our Nature: A History of Violence and Humanity* (London: Penguin, 2012).

But, quite apart from horrors inflicted by dogma, throughout history, superstition and sheer ignorance have played a major part in the denial of human rights. We rightly associate progress on human rights with people such as Wilberforce, who championed slaves; Mary Wollstonecraft, who championed women's rights; Martin Luther King, who fought for the rights of black people, and so on. But why were these rights denied in the first place? Through prejudice, based on ignorance and superstition. It was believed that because they were smaller, women's brains were therefore inferior and that black people belonged to an inferior species. These prejudices still of course persist. But they are nowhere near as widespread as they used to be and are treated with ignominy when they appear. Since the Enlightenment, science has promoted human rights by its exposure of superstition and ignorance, as well as by its repugnance to dogma.

Tribalism and nationalism are two other causes of wars and intolerance. Certainly, many individual scientists have been nationalists, indeed chauvinists, but science itself is international, indeed anti-nationalist and anti-tribalist. Its conferences are international. Its findings are shared internationally. As Chekhov observed, 'There is no national science, just as there is no national multiplication table.' The nationality of a scientist is totally irrelevant. The same, of course, is true of art.

Pinker argues that mankind has made progress over the centuries and that we have gradually become more civilised. He does not claim that we are bound to become more civilised by some iron law of history, or that progress is irreversible, or proceeds by a steady upward graph. There are many blips and temporary reverses. But the trend, he argues, is upwards. When there is the threat of global warming, nuclear weapons in North Korea and

Iran and deadlock in the Middle East, potential break-up of the European Union and the prospect of recession in many parts of the world, it is easy to depict those who believe in progress as little Pollyannas. To be an optimist seems the apogee of naivety. Pessimists seem to be the realists. Gloomsters often convey a spurious aura of intellectual depth (and incidentally, generally have a bad track record). Well, Pinker produces strong evidence in favour of his claim.

Murder rates per head of population, for example, have steadily and dramatically declined. In the fourteenth century they were 110 times higher in England than at the end of the twentieth century. Similar declines are recorded for Italy and the Netherlands. The twentieth century was not the bloodiest in history, though there were certainly some very big blips.

Consider what used to be regarded as public entertainment. What did the Romans ever do for us? Well of course, bread and circuses, which meant seeing people torn apart by wild beasts. Oh, and of course crucifixion, a standard form of imposing the death penalty – automatic for escaping slaves. In England, public executions were public spectacles, to which parents took their children, even to watch someone being hung, drawn and quartered. As late as the seventeenth century, live cats were roasted for entertainment in Paris and people squealed with delight as the cats squealed in agony. We now value human life to the extent that we spare murderers. Capital punishment has been abolished in all member states of the EU and even in fourteen American states. In fact no country can be accepted as an EU member if they retain the death penalty – which for some is an additional reason for leaving it.

It has been argued that it is wrong to claim that science has

made us more civilised because social changes and values influence science, not the converse. We even have a report on Science
and Society in 2000 from a House of Lords Select Committee
(and what could possibly be a more authoritative body?)
that stated:

> Scientists must have morality and values, and must be allowed
> and indeed expected to apply them to their work and its applica-
> tions. By declaring openly the values that underpin their work,
> and by engaging with the values and attitudes of the public, they
> are far more likely to command public support.

Scientists and researchers should certainly declare any conflicting interests. But their values? Should scientists who find that the
impact of pollen from Bt Corn on monarch butterflies in the field
is negligible declare that they have been lifelong Democrats or
Republicans, or Seventh Day Adventists, or that they are against
abortion? Would the public really trust a scientist more if it knew
that he or she hates capitalism, or is an Arsenal supporter?

Indeed, one irrefutable answer to the supposed relevance of a
scientist's background is to ask the question posed by Professor
Robin Fox of Rutgers University: What did it matter whether
Gregor Mendel was a male, white, European, monk? His findings about the heritable characteristics of peas would have been
no less valid if he had been a female plant geneticist from Africa.
(I have slightly adapted his answer.)

With the greatest respect, the House of Lords Committee was
confusing the values of scientists with the values of science. Of
course scientists have moral and social values, but science
does not. although it has very important social consequences.

Ultimately the motives of researchers are unimportant. Scientists may embark on a particular research project because they hope it will help mankind, or make them famous, or will confirm their prejudices, or they may select it because they can get it funded. If they work for a company, no doubt they hope it will help the company make greater profits.

Whatever their motives or their values, in the end the results of their research will be subjected to objective scrutiny. Do the findings stand up to the critical analysis of peer review? Are they reproducible? Can they be verified or falsified? If they stand up, it does not matter whether a scientist works for Greenpeace or Monsanto. If the results are obviously biased by the researcher's prejudices or vested interests, they will be worthless and his or her reputation will suffer. Scientists have a strong incentive not to let their prejudices interfere with their work. Their reputation depends on getting things right. But of course they are human and sometimes hopes will cloud judgement and they will more readily seize on findings that seem to confirm their hypotheses than those that contradict them.

Let me turn to the present. Since the Enlightenment, progress in our understanding of the world around us has been astonishing. But where do we stand today?

I founded Sense About Science in 2002 out of frustration with the misinformation, misrepresentation and basic lack of understanding of science that pervaded politics, much of the media, and public opinion. There seemed to be a dimming of the Enlightenment. There was widespread hostility to GM crops. Their every trial in the UK and Europe had been trashed. There were excessive fears of radiation, not only from nuclear waste, but from mobile phones and phone masts. Several universities offered BSc degrees in Ayurveda, reflexology and chiropractics. There was a general assumption that organic food is better for health. Parents rejected the MMR vaccine. Creationism was beginning to be taught in some of the new academies. There were even TV programmes on how to cleanse your body of all chemicals.

Since then there has been substantial progress. We seem to be at a turning point in public attitudes to transgenic crops, not only in this country, but importantly in Africa, partly because of the work of the Gates Foundation. This government has firmly declared its support for GM crop trials. In Britain most people now accept the need for nuclear power and there has been no hysterical reaction to the Fukushima disaster as there has been elsewhere. The NHS has largely ceased funding homeopathy, which is increasingly becoming a joke, to judge by comedians on television and radio. Schools have been stopped from teaching creationism. Especially important are the government's appointment of chief scientists to all its departments and the review carried out for the BBC Trust by Steve Jones on the impartiality and accuracy of the BBC coverage of science. Polls show that 84 per cent of the public gets its information about science from television. Now the BBC has agreed to appoint a science editor for BBC News; and there are new guidelines on 'due weight' in observing impartiality in its treatment of science issues. There is to be training for journalists. It seems likely that 'balance' will no longer mean equal time for sense and nonsense.

Every time bogus science is pulled apart, it reveals how good science works. The SAS leaflet 'I Don't Know What to Believe' explained the importance of peer review. It has had a big impact, with over half a million downloads and wide distribution in schools. Our campaign 'Ask for the Evidence' is growing in momentum and goes to the root of the scientific way of thinking. As for public interest, there are few more effective communicators to inspire future scientists than David Attenborough and Brian Cox. The Voice of Young Science, a movement of young research workers developed by SAS young staff, has stimulated other young scientists to promote good science. It has spread like wildfire and is now being copied in several other countries.

There have been few things I have enjoyed more in my career (so far) than working with SAS for a cause that Popper and Medawar have both described as 'the greatest adventure of mankind'.

INDEX

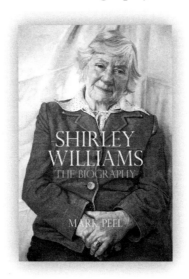